Gluten-Free
Baking
Classics
Second Edition

ANNALISE G. ROBERTS

SURREY BOOKS
CHICAGO

Designed by Joan Sommers Design, Chicago
Photographs on viii, x, 18, 208 © Tom DiBella
Photographs on 104, 130 © iStockphoto
Some recipes were originally published in *Gourmet Magazine*
Excerpts from Chapter 2 first appeared on www.foodphilosopher.com by
Annalise Roberts and Claudia Pillow

Printed in the United States.

Library of Congress Cataloging-in-Publication Data

Roberts, Annalise G.
 Gluten-free baking classics / Annalise G. Roberts. -- 2nd ed.
     p. cm.
 Includes index.
 Summary: "Recipes for gluten-free pastries, breads, sweets, savories and other baked dishes. Includes recipes for wheat-free flour mixes"--Provided by publisher.
 ISBN-13: 978-1-57284-099-7 (pbk.)
 ISBN-10: 1-57284-099-4 (pbk.)
 1. Gluten-free diet--Recipes. 2. Baking. I. Title.
 RM237.86.R58 2008
 641.5'638--dc22

                    2008027238

10 9 8 7 6 5 4 3 2 1

Surrey Books is an imprint of Agate Publishing. Agate books are available in bulk at discount prices. Single copies are available prepaid direct from the publisher. For more information visit agatepublishing.com.

To Conrad—
Who made it possible for me to take my own "road not taken"

ACKNOWLEDGMENTS

Love and thanks to my sister Claudia for joining me in bringing our Food Philosopher dreams to life.

Thanks to Douglas Seibold, president of Agate Publishing for all his encouragement and for giving me the opportunity to see this second edition come to life.

Thanks to Susan Schwartz, who published the first edition of this book, for seeing the value and potential of my work.

Thanks to Tom DiBella, the food photographer who gave his exceptional creative skills and technical talent to this project. Your dedication touched my heart.

Thanks to Ruth Reichl and her staff at *Gourmet Magazine* who tasted my cupcakes and cookies and gave me a chance to share them with their readers.

Thanks to Shelly, David, Jack, and Rivka—your caring made all the difference.

A giant gluten-free thank you to my many willing tasters, especially Alex and Bradford; Herb and Ev; Tim, Cory, and Monica; Don and Macie; Susan and Fritz Zeigler; Daria Ewanik; Mary and Greg Frazier; Carl Scariatti; Madhuri Shukla; the whole Loretti clan; the Krafts; and all the others I fed and questioned endlessly until I got it right.

Another huge thank you to my many willing field testers who offered up their time and kitchens to test recipes for this book: Shawn McBride, Jennifer Granich, Jennifer Cross, Monica Di Bisceglie, Amy Luczak, the Scheps family, Rebecca Armstrong, Jeanne Cobetto, Susan Riedinger, Sue Lampropoulos, Diana Gitig, Susan Goodstadt-Levin, Mary Jane Thomas, Patti Lou Smith, Ed Perell, Gayle Gorga, Nancy Shedrofsky, Pam Philips, Maryse Lalonde, Jason Dietel, Vicki Hunt and her family, and Rita Yohalem.

To Evan Fogelman for all his enthusiasm, support, and efforts on my behalf.

To Sean Budlong, my Website wizard, for all of his hard work and caring.

To Marj Scariati and Keum Park, my caring, self-sacrificing intellectual property support team.

To Dr. Peter Green and Ann Roland Lee at Columbia University, whose efforts and work on gluten intolerance have guided me.

And a heartfelt thanks to the many others who have cheered me on and supported my writing and work.

TABLE OF CONTENTS

NOTES ABOUT THE SECOND EDITION vii

FOREWORD ix

1. WHAT ARE YOU HUNGRY FOR? 1

2. GLUTEN REALITY 3

3. GETTING STARTED 5

4. MUFFINS, SWEET BREADS, SCONES, AND SWEET ROLLS   19

5. CAKES 43

6. PIES AND TARTS 85

7. COOKIES 105

8. OTHER SWEET TREATS 131

9. BREADS, BREAD CRUMBS, PIZZA, AND MORE 155

10. OTHER SAVORIES 195

MEASUREMENTS/EQUIVALENTS 207

INDEX 209

NOTES ON THE SECOND EDITION

THE GLUTEN-FREE "EXPERIENCE" has changed a great deal since I started writing about food and teaching gluten-free cooking and baking classes. Supermarkets, restaurants, and the mass media have all begun to embrace the concerns of those who are gluten sensitive and bring them out into the open. In my classes, I see more and more people who say they are avoiding wheat and gluten because of arthritis, headaches, ADHD, depression, pregnancy problems, and an incredible array of autoimmune ailments, including fibromyalgia, lupus, multiple sclerosis, and thyroid disease. Many have never been tested for celiac; many do not even care if they have it. They just know they feel better when they don't eat wheat.

There is something to be said for thinking about gluten sensitivity as if it were on a spectrum, with celiac (the most severe) on top and various levels of intolerance below. I have come to believe that most people on the planet would be better off if they ate less wheat and gluten, and in many cases, avoided it entirely. Every celiac I meet, it seems, has an intriguing history of family members with ailments that look like, and maybe are, symptoms of gluten sensitivity. They all might feel better on a gluten-free diet.

When I wrote the first edition of *Gluten-Free Baking Classics*, my goal was to bring together all the basic, classic recipes for baked goods that individuals with celiac, gluten sensitivity, and wheat allergies might look for in one book. I wanted the recipes to be simple and foolproof, so people could depend on them and even use them as a foundation to convert their own family favorites, if they so desired.

In retrospect, I have to admit I missed a few things. Who knew that one day I would wake up and realize I had to have a doughnut? And then, I started to miss pecan raisin artisan bread, popovers, and hot cross buns studded with citron. I didn't even see it coming, but suddenly I was immersed in creating more recipes for baked goods I had to have. I even recreated my favorite birthday cake, a hazelnut layer cake with praline buttercream frosting and dark chocolate curls. Along with all this came requests from my readers and baking students for flour tortillas, bagels, challah, gingerbread men, fresh egg pasta, Irish soda bread, soft pretzels, banana muffins, and black and white cookies.

So this second edition evolved as all good things do—over time. Before I knew it, I had 42 new recipes to add to my collection. I am proud to say that they are all are rigorously tested and delicious. I have also reworked and broadened Chapter 3: Getting Started to detail more about the art and science of gluten-free baking and to answer frequently asked questions. I hope this work, which has stayed true to my original goal of keeping all the recipes in one book, encourages you to take out your mixer and create some wonderful food memories for yourself, your family, and your friends.

—*Annalise Roberts, May 2008*

FOREWORD

CELIAC DISEASE IS MORE COMMON than most people realize. In fact, it affects about 1% of the population, or close to 3 million individuals, in the United States. But less than 3% of those with celiac disease are correctly diagnosed: the majority is unaware that they even have this condition. A result of this massive under-diagnosis is that Americans with celiac disease suffer from inadequate support systems. There is a lack of reliable food labeling, a lack of awareness in the food and grocery industry, inadequate knowledge among professional chefs, and a general lack of availability of gluten-free products. This is in marked contrast to the rest of the world!

At the Celiac Disease Center at Columbia University in New York City, we are educating health care professionals and facilitating a great variety of research projects with the goal of increasing the quality of patient care. It is through physician, dietitian, and nurse education that more people with celiac disease will be correctly diagnosed, and thus their lives improved.

We also know that good-tasting, gluten-free baked goods are difficult to find and very often expensive for individuals who need to maintain a gluten-free diet. But this wonderful book by Annalise Roberts helps fill the void. Chock full of accurate information and excellent recipes, it will help decrease the burden of the disease. It is a very readable book, and the recipes taste great!

Peter H. R. Green, M.D.
Anne R. Lee, R.D.
Celiac Disease Center at Columbia University, New York City
www.celiacdiseasecenter.columbia.edu

CHAPTER I

What Are You Hungry For?

Well, and what then shall I tell you, my Lady, of the secrets of nature that I have learned while cooking? . . . One can philosophize quite well while preparing supper. I often say, when I make these little observations, "Had Aristotle cooked, he would have written a great deal more." —Sor Juana Ines de la Cruz[*]

WHEN I TEACH GLUTEN-FREE baking classes or advise newly diagnosed celiacs on how to cook, I always ask them what foods they miss most. In response, I always hear the same few answers: they miss the basics—bread, pizza, cake, pie, cookies. But I also hear the sheer longing in people's voices and the qualifying adjectives they feel compelled to include: *real* pizza; *really good* bread for sandwiches that tastes good and won't crumble; *real* crusty, chewy Italian or French bread; *really good* cake that's not dense and gritty; *really good* pie crust that doesn't taste like cardboard.

Perhaps you've said the same thing. Perhaps you're still hungry for the taste, the texture of something you once either took for granted or cherished every time you took a bite. If you *are* hungry for gluten-free recipes so good that no one will miss the wheat, read on.

For most of us, the search for a decent gluten-free recipe requires time, patience, compromise, and emotional strength. After my own diagnosis of celiac over six years ago, I thought I would never eat a really delicious piece of cake or a good hot, fresh muffin again. But I grew up baking, and I was determined to make gluten-free foods that were as wonderful as those I was used to. It became even more important when one of my sons was diagnosed with gluten intolerance.

The result is this collection of delicious, dependable gluten-free recipes for classic baked goods that look, feel, and taste as good as, or better than, their wheat-containing counterparts. They are all here, in this one book.

HOW OLD ARE YOUR MUFFINS?

Although gluten-free baked goods are available in natural food stores and online, they are usually frozen, often old-tasting, and almost always shrink wrapped for "sell by" dates months in advance. But the worst part is that they are always expensive. This is especially

[*] *La respuesta / Sor Juana Ines de la Cruz.* Critical edition and translation by Electa Arenal and Amanda Powell. New York: Feminist Press at the City University of New York, 1994.

true when you are able to find them fresh. As more individuals are correctly diagnosed and more suppliers move into this potentially lucrative market, prices may come down. But for now, raw material prices, manufacturing constraints, and an incredibly poor distribution system combine to keep prices high.

Moreover, in order for mass-production bakeries to make baked goods that stay fresh on the shelf as long as possible, they need to use more fat and sugar than you would use to make the same kind of baked goods at home. As distribution and pricing improve, gluten-free baked goods will no doubt fall prey to the fattening forces of even larger-scale mass production. They will have even more added fat and sugar than they have now.

Time and effort aside, if you are going to eat and enjoy cake or muffins, you're better off making them yourself. They will be fresher, cost less, and have less fat and sugar than ones you buy at the store—wheat or no wheat.

BUT I DON'T HAVE TIME TO BAKE

I believe that what and how we eat affects our quality of life. Food can make us happier and healthier, and it is a manageable ingredient in our daily lives. Make the time to cook and bake. If you are too busy to cook, maybe you are just plain too busy. Noted social theorist Dr. Robin Fox wrote, "All animals eat, but we are the only animal that cooks. It is what makes us human."

For the gluten-intolerant, the need to cook without gluten cannot be ignored. Good take-out pizza is never a phone call away. But our gluten-free food should do more than simply nourish our bodies; it should also nurture our spirit. You cannot overestimate the happiness home-baked treats can bring to yourself and others. The carefully crafted recipes in this book will provide a foundation for a gluten-free baking repertoire that you can personalize and update for years to come.

CHAPTER 2

Gluten Reality

MANY OF OUR FAVORITE FOODS—a slice of pizza, a chocolate chip cookie, a flaky biscuit—were unknown to our ancestors. All of these delicious foods contain wheat, a grain not grown by man until relatively recently—about 7,000 years ago. You must consider that although *Homo sapiens* has been on the planet about 100,000 years, for 90,000 years the species ate only what it could find. This is the equivalent of a 45-year-old man adding wheat to his diet for the first time at about age 41.

Interestingly enough, today wheat has become part of a growing controversy about carbohydrates. Just how much bread, pasta, cake, and pizza can we eat without getting fat? Do these carbo-loaded foods make us sluggish? Are they good for our blood type? The questions are endless. Unfortunately, so are the answers. But one thing is sure: Wheat can make many of us sick. For people who are gluten sensitive—and particularly those with celiac disease—the concerns are far more serious than whether or not wheat will make them fat.

Celiac is a genetic intolerance to gluten, a protein found in wheat, rye, and barley. When people with celiac disease eat foods containing gluten, their immune systems are triggered to attack the lining of their small intestine. This reaction causes inflammation and interferes with the digestion of vitamins, minerals, and other vital nutrients. Currently, the only effective treatment for celiac disease is a lifelong gluten-free diet.

Celiac is thought to be the most common genetic disease in Europe. It has also been identified in people from South America, the Near East, Pakistan, Cuba, and North Africa. Recent studies indicate that as many as 1 in 100 Americans of European descent may have the disease, although the actual diagnosis rate is 1 in 3,600. It is estimated that there are over 1 million people in the United States with undiagnosed celiac. In fact, it is the most misdiagnosed disease in America. Those with symptoms are often told they have other intestinal, digestive, emotional, or dermatologic problems, including irritable bowel syndrome, Crohn's disease, ulcerative colitis, diverticulosis, intestinal infections, arthritis, depression, and chronic fatigue syndrome.

Many doctors not only fail to correctly screen for celiac, but they also fail to consider it in the first place. The average time for an individual to be correctly diagnosed in the United States is over seven years.

Symptoms of celiac (and gluten sensitivity) include diarrhea, constipation, bloating, stomach pain, skin rash, tooth enamel discoloration, joint and muscle pain, and many autoimmune syndromes (including rheumatoid arthritis, multiple sclerosis, lupus, psoriasis, thyroid disease, alopecia areata, and diabetes). Other associated conditions include: asthma, osteoporosis, iron deficiency anemia, short stature in children, female infertility, peripheral neuropathy, ADD, ADHD (and other learning problems), seizures, other neurologic syndromes, depression, and other psychiatric syndromes. In addition, autism is emerging as a syndrome that may improve with a gluten-free diet.

WHY ARE SO MANY PEOPLE SENSITIVE TO GLUTEN?

Early man hunted for meat and fish and gathered fruits, seeds, herbs, tubers, and roots. As civilization progressed, crops of complex carbohydrates were cultivated for the purpose of stabilizing food supplies. Rice was the most cultivated species in Asia, sorghum and millet in Africa, and in America, maize, or corn, was the major crop. Wheat and barley containing very low gluten content were grown only in Southwest Asia. As time went on, farming of wheat and barley spread into Europe. But our ancestors never ate bread as we know it today.

The industrial and agricultural revolutions of the past 200 years have changed our diet faster than we can change genetically. Today, our wheat crops have a high gluten content (50 percent higher than centuries ago, in some cases) for the purpose of improved bread baking, and with it, we see a rise in the prevalence of gluten intolerance. Just as humans are predisposed to store excess calories as fat, the same genetic makeup that tolerated wheat with low gluten levels cannot tolerate modern foods with high gluten levels.

Unfortunately, we Americans have come to rely on wheat to fill our bellies. Instead of dining on the fruits, vegetables, meats, and fish eaten by our ancestors, today our diets are loaded with gluten-laden wheat-based foods: breads, pastas, pizza, cookies, muffins, and bagels. Gluten is also the second most common additive in all packaged foods (sugar is the most common). Its prevalence, combined with an overall lack of knowledge about gluten intolerance, means that many individuals who are believed to have undiagnosed celiac disease are not even aware that gluten could be the root cause of their ailments.

Modernization may have exacerbated gluten sensitivity, but luckily it provided gluten-free flour alternatives so a child with celiac disease can enjoy a cupcake at his or her own birthday party. And now, for less money and in less time than it takes to go out and buy it, you can make a gluten-free dessert that's so delicious, everyone will want some.

CHAPTER 3

Getting Started

CELIAC IS SERIOUS, but baking can be fun. It is part art and part science. It combines careful measurement with creative flavoring and decorating. My thoughts about gluten-free baking are in harmony with my basic philosophy about all cooking: It should be simple and not all-consuming. This chapter provides details on how to buy, mix, and measure gluten-free flours, discusses gluten-free baking know-how, and presents strategies for making time to bake in busy lives. I have much to tell you and secrets to share. So go buy some xanthan gum, and let's get baking!

WHAT CAN YOU EXPECT?

Chances are you didn't grow up watching your mother or grandmother bake gluten-free cookies. Even if you grew up baking, gluten-free flours change everything: how you measure ingredients; how much baking powder, baking soda, liquid, and eggs you use; baking time; and pan size. Although gluten-free baked goods are notoriously heavy and dense, they need not be. You can make gluten-free cakes and muffins that are as light as those made with wheat. You can make delicious cookies that are indistinguishable from their wheat-containing counterparts. You can make perfect pie and tart shells and New York pizza crusts so delicious you will never again feel pizza-deprived. But like all things worth achieving in life, you can expect that it might take a little time, thought, and energy.

The recipes in this book have been meticulously fine-tuned to produce excellent results—if you follow the directions. There are almost no shortcuts in baking; it is not like throwing a pasta dish together. Do not bother to try a new baking recipe unless you have the ingredients on hand, the equipment you need, and the time to concentrate and complete the task. I can't tell you how many times I've heard people tell me that a recipe failed and then admit that they substituted ingredients, didn't measure correctly, or were in a rush and probably left a step out.

Read each recipe completely before you actually begin to bake. Follow directions, measure all ingredients carefully, and check your oven temperature. Baking is the only form of cooking where a little bit too much or too little can ruin a recipe. Save your baking efforts for times when you are prepared. The result will be fabulous baked goods you, your family, and friends will happily consume.

THE SCIENCE OF BAKING WITH GLUTEN-FREE FLOURS

If you think about how most people bake with wheat, you will realize that they usually use two different kinds of flour: an all-purpose flour for cakes, pies, muffins, and other pastries, and a bread flour for baking bread. The recipes in this book use just two flour mixes: the Brown Rice Flour Mix (*my* all-purpose flour) makes cakes, pies, muffins and cookies that look, feel, and taste like those made with wheat, and the Bread Flour Mix (*my* bread flour) makes crusty, chewy artisan loaves and tender sandwich breads.

Few people I know have large amounts of time to bake, much less to grab for four different flours each time they do. Fewer still have room to store three or four different flour mixes in their cabinets. Following my philosophy that cooking should be simple, I want to be able to reach for a gluten-free all-purpose flour or a gluten-free bread flour and know it will work dependably for everything I make. The recipes in this book are carefully calibrated to work with the flour combinations given below. Be aware that if you do in fact substitute flours, it will probably be necessary to adjust the amounts of other ingredients you use (most likely xanthan gum, liquids, and leavening agents).

In order to make good gluten-free bread, you will have to set aside all your preconceived notions about how bread should be made. There will be no kneading: you will spoon the dough into the pan. No long wait times; there will be one rise and then it's in the oven: you can make a rustic multigrain bread in less than an hour and a half. There will be no gluten to hold your bread together and give it the "elasticity" good bread is known for; you will have to use xanthan gum to help provide that elasticity and to keep it from collapsing. There will be no wheat flavor. But the grainy, nutty flavors of millet and sorghum make delicious sandwich and artisan breads that you will take great delight in eating and serving to others.

GLUTEN-FREE ALL-PURPOSE FLOUR FOR CAKES, PIES, MUFFINS, & COOKIES

My "all-purpose" Brown Rice Flour Mix is a combination of *extra finely ground brown rice flour*, potato starch (*not* potato flour), and tapioca flour (also called tapioca starch).

FOOD PHILOSOPHER® GLUTEN-FREE BROWN RICE FLOUR MIX

Brown rice flour (extra finely ground)	2 parts	2 cups	6 cups
Potato starch (*not potato flour*)	²⁄₃ part	²⁄₃ cup	2 cups
Tapioca flour	¹⁄₃ part	¹⁄₃ cup	1 cup

It is very important that you use an extra finely ground brown rice flour (not just any grind), or your baked goods will be gritty, heavy and/or crumbly. At this time, Authentic Foods® in California sells the only one I can find other than those sold in Asian grocery stores. Authentic Foods® rice flour is powdery, just like all-purpose wheat flour. It can be bought online and in natural food stores; the mailing address, e-mail address, and phone number can be found at the end of this chapter. Take note: Authentic Foods® now makes the above Brown Rice Flour Mix already made up under the name *GF Classic Blend*.

The other brands of brown rice flour have a larger grind that you can actually feel between your fingers. They are not powdery (as of this writing), and it really does make a difference. If you want or need to use one of these other brands, try to find one with the finest grind you can. Buy several at a time, if you can. Open the packages and feel the flour. Use the finest grinds for cakes, muffins, cookies, and pie crusts. Use the coarser grinds for pizza.

The potato starch and tapioca flour can be found in local natural food stores, some grocery stores, and online. The brands seem fairly interchangeable and are consistent in quality.

In addition to the Brown Rice Flour Mix above, several recipes call for sweet rice flour, which helps give certain baked goods a better texture. Only a small amount is ever used at a time, because too much results in a denser, tighter, and gummy product. It is available in local natural food stores, some grocery stores, and online. I recommend extra-finely ground Authentic Foods® sweet rice flour, or your baked goods will be gritty.

GLUTEN-FREE FLOURS FOR BREAD

If you are like me, you have baked and eaten more than your fair share of bad gluten-free bread. Over time, I developed recipes and a flour mix for making some of the breads I missed most. The recipes here were all developed using this one mix (with one slight variation) as a replacement for wheat bread flour. It will allow you to make breads that taste good, rise evenly, and won't fall when they come out of the oven. If you follow the detailed instructions, your gluten-free yeast breads will have the "mouth feel" and texture of the wheat breads you are familiar with. Moreover, they do not contain rice flour, so they will not have the gummy, glossy look and feel of many of the gluten-free breads you see in stores or ones that you may have baked in the past. (Exceptions: The Bagels and the Challah contain a tiny bit of sweet rice flour to enhance their texture. The Soft Pretzels require a unique combination of flours in order to achieve the desired texture and flavor.)

My bread flour mix is made up of whole grain flours and starch flours in a ratio of half to half; a combination of millet, sorghum, corn starch, potato starch (not potato flour), and tapioca flour (also called tapioca starch). Millet and sorghum are used to help vary the taste, improve nutrition, and provide structure to the dough. The starches help lighten the texture and improve mouth feel.

Bread Flour Mix A uses more millet than sorghum and has a very slight golden hue. It works well in each of the bread recipes in this book and makes specialty breads that will surpass your wildest expectations.

Bread Flour Mix B uses equal parts millet and sorghum. It makes a lighter-colored bread and has a blander taste. It can be used for the sandwich bread based recipes that are not multigrain (Sandwich Bread, Buttermilk Bread, Cinnamon Swirl Bread, Hamburger Hot Dog Rolls, and Traditional Dinner Rolls). It is a good blend for newly gluten-intolerant children who are used to white bread.

Both flour mixes make a sandwich bread that is much like homemade wheat bread in terms of texture and density. The millet and sorghum flour (both whole grain) help keep the loaves fresher than gluten-free breads made of all starchy flours. But, remember that real homemade wheat breads never have a shelf life as long as the commercially produced loaves sold in grocery stores today, and neither will your homemade gluten-free bread.

Traditional bread bakers usually use a high-gluten bread flour and then mix it with all-purpose flour, rye, or whole wheat in order to alter the taste and texture of their loaves. All of the multigrain loaves in this book use teff flour, a darker, fiber-and-protein-rich, nutty, whole grain flour. Each of the recipes use ¼ cup of teff flour to replace ¼ cup of bread flour mix. In addition to adding extra nutrition, teff adds color, texture, and flavor to the bread. You can replace the teff flour with coarsely ground oatmeal (I use a blender to grind it), which is my favorite other flour to use for multigrain breads. Replace it with amaranth, quinoa, or Montina if you prefer the much stronger taste of those flours.

For variety, you can add up to 2 tablespoons of ground nut flour in addition to all the flour in a recipe in order to enhance the flavor of the more traditional breads (see Pecan Raisin Artisan Bread, page 174). Take note: Whenever you add extra whole-grain flour or ground nut flour, the bread will become slightly denser and heartier. In gluten-free bread baking, less is more, unless you are looking to make a brick.

Make up a large batch of the flour mix so you can bake bread whenever you want by simply reaching into your pantry and grabbing your gluten-free bread flour, just like you might have once reached for wheat bread flour.

FOOD PHILOSOPHER® GLUTEN-FREE BREAD FLOUR MIXES

Bread Flour Mix A

⅓ part millet flour	2 cups	⅔ cup	½ cup
⅙ part sorghum flour	1 cup	⅓ cup	¼ cup
⅙ part cornstarch	1 cup	⅓ cup	¼ cup
⅙ part potato starch	1 cup	⅓ cup	¼ cup
⅙ part tapioca flour	1 cup	⅓ cup	¼ cup
Total	6 cups	2 cups	1½ cups

Bread Flour Mix B

¼ part millet flour	1½ cups	½ cup	⅓ cup plus 1 tablespoon
¼ part sorghum flour	1½ cups	½ cup	⅓ cup plus 1 tablespoon
⅙ part cornstarch	1 cup	⅓ cup	¼ cup
⅙ part potato starch	1 cup	⅓ cup	¼ cup
⅙ part tapioca flour	1 cup	⅓ cup	¼ cup
Total	6 cups	2 cups	1½ cups

The millet, sorghum, teff, potato starch, tapioca flour, and "gluten-free" oatmeal can be found in local natural food stores, some grocery stores, and online. The brands seem fairly interchangeable and are consistent in quality. Corn starch can be found in any grocery store.

GLUTEN-FREE FLOURS FOR PIZZA

The pizza recipe in this book uses the Brown Rice Flour Mix but does not require finely ground brown rice flour. It will actually have an improved texture if made with a coarser-ground flour. Although I usually use my regular Brown Rice Flour Mix above, I will go out of my way to buy brown rice flour with a coarser grind when I know I'm going to bake a lot of pizza crusts for the freezer. Bob's Red Mill® brown rice flour is great for pizza crust, and I am lucky enough to find it at my local grocery store. It can also be found in local natural food stores or ordered online. But there are many other brands of coarser ground brown rice flour, so you will no doubt be able to find one you like. In addition to the Brown Rice Flour Mix, I use millet flour in pizza, although the recipe can be made without it (just substitute more of the brown rice flour). I think millet adds a bit of complexity to the texture and taste, and I like to use it whenever I make pizza.

HOW TO MEASURE AND MIX GLUTEN-FREE FLOURS

To measure flour for making flour mixes: Put the empty measuring cup into a small bowl. Use a soup spoon to spoon the flour from the package into the measuring cup, or pour the flour from the package into the measuring cup. Then use a knife or spoon handle to level the top (do this over the bowl to avoid a messy cleanup; pour the flour left in the bowl back into the package or another container). Do not scoop gluten-free flours directly out of the package with the measuring cup.

As each flour is measured, transfer it into a plastic container large enough to leave four or five inches from the top unfilled. Shake container vigorously to mix flours. I usually make 12 cups of Brown Rice Flour Mix at a time and store and shake it in a 21-cup Rubbermaid® container.

To measure flour for use in recipes: *Shake* storage container vigorously to mix and aerate the flour mix. Put the empty measuring cup into a small bowl, or hold it over the opening of the container if it is large enough. Use a soup spoon to spoon the flour from the container into the measuring cup, then use a knife or spoon handle to level the top. If you do this over a bowl, pour the flour left in the bowl back into the storage container. Do not scoop gluten-free flours out of the storage container with the measuring cup. *Remember: Shake and bake!*

HOW TO PURCHASE AND STORE GLUTEN-FREE FLOURS

Brown rice flour, millet flour, sorghum, and teff flour are whole-grain flours and must be stored carefully. The Brown Rice Flour Mix and the Bread Flour Mix can be stored at room temperature for about four months. If your house is hot and humid, or if you will not be baking for long periods of time, store the mixes in the refrigerator. Store open packages of brown rice flour, millet flour, sorghum, and teff in the refrigerator.

Purchase all these flours from stores or online sellers that have a lot of turnover, so you can be sure you are getting fresh packages. Do not purchase them too far in advance of when you make the flour mixes (more than four months). When you open a new bag, *make sure it does not have a strong odor, an indication that it is rancid or old*. These flours should have a pleasant, grainy, nutty smell. Millet flour in particular tends to get rancid if not stored properly or if it is old (just like whole-wheat flour). Old flours often impart a bitter taste in your baked goods.

Both open and unopened packages of potato starch, tapioca flour, and corn starch can be stored at room temperature for more than a year. They can be purchased in advance of when you will be using them to make the flour mixes.

THE SECRETS OF XANTHAN AND GUAR GUM

In gluten-free baking, it doesn't matter if you are making cakes and cookies or bread; xanthan gum is used to replace the gluten in wheat flour. Gluten helps hold baked goods together and gives them elasticity. When using gluten-free flours, you must add back the elasticity by using xanthan gum, or sometimes guar gum. These gums are water-soluble; technically, they are called hydrocolloids. Because of their water solubility, xanthan and guar gums improve mouth feel and build viscosity. They help retain moisture, provide elasticity, extend shelf life, encapsulate flavors, and stabilize baked goods so they can be successfully frozen and thawed.

If you use too little xanthan or guar gum, your baked goods will fall apart and turn out brittle and hard. If you use too much, your baked goods will condense and shrink after you bake them, growing ever tighter and smaller as the gum works its magic for days after. The amount of xanthan gum needs to be recalibrated for each recipe based on type and amount of flour mix used; what liquids and flavorings are added (acids exaggerate the effect of the gum); the number of eggs, if any; and the desired texture of the baked good you are trying to make. There is no one-size-fits-all rule for xanthan gum in gluten-free baking. I recommend that you avoid flour mixes that include it as an ingredient.

Xanthan gum is easy to find in natural food stores or online, is fairly consistent in quality across brands, and is very stable over a broad range of temperatures. I recommend it as the gum of choice for almost every recipe in the book. However, I recommend guar gum for my Angel Food Cake and the Vanilla and Chocolate Sponge Cakes. Guar gum increases in viscosity when heated and works really well in cakes without a lot of fat to help them stay tender.

THE ART OF BAKING WITH GLUTEN-FREE FLOURS

Baking is much more of a science than cooking because the proportions of liquid, flour, salt, sugar and yeast or other leavening agents are so critical to the outcome of the baked good. That said, there is some room for well thought out maneuvering and creativity. Gluten-free baking isn't harder than baking with wheat flour- once you have a good understanding of how gluten-free flours behave, a dependable flour mix, xanthan gum, and a good recipe. In fact, every recipe in this book is based on a *good* recipe originally made with wheat.

UNDERSTANDING THE ESSENTIAL NATURE OF GLUTEN-FREE FLOURS

You probably never thought about how much flavor wheat really has until you had to give it up. As a result, you may not realize that one of the things you actually miss most is the flavor of wheat. In my bread and pizza recipes, I try to compensate by using millet, a delicious, nutty flavored grain, along with other more transparent flours like tapioca, cornstarch, and potato starch. In sweet baked goods, I try to mask the lack of wheat and cover up the brown rice flavor by accentuating the delicious flavors of other ingredients in the recipes. I use extra pure extracts and flavorings—more, in fact, than a *good* wheat recipe would call for.

The relative transparency of the gluten-free starch-based flours I use allows other flavors to shine through without affecting their taste. You will notice the essence of vanilla, lemon, almond, chocolate, and even butter in a whole new light. But remember, the relative tartness of yogurt or sour cream will also scream through with the same vibrant clarity.

GLUTEN-FREE MANEUVERING

When I converted these recipes to gluten-free, I discovered the amount of liquid and fat in the original wheat-based recipe almost always had to be decreased slightly; wheat flour absorbs relatively more liquid than finely ground brown rice flour, millet, sorghum, and the starches. I often replaced butter with canola oil, because it tends to produce a lighter gluten-free baked good and adds less flavor. I tried to reduce sugar as much as possible, but not enough to negatively impact taste, moisture, and lightness; I stayed true to my goal of creating "*classic*" baked goods versus "sugar-free." I also tended to reduce the amount of salt a bit because it stands out against the transparent flours. I often increased leavening agents, sometimes by only a little, but not always.

I can safely say that my all-purpose Brown Rice Flour Mix can be used in your own treasured family recipes with the kinds of additions and changes noted above. You may want to find a recipe in my book that is similar to the one you want to make and see how much xanthan gum, fat, liquid, eggs, and leavening I used. Then, you can start to convert your own recipes using my measurements as a guideline.

GLUTEN-FREE CREATIVITY

You can also use my very dependable recipes as a starting place and make your own changes or additions. Gluten-free bakers have used my recipes to create Italian cream cake, pina colada sponge roll, oatmeal cookies with dried cranberries and cardamom, white chocolate macadamia nut cookies, zucchini bread, and Scandinavian nut rolls (using my Cinnamon Roll recipe as the starting point). Some readers have also made a number of successful variations to my recipes (eliminating dairy or eggs, for example), and I am always grateful when they let me know, so I can encourage others to try.

The bread recipes are a bit trickier to change. However, in addition to adding a variety of seeds or 2 tablespoons of finely ground nuts, or replacing ¼ cup of the Bread Flour Mix with another whole-grain flour, such as teff (as noted above), you can also add bits of dried fruit or cheese to change the nature of the loaves you bake.

COMMON QUESTIONS

Is it possible to use egg substitutes? Egg yolks add richness, texture, color, and structure. If you use an egg-white substitute, it might be more difficult to get your baked goods to rise, but it is possible. In addition, *Ener-G-Replacer* and another homemade remedy (1½ tablespoons water, 1½ tablespoons canola oil, and 1½ teaspoons baking powder) can produce a good, *but not always ideal,* result in some recipes. When using egg substitutes, try to use milk that is higher in fat in order to compensate for not having yolks. It will improve mouth feel and help keep the baked good fresh.

Is it possible to use rice, soy, or almond milk? Yes, rice, soy, and almond milk have been successfully used by others for many of these recipes. Rice and almond milk add less aftertaste, unless you like the taste of soy. Remember that gluten-free flours are a bit transparent in flavor.

Is it possible to use sugar alternatives? Sugar acts as a liquid in baking, and since sugar substitutes contain varying amounts of liquid, each recipe would have to be recalibrated for dry/wet proportions, cooking time, and maybe even baking temperature, based on the substitute you use. *The recipes in this book were originally all for traditional, classic baked goods made with wheat. They were not based on recipes for special diets or restricted dietary needs.* That said, you could try substituting the sugar alternative of your choice based on your own knowledge of how to make substitutions (for example, rice syrup was used by some as a sugar substitute in some of my recipes, but the total amount of several ingredients had to be adjusted).

If you are interested in reducing the sugar in my recipes, it is possible—but not always easy. I don't recommend taking out more than 1 tablespoon if a recipe uses less than ½ cup total sugar, or more than ¼ to ⅓ cup if the recipe uses 1 cup or more sugar. Depending on the recipe, you may have to adjust liquid (more) and baking time (less), or you will have a dry baked good.

Is white rice flour an acceptable substitution for brown rice flour? Yes, *but* white rice is not a whole grain and therefore is not as nutritious (it is more of a starch). Baked goods stay fresher longer with brown rice flour because it has more complex proteins (as do all whole-grain products); starchier white rice flour will dry out faster. Brown rice flour gives baked goods a little more complexity in terms of taste (which I actually try to mask a bit with extra flavoring). White rice flour gives an "empty" taste; it is transparent, like the other starches in the mix.

What can be used to replace gelatin in the sandwich breads? Although most of the bread recipes in this book do not use gelatin, the sandwich breads and dinner rolls do call for it in order to add extra body and structure. If you can't use gelatin, or don't like it, add an extra egg yolk.

Why store gluten-free baked goods in the refrigerator? Gluten-free baked goods tend to stay fresher when stored in the refrigerator.

First, brown rice flour is more fragile than highly processed all-purpose wheat flour and more like whole-wheat flour (which people tend to refrigerate in order to keep fresh). Have you ever kept *real, homemade* whole-wheat bread, or even white bread, for that matter, around for more than a day? They both dry out within a relatively short time. Before the advent of commercially baked breads made with enough preservatives and extra added gluten to keep them fresh for several weeks, people used to make bread or go to a bakery every day.

Second, the tapioca flour, potato starch, and corn starch are highly processed flours (starches, actually) that dry out when used in baked goods. Keeping gluten-free baked goods tightly wrapped in the fridge at a constant temperature tends to slow the evaporation process.

Third, my recipes use as little sugar and fat as possible (and much less than you would get in a store-bought baked good with a long shelf life). Since sugar and fat help keep baked goods moist, keeping them refrigerated helps compensate for their absence.

Finally, except for the xanthan gum (these recipes use as little of it as possible; in fact, they use much less than you will find in most gluten-free recipes), there are no preservatives in these baked goods to help stabilize them.

HOW TO MEASURE INGREDIENTS FOR RECIPES IN THIS BOOK

Measure flour in nesting cups of 1, ½, ⅓, and ¼ cup capacity. Spoon ingredients into the measuring cup and level them off with the edge of a knife or the back of the spoon you used to transfer the ingredients. Measure other dry ingredients in measuring spoons the same way. Take care to be accurate. For instance, as much as ⅛ teaspoon too much xanthan gum will affect your baked goods! Measure liquids in glass or plastic measuring cups. Check at eye level.

INVEST IN QUALITY EQUIPMENT

I suggest you invest in good quality baking pans if you do not already have them. It will make a difference in your baked goods. Pans do not have to be professional quality. I use good, made-for-home bakeware that is readily available in stores everywhere, online, or in catalogs.

I use light-colored metal baking pans for recipe development, so if you have black metal pans, you will have to adjust the baking time. Food baked in black pans bakes faster because the dark surfaces absorb more of the radiant heat coming from the oven walls (as compared to pans with light, shiny surfaces, which tend to reflect, rather than absorb, radiant energy). Therefore, baking times must be decreased for black pans.

I strongly recommend that you buy an instant-read thermometer, because it will help you make good bread (as well as several other recipes in this book). You can buy them for under $5 at your grocery store. You do not need a fancy, expensive one.

HOW TO MELT CHOCOLATE FOR RECIPES IN THIS BOOK

The most commonly recommended method used to melt chocolate is in a double boiler. However, I find the quickest and easiest way is over direct heat, and although it demands more concentration and a heavy saucepan, it requires less time. Simply place coarsely chopped chocolate in a *heavy* saucepan over *low* heat. Stir constantly until melted. Immediately remove chocolate from heat to prevent scorching. Chocolate should never be heated beyond 120° to 125°F, and you should not add it to other ingredients until it cools down to about 105°F.

In addition, small amounts of chocolate can be melted in the microwave. Place coarsely chopped chocolate in a glass bowl. Microwave on medium/high for 1 to 1 ½ minutes for 1 to 3 ounces of chocolate. Stir every 30 seconds with a rubber spatula while melting. When melted, cover with plastic wrap until needed.

MAKING HALF THE RECIPE

Almost all of the recipes in this book can be cut in half. In fact, when I test recipes, I almost always make half a recipe first, so I know it can be done. Invest in measuring spoons that include a ⅛ teaspoon, and measure carefully. Remember, a large egg is equal to 3–4 table-spoons (beat it well before measuring), and 1 tablespoon is equal to 3 teaspoons. You may want to write down the quantities for the recipe and cut them in half before you start (like I do) to avoid mistakes. You also may have to adjust baking times and pan sizes (sweet breads, for instance, can be baked in mini-loaf pans).

STRATEGIES FOR MAKING TIME TO BAKE

- Prepare a fresh batch of the Brown Rice Flour Mix whenever you run low, so you'll always have it available. If you have easy access to baking flour, you are more likely to bake whenever time is available or the urge strikes.

- Make sure you have what you need in your baking pantry to make the recipes you want (see pantry recommendations below).

- Make enough pizza crusts and cookie dough to freeze and use over a month's time. I especially like to freeze cookie dough (each recipe includes freezing instructions), so I can bake a small batch of fresh cookies every week without starting from scratch.

- Pre-measure and mix ingredients for breads you know you'll want to make in the course of a month (*do not add the yeast until you are ready to bake*). You're more likely to make a loaf of bread if most of the steps have already been completed. There are two ways to do this: The way I recommend is to pre-measure and mix enough Bread Flour Mix to use for a month or more. Or you might consider mixing and storing all the dry ingredients needed for individual breads (*except the yeast*) in separate, clearly marked containers.

- I often try to pre-measure and mix dry ingredients for recipes ahead of time, so all I have to do is toss in the butter, eggs, and liquids when I am ready to bake. Sometimes, I even pre-measure liquid ingredients and keep them covered (and refrigerated when necessary). I usually store pre-measured or pre-mixed dry ingredients in a tightly covered, labeled plastic container, but depending on what and when I plan on baking, I might just put them in a mixing bowl and cover it with plastic wrap. This is especially nice when I want to make fresh muffins or scones in the morning, or serve fresh rustic flat bread or fruit crisp at dinner.

GLUTEN-FREE BAKING PANTRY

Non-Refrigerated
Extra-fine brown rice flour (recommended: Authentic Foods)*
Regular brown rice flour (optional for pizza)*
Extra-finely ground sweet rice flour (recommended: Authentic Foods)
White rice flour (optional to dust baking pans)
Potato starch (not potato flour)
Tapioca flour (also called tapioca starch)
Cornstarch
Sorghum flour*
Millet flour*
Teff flour*
"Gluten-free" oatmeal

Xantham gum
Guar gum

Granulated sugar
Confectioners' sugar
Dark brown sugar
Light brown sugar

Dried buttermilk powder (keep refrigerated after opening)
Dried egg white powder
Molasses
Light corn syrup

Powdered cocoa
Semisweet chocolate morsels
Semisweet baking chocolate
Unsweetened baking chocolate
German sweet chocolate

Pure vanilla extract
Other pure extracts you use often: almond, lemon, etc.
Baking soda
Baking powder
Cream of tartar
Iodized salt
Sea salt
Mixed whole peppercorns and black ground pepper
A variety of dried herbs and spices, including allspice, basil, cardamom, cinnamon, ground cloves, crushed red pepper, dill weed, fennel seed, ground ginger, nutmeg, oregano, paprika, rosemary, sage, and tarragon
A variety of seeds to use in multigrain breads, including caraway, poppy, sesame, flax, and sunflower
Canola oil
Olive oil
Jars of your favorite pasta sauce or tomato sauce for pizza

Refrigerated
Butter or margarine
Heavy cream
Light cream
Eggs
Milk (I use fat-free for most recipes, but you can use 2% or whole)
Fresh lemons (grated zest can be stored in freezer)
Prepared pesto (can be stored in freezer) for quiches, tarts, and pesto pizza
Bottled lemon juice
Bottled key lime juice
Assorted nuts for baking recipes, including walnuts, almonds, and pecans

* Store open packages of whole-grain flour in refrigerator.

THE LAST WORD ON BAKED GOODS

Baked goods are not the largest group recommended for consumption on the food pyramid, and they should not make up a significantly large part of your diet. Try to eat mostly fresh fruits, vegetables, meat, poultry, fish, beans, gluten-free whole grains like quinoa and buckwheat, and low-fat dairy products (but splurge on good cheese if you can!). However, when you do indulge in baked goods, they should be delicious, make you happy, and soothe your longing. Why waste the calories otherwise?

A recommended source for gluten-free flour:
Authentic Foods®
1860 W. 169th St., Suite B
Gardena, CA 90247
800-806-4737
www.authenticfoods.com

CHAPTER 4

Muffins, Sweet Breads, Scones, and Sweet Rolls

CORNBREAD or CORN MUFFINS

BLUEBERRY MUFFINS
Chocolate Chip Muffins

APPLE CINNAMON MUFFINS
Peach Ginger Muffins

LEMON COCONUT MUFFINS
Lemon Poppy Seed Muffins

BANANA NUT MUFFINS

CHOCOLATE RICOTTA MUFFINS

CARROT SPICE MUFFINS

CRANBERRY NUT BREAD

PUMPKIN BREAD or MUFFINS

TRIPLE GINGER TEA LOAF

LEMON POPPY SEED
TEA LOAVES
Lemon Walnut Tea Loaf

ORANGE JUICE BREAD
Orange Juice Pecan Bread

TRADITIONAL SCONES

LEMON CORNMEAL SCONES

CINNAMON ROLLS

HOT CROSS BUNS

WARM FRAGRANT MUFFINS, sweet breads, scones, and sweet rolls fresh from the oven can transform even the simplest breakfast or brunch into something very special. The recipes in this section were carefully developed to create delicious gluten-free baked goods you will be able to look forward to making and eating over and over.

Now, I didn't say they were fat-free, sugar-free nut-and-seed health muffins you can eat with utter abandon. No, these are the real thing. But remember that baked goods you make at home will typically have less fat and sugar than their store-bought counterparts (see Chapter 1). In fact, all the muffins and two of the sweet breads use canola oil rather than butter. Moreover, I used fat-free milk when I developed the recipes, so you can use the same (or low-fat milk) unless a recipe calls for a specific fat content.

On the other hand, I only use fresh eggs rather than egg substitutes. When a large egg is specified, it means that the fats in the yolk, as well as the whites, are needed to help ensure a sound structure and a good rise.

When you want to have fresh muffins or scones in the morning, I recommend you measure and combine the dry ingredients the night before (keep them tightly sealed). You can even pre-measure the liquids. Take out the pans so they will be on the counter when you need to prep them in the morning. Conversely, the sweet breads are best when they are made the day before because they are easier to slice when cold. Their flavor is best at room temperature. The sweet rolls will take a bit more time because you have to let them rise, but they are worth getting up early for.

This chapter uses the following pans:
• 12-cup muffin pan
• 9 x 5-inch loaf pan
• 8 ½ x 4 ½-inch loaf pan
• four 5 x 3-inch loaf pans
• 8-inch round cake pan
• 9-inch round cake pan
• 12-cup square muffin pan (see Hot Cross Buns recipe, p. 40, for details)
• Large, heavy baking sheet

THE LAST WORD ON MUFFINS
• Set up before starting the recipe: assemble all ingredients
• Measure carefully (see Chapter 3)
• Use the right size pan
• Preheat the oven to the proper temperature (make sure the oven is calibrated correctly)
• Do not open the oven door more than necessary
• Use a timer because you can get distracted

Once you mix the liquids into the dry ingredients, you need to get your muffins, sweet breads, or scones into the oven quickly. The baking powder leaps into action once it is combined with the liquid and creates the air pockets that will help your baked goods rise. So make sure your oven is preheated and your pans are prepared; it will make a difference in the texture and lightness of your baked goods.

Take note: The Blueberry and Apple Muffins are baked at 375°F rather than 350°F (most of the other muffins bake at 350°F). This is to compensate for the relatively cooler temperature and extra moisture of the fruit you add. You can bake them at 350°F, but the outsides will be softer and less firm.

CORNBREAD OR CORN MUFFINS

Makes 9 muffins or one 8-inch round bread.

Cornbread is an American classic. One version or another can be found in every basic cookbook. I'd been making cornbread for decades and taking it for granted—that is, until I could no longer eat it. This is my favorite recipe—but with gluten-free flours. As a bread, this recipe is delicious on its own or with bowls of steamy chili. I also love to make it as corn muffins, served warm from the oven for breakfast with fresh creamy butter or fruit preserves. Either way, cornbread is one of those recipes you'll be happy to have in your repertoire.

    1 cup cornmeal
    1 cup Brown Rice Flour Mix (see p. 6)
    $\frac{1}{2}$ teaspoon xanthan gum
    $\frac{1}{4}$ cup granulated sugar
    $3\frac{1}{2}$ teaspoons baking powder
    $\frac{1}{4}$ teaspoon salt
    $\frac{1}{4}$ cup canola oil
    1 cup milk minus 1 tablespoon
    1 large egg, well beaten
    $\frac{1}{4}$ teaspoon pure vanilla extract

1. Preheat oven to 400°F. Position rack in center of oven. Grease muffin pan or 8-inch round cake pan with cooking spray.

2. Mix dry ingredients in medium mixing bowl. Combine oil, milk, egg, and vanilla in another small bowl. Add wet ingredients to dry and gently stir to combine. Do not over mix. Pour batter into muffin pan or 8-inch round cake pan.

3. Bake about 20 minutes for muffins or about 25 minutes for bread. Remove from pan and serve immediately.

Muffins can be stored in a tightly sealed plastic container in refrigerator or covered with plastic wrap and then with foil and stored in freezer for up to three weeks. Best when eaten within four days of baking. Rewarm briefly in microwave.

BLUEBERRY MUFFINS

Makes 12 muffins.

This is the first muffin recipe I converted to gluten-free because it had always been one of my favorites. The muffins are light and delicious, and just like I remember them. Although the original recipe didn't include vanilla extract, I added it here to mask the brown rice flavor, which peeks through when the muffins are rewarmed in the microwave. Occasionally, I like to put on a Streusel Topping (recipe follows), because that is how my mother made them for Sunday brunch.

My children weren't wild about blueberry muffins when they were small, so I made the same basic recipe for them but put in chocolate chips instead of blueberries. They were an instant hit. The recipe for Chocolate Chip Muffins, also converted from the original, is on the opposite page.

Muffins can be stored in a tightly sealed plastic container in refrigerator or covered with plastic wrap and then with foil and stored in freezer for up to three weeks. Best when eaten within three days of baking. Rewarm briefly in a microwave.

* To make cinnamon sugar, combine 2 tablespoons sugar with $\frac{1}{2}$ teaspoon cinnamon.

2 cups Brown Rice Flour Mix (see p. 6)

$\frac{2}{3}$ cup granulated sugar

1 tablespoon baking powder

1 teaspoon baking soda

$\frac{3}{4}$ teaspoon xanthan gum

$\frac{1}{4}$ teaspoon salt

$\frac{1}{4}$–$\frac{1}{2}$ teaspoon nutmeg, to taste

1 $\frac{1}{2}$ cups unsweetened fresh dry blueberries

$\frac{1}{2}$ cup milk

$\frac{1}{2}$ cup canola oil

2 large eggs

$\frac{1}{2}$ teaspoon pure vanilla extract

Cinnamon sugar* for garnish *or* optional Streusel Topping, recipe follows

1. Preheat oven to 375°F. Position rack in center of oven. Grease muffin pan with cooking spray.

2. Mix flour, sugar, baking powder, baking soda, xanthan gum, salt, and nutmeg in large mixing bowl. Add blueberries; stir to coat evenly.

3. Combine milk and oil in small bowl; remove 1 tablespoon of combined liquid and discard it. Beat in eggs and vanilla. Add liquids to blueberry mixture and stir until just blended.

4. Fill muffin pans $\frac{2}{3}$ full. Sprinkle top with cinnamon sugar or Streusel Topping (below). Bake 18–25 minutes until light golden. Remove muffins from pan and serve immediately or cool on a rack.

CHOCOLATE CHIP MUFFINS

Omit blueberries, nutmeg, and cinnamon sugar topping. Add 1 cup chocolate chips. Sprinkle top with granulated sugar or Streusel Topping. Bake at 350°F rather than 375°F.

STREUSEL TOPPING

$\frac{1}{2}$ cup Brown Rice Flour Mix (see p. 6)

$\frac{1}{3}$ cup brown sugar

$\frac{1}{2}$ teaspoon cinnamon

$\frac{1}{4}$ teaspoon xanthan gum

3 tablespoons unsalted butter, melted

1. Combine flour, brown sugar, cinnamon, and xanthan gum in a small bowl; stir to blend. Pour in butter and stir until all dry ingredients are moistened. Break into small pieces with spoon.

APPLE CINNAMON MUFFINS WITH STREUSEL TOPPING

Makes 12 muffins.

I like to make these muffins in the fall and winter, because a warm cinnamon-apple aroma floats out of the oven and fills the house. They require relatively little effort but give back a huge return in terms of making people happy. Even better, my family and friends still love them in their new gluten-free version. In the summer when fresh ripe peaches are available, you can make the same basic recipe using peaches and ground ginger instead of apples and cinnamon for another delicious breakfast treat.

Muffins can be stored in a tightly sealed plastic container in refrigerator or covered with plastic wrap and then with foil and stored in freezer for up to three weeks. Best when eaten within three days of baking. Rewarm briefly in microwave.

* To make cinnamon sugar, combine 2 tablespoons granulated sugar with 1/2 teaspoon cinnamon.

2 cups Brown Rice Flour Mix (see p. 6)

$\frac{2}{3}$ cup granulated sugar

1 tablespoon baking powder

1 teaspoon baking soda

$\frac{3}{4}$ teaspoon xanthan gum

$\frac{1}{4}$ teaspoon salt

2 teaspoons ground cinnamon

1 cup peeled, chopped apple

$\frac{1}{2}$ cup chopped walnuts, optional

$\frac{1}{2}$ cup milk

$\frac{1}{2}$ cup canola oil

2 large eggs

Streusel Topping (recipe follows) *or* cinnamon sugar* for garnish

1. Preheat oven to 375°F. Position rack in center of oven. Grease muffin pan with cooking spray.

2. Mix flour, sugar, baking powder, baking soda, xanthan gum, salt, and cinnamon in large mixing bowl. Add apples and walnuts; stir to coat evenly.

3. Combine milk and oil in small bowl; remove 1 tablespoon of combined liquid and discard it. Beat in eggs. Add liquids to apple mixture and stir until just blended.

4. Fill muffin pans $\frac{2}{3}$ full. Top with streusel. Bake 18–25 minutes until light golden. Remove from pan and serve immediately or cool on a rack.

PEACH GINGER MUFFINS

Omit apples, walnuts, and cinnamon. Add 2 cups peeled and chopped fresh peaches, $\frac{1}{2}$ teaspoon pure vanilla extract, and $\frac{1}{2}$ teaspoon (or to taste) ground ginger. Sprinkle muffin tops with granulated sugar.

STREUSEL TOPPING

$\frac{1}{2}$ cup Brown Rice Flour Mix (see p. 6)

$\frac{1}{3}$ cup brown sugar

$\frac{1}{2}$ teaspoon cinnamon

$\frac{1}{4}$ teaspoon xanthan gum

3 tablespoons unsalted butter, melted

1. Combine flour, brown sugar, cinnamon, and xanthan gum in a small bowl; stir to blend. Pour in butter and stir until all dry ingredients are moistened. Break into small pieces with spoon.

Peach muffins do not keep well because fresh peaches are so wet they can make the muffins a bit soggy. They are best when eaten within two days of baking. Try making half the recipe if you won't be able to eat them within this time frame.

LEMON COCONUT MUFFINS

Makes 12 muffins.

Years ago, I used to love going through the Union Square Green Market in New York City on my way to work. One of my favorite stands was The Muffin Man, who offered up a table of delicious fresh muffins; my absolute favorite was his lemon coconut muffin. When I stopped working in the City, I searched all over to find one as good as his, to no avail. So I made them myself.

Fragrant with lemon and coconut, delicate yet with more body than a blueberry muffin, I still crave them. Fortunately, I was able to satisfy that craving with this true-to-the-original gluten-free version. Take note that the natural acidity of the lemon works with xanthan gum to tighten the muffin a bit more than muffins without lemon. They will be slightly smaller after the first day or if you freeze them.

Muffins can be stored in a tightly sealed plastic container in refrigerator or covered with plastic wrap and then with foil and stored in freezer for up to three weeks. Best when eaten within three days of baking. Rewarm briefly in microwave.

> 2 cups Brown Rice Flour Mix (see p. 6)
> $\frac{2}{3}$ cup granulated sugar
> 1 tablespoon baking powder
> 1 teaspoon baking soda
> $\frac{3}{4}$ teaspoon xanthan gum
> $\frac{1}{4}$ teaspoon salt
> 1 cup sweetened flaked coconut
> 1 packed tablespoon grated lemon rind
> $\frac{1}{2}$ cup milk
> $\frac{1}{2}$ cup canola oil
> 2 large eggs

1. Preheat oven to 350°F. Position rack in center of oven. Grease muffin pan with cooking spray.

2. Mix flour, sugar, baking powder, baking soda, xanthan gum, and salt in large mixing bowl. Add coconut and lemon rind and stir to combine.

3. Combine milk and oil in small bowl; remove 1 tablespoon of combined liquid and discard it. Beat in eggs. Add liquids to flour mixture and stir until just blended.

4. Fill muffin pans $\frac{2}{3}$ full. Sprinkle top with granulated sugar. Bake 18–25 minutes until light golden. Remove from pan and serve immediately.

LEMON POPPY SEED MUFFINS

Omit coconut. Add $\frac{1}{4}$ cup poppy seeds and 2 packed tablespoons grated lemon rind. Sprinkle top with granulated sugar.

BANANA NUT MUFFINS

Bring a basket of old-fashioned banana nut muffins to your breakfast table and watch them disappear. They are a delicious way to start the morning, and they smell heavenly while baking in the oven. Even if you didn't think you were a banana bread lover, this simple, flavorful recipe will convert you. Loaded with ripe bananas and sweet walnuts, these muffins are full of vitamin B, vitamin C, potassium, dietary fiber, and omega-3 fatty acids. They take just a few minutes to make and they keep well in the refrigerator and freezer so you can enjoy them for several days, or even weeks after you make them.

Makes 12 muffins or three 5 x 3-inch loaves.

    2 cups Brown Rice Flour Mix (see p. 6)
 2/3 cup granulated sugar
    1 tablespoon baking powder
    1 teaspoon baking soda
 3/4 teaspoon xanthan gum
 1/4 teaspoon salt
    1 teaspoon cinnamon
    1 packed cup very ripe chopped banana
      (about 2 medium bananas)
 1/2 cup chopped walnuts, optional
    2 large eggs
 1/2 cup milk
 1/2 cup canola oil
      Granulated sugar for garnish, optional

1. Preheat oven to 350°F. Position rack in center of oven. Grease muffin pan with cooking spray (or three 5 x 3 inch loaf pans).

2. Mix flour, sugar, baking powder, baking soda, xanthan gum, salt and cinnamon in large mixing bowl. Add bananas and walnuts; stir to coat evenly.

3. Combine milk and oil in small bowl; remove 1 tablespoon of combined liquid and discard it. Beat in eggs. Add liquids to banana mixture and stir until just blended.

4. Fill muffin pans 2/3 full. Bake 18–25 minutes until golden brown (35–44 minutes for loaf pans). Remove from pan and serve immediately or cool on a rack.

Muffins and bread can be stored in a tightly sealed plastic container in refrigerator or covered with plastic wrap and then with foil, and stored in freezer for up to three weeks.

Best when eaten within three days of baking. Rewarm briefly in microwave.

CHOCOLATE RICOTTA MUFFINS

Makes 10 muffins.

These muffins are so good you won't be able to keep people from eating the entire batch after you take them out of the oven. They are excellent for an afternoon snack or a with a cup of coffee in the late morning. They have a rich chocolate flavor and a tender texture. Although I always make them with fat-free milk and low-fat ricotta cheese, you could use a higher-fat milk and whole-milk ricotta, and they would still be delicious.

$1\frac{1}{4}$ cups Brown Rice Flour Mix (see p. 6)

$\frac{1}{4}$ cup unsweetened cocoa powder

$\frac{1}{2}$ cup granulated sugar

$1\frac{1}{2}$ teaspoons baking powder

$\frac{1}{2}$ teaspoon baking soda

$\frac{1}{4}$ teaspoon xanthan gum

$\frac{1}{4}$ teaspoon salt

$\frac{2}{3}$ cup semisweet chocolate chips

1 large egg

$\frac{1}{2}$ cup ricotta cheese, part skim

$\frac{2}{3}$ cup milk

2 tablespoons canola oil

2 teaspoons pure vanilla extract

1. Preheat oven to 350°F. Position rack in center of oven. Grease muffin pan with cooking spray or line with paper baking cup liners.

2. Whisk flour, cocoa, sugar, baking powder, baking soda, xanthan gum, and salt together in a large mixing bowl. Stir in chocolate chips.

3. In another medium mixing bowl, whisk egg, ricotta, milk, oil, and vanilla together until well blended.

4. Pour the milk mixture into the flour mixture and combine until well blended. Do not over beat.

5. Spoon batter into prepared muffin cups and place in center of oven. Bake for 18–20 minutes until toothpick inserted in center of a muffin comes out clean. Remove from pan and serve immediately or cool on a rack.

Muffins can be stored in a tightly sealed plastic container in refrigerator or covered with plastic wrap and then with foil and stored in freezer for up to three weeks. Best when eaten within four days of baking. Rewarm briefly in microwave.

CARROT SPICE MUFFINS

I have to admit that I only started making these muffins recently, but they have become a favorite in my household. The delicate flavor of carrot, combined with crunchy walnuts, sweet coconut, cinnamon, and nutmeg, can really brighten up a morning. If you like carrot cake, you will undoubtedly enjoy eating these muffins. The only problem will be trying not to eat too many.

2 cups Brown Rice Flour Mix (see p. 6)

⅔ cup granulated sugar

1 tablespoon baking powder

1 teaspoon baking soda

¾ teaspoon xanthan gum

2 teaspoons cinnamon

½ teaspoon nutmeg

¼ teaspoon salt

1 cup finely shredded carrot

½ cup finely chopped walnuts

½ cup sweetened shredded coconut

½ cup milk

½ cup canola oil

2 large eggs

1 teaspoon pure vanilla extract

Cinnamon sugar* for garnish

1. Preheat oven to 350°F. Position rack in center of oven. Grease muffin pan with cooking spray.

2. Mix flour, sugar, baking powder, baking soda, xanthan gum, cinnamon, nutmeg, and salt in large mixing bowl. Add carrots, walnuts, and coconut; stir to coat evenly.

3. Combine milk and oil in small bowl; remove 1 tablespoon of combined liquid and discard it. Beat in eggs and vanilla. Add liquids to flour mixture and stir until just blended.

4. Fill muffin pans ⅔ full. Sprinkle top with cinnamon sugar. Bake 18–25 minutes until light golden. Remove from pan and serve immediately or cool on a rack.

Makes 12 muffins.

Muffins can be stored in a tightly sealed plastic container in refrigerator or covered with plastic wrap and then with foil and stored in freezer for up to three weeks. Best when eaten within four days of baking. Rewarm briefly in microwave.

* To make cinnamon sugar, combine 2 tablespoons sugar with ½ teaspoon cinnamon.

CRANBERRY NUT BREAD

Makes one 9 x 5-inch
loaf or three
5 x 3-inch loaves.

It wouldn't be Thanksgiving in my home without this bread. I make it in the traditional way, flavored with sweet orange and crunchy walnuts. My mother served the original version every year, and it was the first sweet bread I tried to convert from my recipe box. The first year that I was brave enough to serve it at Thanksgiving in its new gluten-free version, I didn't say a word to anyone. Eventually, my mother noticed me eating a piece and asked me if I would get sick from the wheat. I knew then that I could stop testing the recipe.

Store bread covered tightly with plastic wrap in refrigerator for up to five days. Can be covered with plastic wrap and then with foil and stored in freezer for up to six weeks. Best when eaten within four days of baking.

2 cups Brown Rice Flour Mix (see p. 6)
1 cup granulated sugar
2 teaspoons baking powder
$\frac{3}{4}$ teaspoon xanthan gum
$\frac{3}{4}$ teaspoon salt
$\frac{1}{2}$ teaspoon baking soda
$\frac{1}{4}$ cup shortening
$\frac{2}{3}$ cup fresh orange juice
1 large egg, slightly beaten
2 cups fresh cranberries, coarsely chopped
$\frac{1}{2}$ cup shelled walnuts, coarsely chopped
1 tablespoon freshly grated orange rind
Granulated sugar, optional

1. Preheat oven to 350°F. Position rack in center of oven. Grease 9 x 5-inch loaf pan or three 5 x 3-inch loaf pans with cooking spray.

2. Mix flour, sugar, baking powder, xanthan gum, salt, and baking soda in large bowl of electric mixer.

3. Blend in shortening until mixture resembles fine cornmeal. Pour in orange juice and egg and mix just until moistened. Fold in cranberries, walnuts, and orange rind.

4. Pour batter into prepared pan, sprinkle with granulated sugar, optional, and place in center of oven. Bake about 1 hour for 9 x 5-inch loaf or 45 minutes for 5 x 3-inch loaves (until knife inserted in center comes out clean.)

5. Cool bread for 10 minutes and then remove from pan. Cool completely on rack before serving or wrapping for storage. Easiest to slice when chilled.

PUMPKIN BREAD OR MUFFINS

I like to make Pumpkin Bread in the autumn, when the fall colors are peeking through my window. It seems so perfect for morning coffee or afternoon snacks once the weather starts to get cool. Your home will be filled with the warm aroma of sweet cinnamon, ginger, nutmeg, and cloves. This recipe makes traditionally moist, tender mini-loaves or muffins. Both freeze well, so you can make some for the holidays several weeks ahead.

Makes 12 muffins or three 5 x 3-inch loaves.

1¾ cups Brown Rice Flour Mix (see p. 6)

1 cup granulated sugar

1 teaspoon baking soda

¾ teaspoon xanthan gum

¾ teaspoon salt

½ teaspoon baking powder

½ teaspoon cinnamon

½ teaspoon nutmeg

½ teaspoon ground ginger

¼ teaspoon ground cloves

2 large eggs

¼ cup water

⅓ cup plus 2 tablespoons canola oil

2 tablespoons molasses

1 cup pumpkin puree

Store bread covered tightly with plastic wrap in refrigerator for up to five days. Muffins can be stored in a tightly sealed plastic container. Pumpkin Bread or Muffins can be covered with plastic wrap and then with foil and stored in freezer for up to six weeks. Best when eaten within four days of baking.

1. Preheat oven to 350°F. Position rack in center of oven. Grease three 5 x 3-inch loaf pans or muffin pan with cooking spray.

2. Mix flour, sugar, baking soda, xanthan gum, salt, baking powder, cinnamon, nutmeg, ginger, and cloves together in large mixing bowl of electric mixer.

3. Combine eggs, water, oil, molasses, and pumpkin in a separate bowl. Whisk to blend.

4. Pour the wet ingredients into dry and mix until well blended. Do not over beat.

5. Pour batter evenly into pans and bake 45–55 minutes for loaves and about 20–25 minutes for muffins or until toothpick inserted in center comes out clean.

6. Cool loaves for 8 minutes and then remove from pans. Remove muffins from pan immediately. Cool completely on rack before serving or wrapping for storage. Easiest to slice when chilled.

TRIPLE GINGER TEA LOAF

Makes one 8 ½ x 4 ½-inch loaf or three 5 x 3-inch loaves.

I first tasted this tender tea bread more than ten years ago, when a friend brought me one for Christmas. I've been making it ever since and serving it throughout the holidays. It features a delicious blend of crystallized, fresh, and ground ginger in a fragrant loaf sweetened with light brown sugar. The bread slices more easily when chilled, so make it at least one day before you want to serve it. In fact, my gluten-free version of Triple Ginger Tea Loaf can be made well in advance (follow storage instructions below), because it stores well.

1⅔ cups Brown Rice Flour Mix (see p. 6)

2 tablespoons buttermilk powder

1½ teaspoons baking soda

½ teaspoon xanthan gum

1 teaspoon ground ginger

1 teaspoon ground cinnamon

½ teaspoon ground cardamom

½ teaspoon salt

6 tablespoons minced crystallized ginger (about 2 ounces), divided

½ cup unsalted butter, room temperature

½ cup granulated sugar

½ cup golden light brown sugar

2 large eggs

2 tablespoons grated peeled fresh ginger

½ cup water

1. Preheat oven to 350°F. Position rack in center of oven. Grease 8 ½ x 4 ½-inch loaf pan or three 5 x 3-inch loaf pans with cooking spray.

2. Mix flour, buttermilk powder, baking soda, xanthan gum, ground ginger, cinnamon, cardamom, salt, and 3 tablespoons crystallized ginger in medium bowl. Set aside.

3. Beat butter and both sugars in large bowl of electric mixer until light and fluffy. Beat in eggs one at a time. Mix in grated fresh ginger. Add flour mixture and water and mix just until blended.

4. Pour batter into prepared pans and sprinkle top with remaining 3 tablespoons minced crystallized ginger. Press ginger lightly into batter. Place in center of oven and bake 35–40 minutes for small loaves or until knife inserted in center comes out clean. Bake 50

minutes for large loaf; if necessary, turn oven to 250°F and bake another 5–10 minutes until knife inserted in center comes out clean.

5. Cool bread for 8 minutes and then remove from pans. Cool completely on rack before serving or wrapping for storage. Easiest to slice when chilled.

Store bread covered tightly with plastic wrap in refrigerator for up to five days. Can be covered with plastic wrap and then with foil and stored in freezer for up to six weeks. Best when eaten within four days of baking.

LEMON POPPY SEED TEA LOAVES

*Makes four
5 x 3-inch loaves.*

These are the kind of delicate little lemon breads you're served with your morning meal at old-fashioned bed and breakfasts. Light and bursting with lemon flavor and crunchy poppy seeds, they are one of life's pleasures. Bake up a batch to serve for a Sunday brunch or afternoon tea. In their new gluten-free form, they stay fresh for days in the refrigerator and freeze so well that you'll be able to enjoy them several weeks later.

Store breads covered tightly with plastic wrap in refrigerator for up to five days. Breads can be covered with plastic wrap and then with foil and stored in freezer for up to six weeks. Best when eaten within four days of baking.

2 cups Brown Rice Flour Mix (see p. 6)

2 teaspoons baking powder

¾ teaspoon xanthan gum

½ teaspoon salt

¼ cup poppy seeds

2 packed tablespoons grated lemon rind

1 cup granulated sugar

½ cup canola oil

3 large eggs

½ teaspoon lemon extract

¾ cup milk

Granulated sugar

1. Preheat oven to 350°F. Position rack in center of oven. Grease four 5 x 3-inch loaf pans with cooking spray.

2. Mix flour, baking powder, xanthan gum, salt, poppy seeds, and lemon rind in medium mixing bowl. Set aside.

3. Combine sugar, oil, eggs, and lemon extract in large bowl of electric mixer. Beat for 1 minute at medium-high speed. Add flour mixture and milk and mix until just blended.

4. Fill loaf pans with batter. Sprinkle tops with granulated sugar. Bake 35–40 minutes or until toothpick inserted in center comes out clean.

5. Cool breads for 10 minutes and then remove from pans. Cool completely on rack before serving or wrapping for storage. Easiest to slice when chilled.

LEMON WALNUT TEA LOAVES

Omit poppy seeds. Add ¾ cup finely chopped walnuts.

ORANGE JUICE BREAD

I have been making this bread for longer than I can remember, and it never fails to surprise me how delicate and fragrant it is. The essence of sweet orange fills the kitchen when it's baking, and then the loaf stays fresh and flavorful for days after, even in its new gluten-free form. This tender bread makes a delicious treat for cold winter mornings with your last cup of coffee or as a special accompaniment to a cup of afternoon tea.

1 1/2 cups Brown Rice Flour Mix (see p. 6)

1 1/2 teaspoons baking powder

1/2 teaspoon xanthan gum

1/4 teaspoon salt

    Grated rind from 1 large orange

1 tablespoon grated lemon rind

1/2 cup unsalted butter, room temperature

1 cup granulated sugar

2 large eggs

1/2 cup fresh orange juice

1/4 teaspoon lemon extract

    Granulated sugar

1. Preheat oven to 350°F. Position rack in center of oven. Grease 9 x 5-inch loaf pan with cooking spray.

2. Mix flour, baking powder, xanthan gum, salt, and orange and lemon rind in medium bowl. Set aside.

3. Beat butter and sugar in large bowl of electric mixer until light and fluffy. Beat in eggs one at a time. Add flour mixture, orange juice, and lemon extract and mix just until blended.

4. Pour batter into prepared pan and sprinkle top with granulated sugar. Place pan in center of oven and bake for 45 minutes or until knife inserted in center comes out clean.

5. Cool bread for 10 minutes and then remove from pan. Cool completely on rack before serving or wrapping for storage. Easiest to slice when chilled.

ORANGE JUICE PECAN BREAD

Add 3/4 cup chopped pecans.

*Makes one
9 x 5-inch loaf.*

Store bread covered tightly with plastic wrap in refrigerator for up to five days. Can be covered with plastic wrap and then with foil and stored in freezer for up to six weeks. Best when eaten within four days of baking.

TRADITIONAL SCONES

Makes 9–10 scones.

Scones have become popular in this country, although most American versions tends to be sweeter and heavier than their traditional English relatives. The best traditional scones I've had on this side of the Atlantic were in a New York City restaurant called Sarabeth's Kitchen. When I saw her recipe in a magazine many years ago, I cut it out and it became a favorite in my household.

After repeated attempts to recreate it in a gluten-free form, I came up with this recipe for a delicious traditional-style scone that soothed my longing. The trick is to make sure you really beat the eggs until they are very light and foamy. Just follow the directions carefully—no shortcuts—and you'll have a scone you could proudly serve at an English high tea.

Store leftover scones in an airtight container in refrigerator, or cover scones with plastic wrap and then with foil and store in freezer for up to three weeks. Best when eaten within four days of baking. Rewarm in a preheated 350°F oven for 5 to 10 minutes. Do not use a microwave!

$\frac{1}{2}$ cup milk

$\frac{1}{2}$ cup raisins

2 cups Brown Rice Flour Mix (see p. 6)

1 tablespoon granulated sugar

1 tablespoon baking powder

$\frac{3}{4}$ teaspoon xanthan gum

$\frac{1}{2}$ teaspoon salt

5 tablespoons unsalted butter, cut into small pieces

2 large eggs

1. Preheat oven to 425°F. Position rack in center of oven. Line heavy baking sheet with parchment paper.

2. Combine milk and raisins in glass measuring cup and set aside.

3. Combine flour, sugar, baking powder, xanthan gum, and salt in large bowl of electric mixer. With mixer on low, cut butter into flour mixture until it resembles a coarse meal. Put mixture into a small bowl and set aside.

4. Beat eggs in the same large bowl of electric mixer until *very light and foamy*. Add milk and flour mixtures all at once, and mix at medium-low speed for 1 minute. Use lightly floured hands to pat out dough into a large, 1-inch-thick round on lightly floured surface. Cut out scones with a 2$\frac{1}{2}$-inch round cookie cutter. Press dough scraps together and repeat.

5. Place dough on prepared baking sheet and put in center of oven. Turn oven temperature down to 375°F and bake 20–25 minutes until golden and cooked through. Serve warm with butter or preserves.

LEMON CORNMEAL SCONES

These fragrant, crunchy scones are bursting with lemon flavor. Traditional in shape and not too sweet, they're perfect for breakfast or afternoon tea with jam or preserves. Make sure you beat the eggs until they are very light and foamy, and follow the directions carefully. These scones keep well in the refrigerator for several days and reheat easily in a preheated oven (do not use a microwave!). They are sure to become a favorite you'll make often.

Makes 14 scones.

½ cup milk

1 cup golden raisins

1¾ cups Brown Rice Flour Mix (see p. 6)

1 cup stone-ground yellow cornmeal

¼ cup granulated sugar

4 teaspoons baking powder

¾ teaspoon xanthan gum

½ teaspoon salt

6 tablespoons unsalted butter, cut into small pieces

2 large eggs

1 teaspoon grated lemon rind

2 teaspoons pure vanilla extract

½ teaspoon pure lemon extract

Store leftover scones in an airtight container in refrigerator. Or cover them with plastic wrap and then with foil and store in freezer for up to three weeks. Best when eaten within four days of baking. Rewarm in a preheated 350°F oven for 5 to 10 minutes.

1. Preheat oven to 425°F. Position rack in center of oven. Line heavy baking sheet with parchment paper.

2. Combine milk and raisins in glass measuring cup and set aside.

3. Combine flour, cornmeal, sugar, baking powder, xanthan gum, and salt in large bowl of electric mixer. With mixer on low, cut butter into flour mixture until it resembles a coarse meal. Put mixture into a small bowl and set aside.

4. Beat eggs in the same large bowl of electric mixer until *very light and foamy*. Add milk and flour mixtures, grated lemon rind, and vanilla and lemon extracts all at once and mix at medium-low speed for 1 minute. Use lightly floured hands to pat out dough into a large, 1-inch-thick round on lightly floured surface. Cut out scones with a 2½-inch round cookie cutter. Press dough scraps together and repeat.

5. Place dough on prepared baking sheet and put in center of oven. Turn oven temperature down to 375°F and bake 20–25 minutes until golden and cooked through. Serve warm with jam or preserves.

CINNAMON ROLLS

Makes 8 rolls

Good-quality yeast doughs are particularly hard to recreate with gluten-free flours. After all, wheat has always been highly favored over other grains for its ability to produce a springy texture in baked goods. The problem seems to be compounded when we try to recreate sweet yeast doughs because of their extra fat and sugar.

Take heart: You can make homemade cinnamon rolls just like you remember them—small, warm rounds of springy dough bursting with cinnamon and topped with an old-fashioned sugar glaze. These are not the huge cinnamon buns you'll find at the mall that weigh in at more than half a pound and include several days' worth of fat and sugar. Mine are perfectly sized for comfort and so good you'll still be able to feel a little guilty. In order to come up with a soft dough, I've taken out some of the fat and sugar and used a bit of sweet rice flour. Follow the directions carefully, and you'll have everyone in the house swarming the kitchen waiting for you to pull them out of the oven.

Rolls can be prepared in advance. Bake according to directions, remove from oven, and allow to cool in pan on a rack. Store in a tightly sealed plastic container in refrigerator for up to three days. Wrap well in plastic wrap and then foil to store in freezer for up to three weeks. Wrap in foil and rewarm in 350°F preheated oven, or reheat briefly in microwave.

Filling

$1/3$ cup packed dark brown sugar

$3/4$ teaspoon cinnamon

$1/4$ teaspoon nutmeg, optional

Dough

7 tablespoons skim or 2% milk, heated to 110°F

1 tablespoon dry yeast granules (not quick-rise)

$1/4$ cup sweet rice flour (see p. 7), separated

$1/4$ cup granulated sugar, separated

2 large eggs (room temperature is best)

2 tablespoons canola oil

$1^3/4$ cups Brown Rice Flour Mix (see p. 6)

$1^1/4$ teaspoon xanthan gum

$1/2$ teaspoon salt

Rice flour (about 2 tablespoons, used to flour board)

1 tablespoon melted unsalted butter

Glaze

$3/4$ cup confectioners' sugar

1 tablespoon milk or half and half

$1/2$ teaspoon pure vanilla extract

1. Combine brown sugar, cinnamon, and nutmeg (optional) in a small bowl and set aside.

2. Combine warm milk (110°F), yeast, 1 tablespoon of the sweet rice flour, and 1 tablespoon of the sugar in a measuring cup; stir until well blended. Cover with a towel and set aside for 5 to 10 minutes until mixture becomes foamy.

3. Mix eggs and canola oil together in a small bowl and set aside.

4. Lightly grease a 9-inch round cake pan with cooking spray.

5. Mix brown rice flour mix, xanthan gum, salt, and remaining 3 tablespoons sweet rice flour and 3 tablespoons sugar in large bowl of electric mixer. Add warm milk/yeast mixture, egg and oil to the bowl; mix until just blended. Scrape bowl and beaters and then beat at high speed for 3 minutes.

6. Liberally spread rice flour over surface of a wooden board and lightly flour hands. Use a spatula to move dough out onto the wooden board in a ball shape. Dough will be sticky. Roll dough around in the rice flour until it is lightly covered. Gently press into a 12 x 8-inch rectangle with your hands.

7. Lightly brush melted butter over top of rolled dough and sprinkle with brown sugar and cinnamon mixture. Starting with 8-inch side, carefully roll dough jelly-roll fashion. Do not roll dough tightly; the individual rolls will rise better if they are more loosely rolled.

8. Use a small, sharp knife to cut 8-inch roll of dough into eight 1-inch slices. (Don't worry if slices seem loosely rolled). Coat knife with rice flour if dough is sticking to it.

9. Carefully arrange slices in prepared cake pan so that they do not touch (put six around the outside of the pan and two in the middle). Cover with a light cloth and let rise in a warm place until rolls have doubled or more in size and have filled pan (80°F is ideal and almost essential for this very heavy dough to rise in 1 to 1 ½ hours).

10. Preheat oven to 375°F. Position rack in center of oven. Place rolls in center of oven and bake about 20 minutes, until light golden and cooked through.

11. Combine confectioners' sugar, milk, and vanilla in a small bowl and stir until smooth and creamy. Spoon over top of rolls. Serve warm.

Cook's Note: Dry ingredients can be mixed ahead and stored in plastic containers for future use, but do not add yeast until ready to bake rolls.

HOT CROSS BUNS

Makes 9 buns

I have vivid memories of my father making hot cross buns for my mother at Easter time. After several years of ignoring my desire for this traditional holiday food, I succumbed and attempted to make them gluten-free. You may (or may not) be able to imagine how many rounds of testing it took before I discovered a way to make a soft, delicate, somewhat chewy bun, but I am thankful I had friends and family to share all the not-so-perfect versions. I am also thankful that I was able to find a square cupcake pan to inspire me to try the recipe. I flavor my buns with plump raisins and candied orange peel the way my father did, but you may make your own version flavored with cherries or cinnamon. No matter what you add to your dough, you'll find that making gluten-free hot cross buns is easier and faster than making them with wheat—and, according to my father, just as delicious.

Dough

- 1 cup skim or 2% milk, heated to 110°F
- 1 packet (¼ oz.) active dry yeast granules (not quick-rise)
- 2 tablespoons sweet rice flour (see p. 7), separated
- ¼ cup granulated sugar, separated
- 2 large eggs (room temperature is best)
- 2 tablespoons canola oil
- 1¾ cups Brown Rice Flour Mix (see p. 6)
- 1¼ teaspoon xanthan gum
- ½ teaspoon salt
- ½ cup golden raisins
- ⅓ cup candied orange peel*

Icing

- ¾ cup confectioners' sugar
- 1 tablespoon milk
- ½ teaspoon pure vanilla extract

1. Combine warm milk (110°F), yeast, 1 tablespoon of the sweet rice flour mix, and 1 tablespoon of the sugar in a measuring cup; stir until well blended. Cover with a towel and set aside for 5 to 10 minutes until mixture becomes foamy.

2. Mix eggs and canola oil together in a small bowl and set aside.

3. Lightly grease 9 cups of a 12-cup square muffin pan (if you use a square cupcake pan, your Hot Cross Buns will look just like wheat

Buns are best when fresh but can be prepared in advance. Bake according to directions, remove from oven, and allow to cool in pan on a rack. Store in a tightly sealed plastic container in refrigerator for up to three days. Wrap well in plastic wrap and then foil to store in freezer for up to two weeks. To reheat, freshen buns by sprinkling bottom and sides with a bit of water, wrap in foil, and warm in preheated 350°F oven about 15 minutes, or reheat briefly in microwave. Icing may melt a bit when reheated. For best presentation when preparing ahead, ice after reheating.

Cook's Note: Dry ingredients can be mixed ahead and stored in plastic containers for future use, but do not add yeast until ready to bake rolls.

ones—see Cook's Note on this page) or 12-cup cupcake pan with cooking spray. If you use a regular cupcake pan, this recipe will make 10–12 buns; be sure to fill each cupcake form no more than half way.

4. Mix brown rice flour mix, xanthan gum, salt, remaining 1 tablespoon sweet rice flour, and remaining 3 tablespoons sugar in large bowl of electric mixer. Add warm milk/yeast mixture and egg and oil mixture to the bowl; mix until just blended. Scrape bowl and beaters and then beat at high speed for 3 minutes. Mix in raisins and candied orange peel.

5. Pour dough into prepared muffin or cupcake pan. Cover with a light cloth and let rise in a warm place until buns have doubled or more in size and have filled pan (80°F is ideal and almost essential for this very heavy dough to rise in about 1 hour).

6. Preheat oven to 375°F. Position rack in center of oven. Place buns in center of oven and bake about 20–25 minutes (15–20 minutes if you use a regular cupcake pan), until golden brown and cooked through.

7. Use a sharp, pointed knife to go around the edges of the buns. Remove them from the baking pan and cool on a rack about 30 minutes.

8. Combine confectioners' sugar, milk, and vanilla in a small bowl and stir until smooth and creamy. Spoon icing into small pastry tube fitted with a medium size tip. Pipe onto buns in the shape of a cross.

Cook's Note: A square muffin pan is a square cupcake pan with 12 individual square forms. Size: 16" x 11". It is available at fine cookware stores or online retailers (Amazon).

* I recommend a high quality candied orange peel like the one available in The Baker's Catalogue from King Arthur Flour (1-800-827-6836, or bakerscatalogue.com).

CHAPTER 5

Cakes

YELLOW LAYER CAKE

VANILLA CUPCAKES

VANILLA (BUTTER) LAYER CAKE

LEMON LAYER CAKE

MAPLE WALNUT CAKE

COCONUT LAYER CAKE

HAZELNUT CAKE

CHOCOLATE FUDGE CAKE

GERMAN CHOCOLATE CAKE

FLOURLESS CHOCOLATE CAKE

ANGEL FOOD CAKE

VANILLA SPONGE CAKE or
JELLY ROLL

CHOCOLATE SPONGE CAKE or
JELLY ROLL

CARROT CAKE

GINGERBREAD

NEW YORK CHEESECAKE

CLASSIC CHEESECAKE

CUSTARD CAKE WITH FRUIT
Custard Cake with Cherries

SOUR CREAM COFFEE CAKE

CRUMB CAKE

VANILLA POUND CAKE
Chocolate Chip Pound Cake

LEMON POUND CAKE
Lemon Blueberry Pound Cake
Lemon Poppy Seed Pound Cake

EUROPEAN-STYLE YEAST
COFFEE CAKE (CHEESE FILLED)

WE ARE LUCKY. Cake comes in so many shapes, sizes, textures, and flavors that we are sure to have a favorite, no matter how particular we are. The trick is converting that favorite to gluten-free. I found after much trial and error that there are tricks to making a great gluten-free cake. Some are common sense and basic, and others will start to make sense once you understand the nature of the ingredients.

Since gluten-free flours tend to be heavier and grainier than wheat, it is important to use finely ground brown rice flour for cake. Because the flours can produce a denser crumb, we often use canola oil instead of butter with great results (and we often use slightly less fat in general). We typically use less liquid and a little more leavening. We have to adjust flavors: reduce salt, for example, because it will stand out, and increase vanilla or other extracts to cover up the lack of wheat. We also use the smallest pan possible to get a good rise because no matter how hard you try, it will be difficult to get a round 12-inch or a 9 x 12-inch gluten-free cake to rise correctly with layers of traditional thickness. If you want to make very large rounds for a wedding cake (12 or 16-inch rounds), make *thin* layers and carefully adjust your baking time (it will take slightly less time).

There are a wide variety of cakes in this chapter. Some are so simple, like Vanilla Cupcakes and Chocolate Chip Pound Cake, that you might make them all the time. Others, such as the Angel Food Cake, might seem more complicated. But if you follow the directions, you will be able to make a fabulous cake that you'll be delighted to serve. If you are new to baking cakes from scratch, start with the Vanilla Cupcakes or Yellow Layer Cake. They are so easy that I use them in my Introduction to Gluten-Free Baking class. With one success under your apron, branch out and try some of the others until you can make all your favorites.

This chapter uses the following pans:

- 8-inch round cake pan
- 9-inch round cake pan
- 12-muffin pan
- 9-inch (across the top) kugelhoph crown-shaped mold, or a fluted ring mold that holds 8 to 10 cups filled to the top rim (it is also called a small bundt pan with 4- to 6-cup capacity)
- 9-inch flat-bottom tube pan with removable bottom
- 9-inch round springform pan
- 10-inch springform pan
- Three 5 x 3-inch loaf pans
- Glass (Pyrex) or ceramic deep-dish pie pan (for custard cake)

THE LAST WORD ON CAKES

- Set up before starting the recipe: assemble all the ingredients.
- Separate eggs when they are cold, and then let them warm to room temperature.
- Measure carefully (see Chapter 3).
- *Follow the directions carefully.* When it says beat the eggs until foamy before adding sugar, or add sugar to the eggs (or butter) a little at a time, or beat eggs until thick and lemon colored, or beat butter until light and fluffy—please follow the directions, because there's a reason for them.
- Use the right size pan.
- Preheat the oven to the proper temperature (make sure the oven is calibrated correctly).
- Do not open the oven door more than necessary.
- Use a timer because you can get distracted.
- Once you mix the liquids into the dry ingredients, you need to get your cakes into the oven fairly quickly. The baking powder leaps into action once it is combined with the liquid and creates the air pockets that will help your baked goods to rise. So make sure your oven is preheated and your pans are prepared; it will make a difference in the texture and lightness of your baked goods.
- Typically, a cake cracks or rises and then falls because it is rising too fast. Your oven could be running a bit hot; check it with an oven thermometer. Are you using dark pans (dark pans require lower temperatures because they absorb more radiant heat)? Did you measure the baking powder correctly? Perhaps you're using too much. It is also very important not to overbeat cake batters (particularly the Chocolate Fudge Cake, German Chocolate Cake, Pound Cake, Sour Cream Coffee Cake, and Crumb Cake). They will rise too fast and fall in the middle. This often happens when home bakers use professional-sized mixers (particularly KitchenAid's). These pro mixers are actually too large to make many "home-sized" recipes. The mixing bowl on the mixer is too large for the amount of batter, so it's difficult to beat the batter correctly. Home bakers tend to compensate by overbeating the batter without realizing it.

YELLOW LAYER CAKE

One way to tell the quality of a baker is by how good their most basic cake is—not the icing, mind you, just the cake by itself. The texture, taste, and appearance of this cake will please and delight you if you've been looking for a great yellow cake. It is versatile and can be used with light whipped frostings as well as denser buttercreams and chocolate ganache. It holds up well in the refrigerator and can also be frozen for up to three weeks. You will find this basic yellow cake a welcome addition to your gluten-free baking repertoire.

Makes two 8- or 9-inch rounds or 24 cupcakes.

2 cups granulated sugar

4 large eggs

2½ cups Brown Rice Flour Mix (see p. 6)

½ teaspoon salt

1 tablespoon baking powder

1 teaspoon xanthan gum

1 cup canola oil

1 cup milk

2 teaspoons pure vanilla extract

2 cups of your favorite frosting

1. Preheat oven to 350°F. Position rack in center of oven. Line 2 round 9-inch layer cake pans with parchment or wax paper and spray with cooking spray.

2. Beat sugar and eggs in large bowl of electric mixer at medium speed for 1 minute. Add flour, salt, baking powder, xanthan gum, oil, milk, and vanilla; beat at medium speed for 1 minute.

3. Pour batter into prepared pans. Place in center of oven and bake about 35 minutes (40 minutes for an 8-inch cake, 18–20 minutes for cupcakes) or until center springs back when touched and cake has pulled away from sides of pan.

4. Cool cake layers in the pans on a rack for 5 minutes. Use a small knife to cut around pan sides to loosen cake. Invert cake layers onto a rack, peel off parchment, and cool completely.

5. Place one cake layer on a platter. Spread 1 cup of frosting over top and sides. Place second layer on top. Spread remaining frosting over entire cake.

Serve slightly chilled or at room temperature. Can be made a day ahead. Store frosted cake in refrigerator. Unfrosted cake layers can be covered tightly with plastic wrap and stored in refrigerator for one day. Unfrosted cake layers can also be covered with plastic wrap and then with foil and stored in freezer for up to three weeks. Best when eaten within three days of baking.

To make a four-layer cake: chill unfrosted layers until very cold or freeze briefly. Slice horizontally across each layer.

VANILLA CUPCAKES

Makes 12 cupcakes or one 8- or 9-inch round.

These vanilla cupcakes are delicious and easy to make; they literally take minutes to prepare. Once you try them, you'll think twice about using a cake mix ever again. The recipe is actually the Yellow Layer Cake (preceding recipe) cut in half because that is how I came to use it the most: for a small, quick batch of cupcakes. The texture of the cake is light and flavorful, with a tender crumb. Use your favorite frostings, or create mini-shortcakes with fresh fruit and whipped cream. But no matter how you make them, these cupcakes are sure to become a favorite in your home.

Serve slightly chilled or at room temperature. Can be made a day ahead. Store frosted cupcakes in refrigerator. Unfrosted cupcakes can be covered tightly with plastic wrap and stored in refrigerator for one day. Unfrosted cupcakes can also be covered with plastic wrap and then with foil and stored in freezer for up to three weeks. Best when eaten within three days of baking.

1 cup granulated sugar

2 large eggs

1 ¼ cups Brown Rice Flour Mix (see p. 6)

¼ teaspoon salt

1 ½ teaspoons baking powder

½ teaspoon xanthan gum

½ cup canola oil

½ cup milk

1 teaspoon pure vanilla extract

Prepared frosting

1. Preheat oven to 350°F. Position rack in center of oven. Place cupcake baking liners in a 12-cupcake baking pan.

2. Beat sugar and eggs in large bowl of electric mixer at medium speed for 1 minute. Add flour, salt, baking powder, xanthan gum, oil, milk, and vanilla; beat at medium speed for 1 minute.

3. Pour batter into prepared pan. Place in center of oven and bake for about 20 minutes or until center springs back when touched and cupcakes are very lightly browned (bake about 35 minutes for 9-inch round, 40 minutes for 8-inch round).

4. Cool on rack for 5 minutes. Remove cupcakes from pan onto rack and cool completely before icing.

5. Top with your favorite frosting.

VANILLA (BUTTER) LAYER CAKE

I originally created this cake for a woman who wanted a gluten-free white wedding cake. She was looking for the slightly firmer consistency of cakes used to make the tiered pastry extravaganzas we associate with those festive occasions. The original version used separated eggs, but I found I was able to skip that step and still make a great cake that rose well, had a fine texture, and tasted delicious. Unlike white cakes made with wheat, the egg yolks are needed to give structure, so this cake will not really be white in the purest sense. But it is so good no one will even notice.

1 1/2 cups granulated sugar

1/2 cup unsalted butter, room temperature

4 large eggs, room temperature

2 cups Brown Rice Flour Mix (see p. 6)

1/2 teaspoon salt

1 tablespoon baking powder

1/2 teaspoon xanthan gum

3/4 cup milk (fat-free can be used)

2 teaspoons pure vanilla extract

2 cups of your favorite frosting

1. Preheat oven to 375°F. Position rack in center of oven. Line bottoms of two 8- or 9-inch round cake pans with wax paper or parchment. Very lightly grease and flour sides of pans with baking spray and approximately 1/2 teaspoon rice flour.

2. Beat butter and sugar in large bowl of electric mixer until light and fluffy. Add eggs one at a time, blending each one in before adding the next. Scrape bowl and beaters. Add flour, salt, baking powder, xanthan gum, milk, and vanilla; beat at medium speed for 1 minute.

3. Pour batter into prepared pans. Place in center of oven and bake for about 25 minutes for 8-inch rounds (20 minutes for 9-inch rounds) or until a toothpick inserted into center comes out clean.

4. Cool on rack for 7 minutes. Use a small knife to cut around pan sides to loosen cake. Invert cake layers onto a rack, peel off paper, and cool completely.

5. Place one cake layer on a platter. Spread 1 cup of frosting over top and sides. Place second layer on top. Spread remaining frosting over entire cake.

Makes two 8- or 9-inch rounds. Recipe can be cut in half.

Serve slightly chilled or at room temperature. Can be made a day ahead. Store frosted cake in refrigerator. Unfrosted cake layers can be covered tightly with plastic wrap and stored in refrigerator for one day. Unfrosted cake layers can also be covered with plastic wrap and then with foil and stored in freezer for up to three weeks. Best when eaten within three days of baking.

To make a four-layer cake, chill unfrosted layers until very cold or freeze briefly. Slice horizontally across each layer.

LEMON LAYER CAKE

Makes two 8- or 9-inch rounds or 24 cupcakes. Recipe can be cut in half.

Lemon layer cake was one of my father's favorite birthday cakes when I was little, and I have always loved it as well. This cake is bursting with lemon flavor featured in a variety of melt-in-your-mouth textures: velvety cake, creamy buttercream, and a cool pudding-like lemon curd filling. But don't wait for a birthday party. Make this delicious cake for the lemon lover in your life. It can help turn any meal into a celebration.

Serve slightly chilled or at room temperature. Can be made a day ahead. Store frosted cake in refrigerator. Unfrosted cake layers can be covered tightly with plastic wrap and stored in refrigerator for one day. Unfrosted cake layers can also be covered with plastic wrap and then with foil and stored in freezer for up to three weeks. Best when eaten within three days of baking.

> 2 cups granulated sugar
> 4 large eggs
> 2$\frac{1}{2}$ cups Brown Rice Flour Mix (see p. 6)
> $\frac{1}{2}$ teaspoon salt
> 1 tablespoon baking powder
> 1 teaspoon xanthan gum
> 1 cup canola oil
> 1 cup milk
> 1 teaspoon pure vanilla extract
> 1 teaspoon pure lemon extract
> 1 tablespoon grated lemon rind
> Lemon Curd Filling and Lemon Buttercream Frosting (recipes follow)

1. Preheat oven to 350°F. Position rack in center of oven. Line two round 9-inch layer cake pans with parchment or wax paper and spray lightly with cooking spray.

2. Beat sugar and eggs in large bowl of electric mixer at medium speed for 1 minute. Add flour, salt, baking powder, xanthan gum, oil, milk, vanilla extract, lemon extract, and lemon rind; beat at medium speed for 1 minute.

3. Pour batter into prepared pans. Place in center of oven and bake about 35 minutes (40 minutes for an 8-inch cake; 18–20 minutes for cupcakes) or until center springs back when touched and cake has pulled away from sides of pan.

4. Cool cake layers in the pans on a rack for 5 minutes. Use a small knife to cut around pan sides to loosen cake. Invert cake layers onto a rack, peel off paper, and cool completely.

5. Carefully slice each layer in half horizontally to create four layers (this is more easily done when cake has been chilled). Spread each

of the two bottom layers with ½ of the lemon curd. Cover each bottom layer with one of the two remaining top layers.

6. Place one set of filled layers on a cake plate and spread with about ½ cup frosting. Place the other set of filled layers on top and cover top and sides of cake with remaining frosting.

LEMON CURD FILLING

  3 egg yolks
¼ cup plus 2 tablespoons granulated sugar
¼ cup fresh lemon juice
¼ cup unsalted butter, cut into 4 pieces
¼ teaspoon guar gum*
  2 teaspoons grated lemon rind
¼ teaspoon lemon extract

1. Combine egg yolks, sugar, and lemon juice in a small saucepan and whisk until well blended.

2. Cook over medium-low heat until smooth and so thick that curd coats the back of a wooden spoon (this should take 5–7 minutes). Whisk in butter, one piece at a time, until completely incorporated. Whisk in guar gum, lemon rind, and lemon extract.

3. Pour the curd into a small bowl and cover with wax paper or plastic wrap. Chill until very cold.

Guar gum will add viscosity to the curd and keep it from seeping into the cake layers. You would not use guar gum in a lemon curd tart. It is not necessary to use it here, but the end result will be better.

LEMON BUTTERCREAM FROSTING

  1 cup unsalted butter
3½ cups confectioners' sugar, divided
¼ cup fresh lemon juice
½ teaspoon lemon extract
  2 teaspoons grated lemon rind

1. Beat butter in large bowl of electric mixer until light and fluffy. Add 1 cup confectioners' sugar, lemon juice, lemon extract, and lemon rind; beat to blend. Add remaining sugar and beat until creamy.

MAPLE WALNUT CAKE

Makes two 8- or
9-inch rounds.
Recipe can be
cut in half.

Maple Walnut Cake is a much-requested favorite in my house. This cake blends the taste of sweet summer apricots with autumn walnuts and winter-rich maple flavor. I tend to make it in the cooler months because the flavors are so warm; it is comfort food in the truest sense.

2 cups granulated sugar

4 large eggs

2$\frac{1}{2}$ cups Brown Rice Flour Mix (see p. 6)

$\frac{1}{2}$ teaspoon salt

1 tablespoon baking powder

1 teaspoon xanthan gum

1 cup canola oil

1 cup milk

2 teaspoons pure vanilla extract

$\frac{2}{3}$–1 cup apricot butter or preserves*

Maple Buttercream Frosting (recipe follows)

2 cups crushed walnuts

Serve slightly chilled or at room temperature. Can be made a day ahead. Store frosted cake in refrigerator. Unfrosted cake layers can be covered tightly with plastic wrap and stored in refrigerator for one day. Unfrosted cake layers can be covered with plastic wrap and then with foil and stored in freezer for up to three weeks. Best when eaten within three days of baking.

* We recommend Simon Fischer® Golden Apricot Butter

1. Preheat oven to 350°F. Position rack in center of oven. Line two 9-inch round layer cake pans with parchment or wax paper and spray lightly with cooking spray.

2. Beat sugar and eggs in large bowl of electric mixer at medium speed for 1 minute. Add flour, salt, baking powder, xanthan gum, oil, milk, and vanilla; beat at medium speed for 1 minute.

3. Pour batter into prepared pans. Place in center of oven and bake for 35 minutes (40 minutes for an 8-inch cake) or until center springs back when touched and cake has pulled away from sides of pan.

4. Cool cake layers in the pans on a rack for 5 minutes. Use a small knife to cut around pan sides to loosen cake. Invert cake layers onto a rack, peel off paper, and cool completely.

5. Carefully slice each layer in half to create four layers (this is more easily done when cake has been chilled). Spread each of the two bottom layers with $\frac{1}{3}$ to $\frac{1}{2}$ cup apricot butter or preserves. Cover each bottom layer with one of the two remaining top layers.

6. Place one set of filled layers on a cake plate and spread with about ½ cup frosting. Place the other set of filled layers on top and cover top and sides of cake with remaining frosting. Gently press crushed walnuts onto top and sides of cake.

MAPLE BUTTERCREAM FROSTING

1 cup unsalted butter

3 cups confectioners' sugar, divided

2 tablespoons very strong black coffee

1 tablespoon maple extract

1 tablespoon milk

1. Beat butter in large bowl of electric mixer until light and fluffy. Add 1 cup confectioners' sugar, coffee, and maple extract; beat to blend. Add remaining sugar and milk and beat until creamy.

COCONUT LAYER CAKE

Makes two 8- or 9-inch
rounds or 24 cupcakes.
Recipe can be
cut in half.

Luscious coconut cakes: You see them proudly displayed in quaint cafes, on the long tables of church suppers, and on the covers of food magazines. Many of us have a favorite recipe, and this is mine. I created it years ago, and it converted beautifully to its new gluten-free form. I happily make it for my coconut-loving friends whenever I can.

> 2 cups granulated sugar
> 4 large eggs
> 2$\frac{1}{2}$ cups Brown Rice Flour Mix (see p. 6)
> $\frac{1}{2}$ teaspoon salt
> 1 tablespoon baking powder
> 1 teaspoon xanthan gum
> 1 cup canola oil
> 1 cup unsweetened coconut milk (not low-fat)
> 1 teaspoon pure vanilla extract
> 1 teaspoon coconut extract
> Coconut Frosting (recipe follows)
> $\frac{1}{2}$–$\frac{3}{4}$ cup sweetened flaked coconut, optional

Serve slightly chilled or
at room temperature.
Can be made a day
ahead. Store frosted
cake in refrigerator.
Unfrosted cake layers
can be covered tightly
with plastic wrap and
stored in refrigerator for
one day. Unfrosted cake
layers can also be cov-
ered with plastic wrap
and then with foil and
stored in freezer for up
to three weeks. Best
when eaten within
three days of baking.

To make a four-layer
cake, chill unfrosted layers until very cold or
freeze briefly. Slice horizontally across each
layer.

1. Preheat oven to 350°F. Position rack in center of oven. Line two 8-inch round layer cake pans with parchment or wax paper and spray lightly with cooking spray.

2. Beat sugar and eggs in large bowl of electric mixer at medium speed for 1 minute. Add flour, salt, baking powder, xanthan gum, oil, coconut milk, and vanilla and coconut extracts; beat at medium speed for 1 minute.

3. Pour batter into prepared pans. Place in center of oven and bake about 40 minutes (35 minutes for a 9-inch cake; 18–20 minutes for cupcakes) or until center springs back when touched and cake has pulled away from sides of pan.

4. Cool cake layers in the pans on a rack for 5 minutes. Use a small knife to cut around pan sides to loosen cake. Invert cake layers onto a rack, peel off paper, and cool completely.

5. Place one cake layer on a platter. Spread 1 cup of frosting over top and sides. Place second layer on top. Spread remaining frosting over entire cake. Pat sweetened flaked coconut onto the sides of the cake.

COCONUT FROSTING

$1/2$ cup unsalted butter, room temperature

4 ozs. low-fat cream cheese, room temperature

3 cups confectioners' sugar, sifted if lumpy

$1/4$ cup unsweetened coconut milk

$1/2$ teaspoon pure vanilla extract

$1/2$ teaspoon coconut extract

1. Beat butter and cream cheese in large bowl of electric mixer until light and fluffy.
2. Add confectioners' sugar, coconut milk, vanilla, and coconut extract and beat at low speed until well blended and smooth.

HAZELNUT CAKE

Makes two 9-inch rounds.

Hazelnut cake was always my favorite birthday cake and the only one my family ever purchased (from a favorite bakery). The original wheat version was made with a hazelnut-enhanced genoise, a rich, not-too-sweet hazelnut praline butter-cream, and an abundance of dark chocolate shavings. I was determined to recreate it gluten-free. I knew from teaching baking classes that only the most hardy, experienced bakers don't run in terror from a recipe for genoise. I enhanced my easy-to-make vanilla cake with freshly ground hazelnuts, created a simple butter-cream from a purchased praline and homemade custard base (my homemade praline wasn't as true to the one in the original cake as the brand I recommend), and then I quickly learned how to make chocolate curls without slicing my fingers (actually, my youngest son, Bradford, developed the winning technique I use here). Try my favorite birthday cake for your next birthday.

Serve at room temperature for best flavor. Can be made a day ahead. Store frosted cake in refrigerator. Unfrosted cake layers can be covered tightly with plastic wrap and stored in refrigerator for one day. Unfrosted cake layers can be covered with plastic wrap and then with foil, and stored in freezer for up to three weeks. Best when eaten within three days of baking.

> 2 cups granulated sugar
>
> 4 large eggs
>
> 2 cups Brown Rice Flour Mix (see p. 6)
>
> 1/2 cup very finely ground hazelnuts
>
> 1/2 teaspoon salt
>
> 3 teaspoons baking powder
>
> 1 teaspoon xanthan gum
>
> 1 cup canola oil
>
> 1 cup milk
>
> 2 teaspoons pure vanilla extract
>
> Hazelnut Praline Buttercream (recipe follows)
>
> Chocolate Shavings (recipe follows)

1. Preheat oven to 350°F. Position rack in center of oven. Line two round 9-inch layer cake pans with parchment paper or wax paper and grease with cooking spray.

2. Beat sugar and eggs in large bowl of electric mixer at medium speed for one minute. Add flour, ground hazelnuts, salt, baking powder, xanthan gum, oil, milk, and vanilla; beat at medium speed for one minute.

3. Pour batter into prepared pans. Place in center of oven and bake about 35 minutes or until center springs back to touch and cake has pulled away from sides of the pan.

4. Cool cake layers in the pans on a rack for 5 minutes. Use a small knife to cut around pan sides to loosen cake. Invert cake layers onto

a rack, peel off parchment paper, and cool completely.

5. Carefully slice each layer in half to create four layers (this is more easily done when cake has been chilled). Spread each of the two bottom layers with ½ cup of the Hazelnut Praline Buttercream. Cover with the two remaining top layers.

6. Place one set of layers on a cake plate and spread with about ½ cup Hazelnut Praline Buttercream. Place the other set of layers on top and cover top and sides of cake with remaining frosting. Completely cover top of cake with chocolate curls and sides with Chocolate Shavings (instructions on next page).

HAZELNUT PRALINE BUTTERCREAM

2 large egg yolks

⅓ cup granulated sugar

2 tablespoons corn starch

⅛ teaspoon salt

1 cup milk

1 10-oz. can Love n Bake Hazelnut Praline*

1½ cups unsalted butter

1½ cups confectioners' sugar

Love n Bake Hazelnut Praline is sold in fine grocery stores and specialty shops or online at www.kingarthurflour.com and www.lovenbake.com.

1. Beat egg yolks in large bowl of electric mixer at medium-high speed until foamy. Gradually add sugar a little at a time and continue beating until the mixture is pale yellow and thick. Add the corn starch and salt and beat until well blended.

2. Bring milk to a boil in a large heavy saucepan over medium-high heat while you are beating the egg yolks.

3. With the mixer on low, gradually add hot milk to egg mixture in a thin stream. Quickly scrap sides and bottom of bowl and mix at medium speed until well blended.

4. Pour the custard mixture back into the saucepan and cook it over a medium high heat, stirring constantly with a wire whip, until it comes to a boil and thickens. Lower heat and cook for one minute more. Remove from heat.

5. Put custard in small bowl or plastic container to cool. Cover top with plastic wrap to prevent a skim from forming over the surface and chill in the refrigerator. (Can be stored in refrigerator for up to five days. Keep plastic wrap on surface.)

6. Put hazelnut praline in large bowl of electric mixer and beat with wire whip attachment until well blended (praline separates in the can and needs to be re-blended). Add cooled custard and beat until creamy. Set aside in small bowl and cover top with plastic to prevent a skin from forming.

7. Beat butter in the same large bowl of electric mixer until light and fluffy. Add confectioners' sugar and beat at high speed until well blended and smooth. Add custard praline mixture and beat until light and creamy.

CHOCOLATE SHAVINGS

6 ozs. good quality semisweet chocolate chopped into very small pieces

You can also make simpler (but less impressive) shavings by using a vegetable peeler to cut shavings and curls off a slightly-above-room-temperature bar of semisweet chocolate.

1. Melt chocolate in a small, heavy saucepan over medium-low heat; stir constantly until it is just melted and smooth. Pour melted chocolate onto a large marble slab or a very large baking sheet and smooth out the chocolate into a large rectangle (about 8 x 11 inches) with a long off-set spatula. Allow the chocolate to cool until it is firm enough to allow you to make curls and shavings with a cheese slicer. Separate large "curls" from smaller shavings.

CHOCOLATE FUDGE CAKE

If your mouth has been watering for an old-fashioned chocolate layer cake, then here is just the thing: moist and dense but not heavy; rich and fudgy, but not too sweet. If you follow these easy directions, you can whip up this cake in no time. Even better, no one will be able to tell it is gluten-free. You can make it for a special celebration, use the batter to make cupcakes for birthday parties (bake about 20 minutes), or make it just because you've been craving a fabulous piece of cake. Pour yourself a cold glass of milk or a hot, steamy cup of coffee and dig in!

4 ozs. unsweetened chocolate, chopped

1¾ cups Brown Rice Flour Mix (see p. 6)

¼ cup unsweetened cocoa powder

2 teaspoons baking powder

1 teaspoon baking soda

½ teaspoon salt

¾ teaspoon xanthan gum

½ cup canola oil

1½ cups fat-free milk

2 cups granulated sugar

2 large eggs

2 teaspoons pure vanilla extract

2 cups of your favorite frosting

1. Preheat oven to 350°F. Position rack in center of oven. Line two 9-inch round layer cake pans with parchment or wax paper and spray lightly with cooking spray.

2. Melt chocolate in small, heavy saucepan over low heat, stirring constantly. Remove from heat and cool until lukewarm.

3. Put flour, cocoa powder, baking powder, baking soda, salt, and xanthan gum in medium bowl and whisk until thoroughly combined. Set aside.

4. Place canola oil and milk in a liquid measuring cup and whisk until thoroughly combined. Remove two tablespoons of liquid and discard. Set aside.

5. Beat sugar and eggs in large bowl of electric mixer at medium speed until light and fluffy. Blend in melted chocolate and vanilla. Add dry and wet ingredients in two additions at low speed, then mix at medium speed for 1 more minute.

Makes two 8- or 9-inch rounds or 24 cupcakes. Recipe can be cut in half.

Serve slightly chilled or at room temperature. Can be made a day ahead. Store frosted cake in refrigerator. Unfrosted cake layers can be covered tightly with plastic wrap and stored in refrigerator for one day. Unfrosted cake layers can also be covered with plastic wrap and then with foil and stored in freezer for up to two weeks. Best when eaten within three days of baking.

To make a four-layer cake, chill unfrosted layers until very cold or freeze briefly. Slice horizontally across each layer.

6. Pour batter into prepared pans. Place in center of oven and bake for 30–35 minutes or until a toothpick inserted in the center of a layer comes out clean. (Bake 35–40 minutes for 8-inch rounds; 18–20 minutes for cupcakes).

7. Cool cake layers in the pans on a rack for 5 minutes. Use a small knife to cut around pan sides to loosen cake. Invert cake layers onto a rack, peel off paper, and cool completely.

8. Place one cake layer on a platter. Spread 1 cup of frosting over top and sides. Place second layer on top. Spread remaining frosting over entire cake.

GERMAN CHOCOLATE CAKE

Chocolate and coconut together? It doesn't get better than this cake. In fact, it is so good in its new gluten-free form that no one will even notice the lack of wheat, much less miss it. Serve this fabulous German Chocolate Cake after tangy summer barbecues or savory cold-weather stews. No matter when you bring it to the table, you'll get big smiles.

Makes two 9-inch rounds. Recipe can be cut in half.

6 ozs. Baker's German sweet chocolate, chopped

$^1/_2$ cup water

$2^1/_4$ cups Brown Rice Flour Mix (see p. 6)

2 teaspoons baking soda

$^1/_4$ teaspoon salt

1 teaspoon xanthan gum

$^1/_4$ cup buttermilk powder

1 cup canola oil

$^3/_4$ cup plus 2 tablespoons water

4 large eggs

2 cups granulated sugar

2 teaspoons pure vanilla extract

$1^1/_3$ cups semisweet chocolate chips, divided

German Chocolate Cake Frosting (recipe follows)

Serve slightly chilled or at room temperature. Can be made a day ahead. Store frosted cake in refrigerator. Unfrosted cake layers can be covered tightly with plastic wrap and stored in refrigerator for one day. Frosted and unfrosted cake layers can be covered with plastic wrap and then with foil and stored in freezer for up to three weeks. Best when eaten within three days of baking.

1. Preheat oven to 350°F. Position rack in center of oven. Line two 9-inch round layer cake pans with parchment or wax paper and spray with cooking spray.

2. Bring $^1/_2$ cup water to a simmer in a small saucepan. Turn off heat. Add chopped chocolate and whisk until smooth. Remove from heat and cool until lukewarm.

3. Put flour, baking soda, salt, xanthan gum, and buttermilk powder in medium bowl and whisk until thoroughly combined. Set aside. Combine oil and water in a glass measuring cup. Set aside.

4. Beat eggs in large bowl of electric mixer until lemon colored. Slowly add sugar a little at a time, and beat until mixture turns pale yellow and thick. Beat in melted chocolate and vanilla.

5. Add flour mixture alternately with oil and water mixture in two additions; scrape sides and bottom of bowl, then mix at medium speed for 1 more minute.

6. Pour batter into prepared pans. Sprinkle chocolate chips over the batter in each pan, $\frac{1}{2}$ cup in each (1 cup total). Place pans in center of oven and bake 40–45 minutes or until a toothpick inserted in the center of a layer comes out clean.

7. Cool cake layers in the pans on a rack for 8 minutes. Use a small knife to cut around pan sides to loosen cake. Invert cake layers onto a rack, peel off paper, and cool completely.

8. Frost cake layers separately. Place one cake layer on a platter. Spread $\frac{1}{2}$ of the frosting over top (and sides, if desired). Place second layer on another platter and repeat. Place second layer on top of first. Sprinkle remaining chocolate chips over top of cake.

GERMAN CHOCOLATE CAKE FROSTING

1 12-oz. can evaporated milk
$1\frac{1}{2}$ cups granulated sugar
$\frac{1}{2}$ cup unsalted butter
4 large egg yolks
$\frac{1}{4}$–$\frac{1}{2}$ teaspoon almond extract, to taste
1 7-oz. package sweetened shredded coconut
$1\frac{1}{2}$ cups coarsely chopped pecans

1. Combine evaporated milk, sugar, butter, and egg yolks in a medium saucepan. Whisk over medium-high heat until mixture is smooth and thick enough to see an indentation from your finger on a frosting-coated wooden spoon. This will take about 15 minutes.

2. Stir in almond extract, coconut, and pecans. Allow to sit at room temperature for one hour before frosting cake.

FLOURLESS CHOCOLATE CAKE

Makes one 9-inch round cake.

There is a wonderful variety of flourless chocolate cakes for us to enjoy. Some are heavy and dense and use incredible quantities of melted chocolate. Some feature ground nuts or fruit flavors. Mine has a light soufflé-like texture and a rich chocolate flavor that is almost brownie-like. Serve it with sweetened whipped cream and fresh berries on the side. This cake is utterly simple to make, delightful to eat, and sure to become a favorite.

8 ozs. semisweet chocolate

8 tablespoons unsalted butter, room temperature

¾ cup granulated sugar

7 large eggs, separated, room temperature

1 teaspoon pure vanilla extract

1. Preheat oven to 350°F. Position rack in center of oven. Line 9-inch springform pan with parchment or wax paper and spray lightly with cooking spray.

2. Melt chocolate in small, heavy saucepan over low heat, stirring constantly. Remove from heat and cool until lukewarm.

3. Beat butter and sugar in electric mixer 4–5 minutes. Add egg yolks, one at a time, beating after each addition. Beat in the chocolate and vanilla.

4. Using clean beaters and another large bowl, beat egg whites until soft peaks form. Use a spatula to fold ⅓ of the egg whites into the batter to lighten it. Then fold in remaining egg whites.

5. Pour batter into prepared pan and bake in center of oven for 40–45 minutes or until cake is puffed and the center is firm and elastic to touch.

6. Cool cake in pan for 5 minutes (cake will fall). Use a small knife to cut around pan sides to loosen cake. Remove sides of pan and invert the cake onto a rack. Peel off paper. Cool completely and slide onto a plate.

Serve at room temperature. Cake can be made ahead up to two days before serving. Wrap tightly in plastic to refrigerate. Bring to room temperature before serving.

ANGEL FOOD CAKE

*Makes one
10-inch cake.*

If you know and miss the pleasures of angel food cake, try this remarkable gluten-free version. It looks, tastes, and feels as good as most wheat-containing angel food, and better than those chemically preserved cakes you see in your grocery store. Lacking butter, oil, and egg yolks, all angel food cakes rely on sugar to keep them moist. They are slightly less tender than their sponge counterparts because the egg whites give them so much structure. No matter, you will still need guar gum or xanthan gum to ensure a successful gluten-free cake. Guar gum results in a slightly more tender cake, but xanthan gum will still give you a good texture. So crack some eggs today and start baking!

1 1/4 cups confectioners' sugar

1 cup Brown Rice Flour Mix (see p. 6), *sifted 3 times before measuring*

1/2 teaspoon guar gum *or* xanthan gum if guar gum is unavailable

1 1/2 cups (about 12) egg whites, room temperature

1 1/2 teaspoons cream of tartar

1/4 teaspoon salt

2 teaspoons pure vanilla extract

1/2 teaspoon pure almond extract

1 cup granulated sugar

Serve at room temperature. Can be made 'a day ahead. Cover tightly with plastic wrap to store in refrigerator. Cannot be frozen. Best when eaten within three days of baking.

1. Preheat oven to 400°F. Position rack on second shelf from bottom. Have ready a clean 10-inch tube pan with a removable bottom.

2. Combine and then sift confectioners' sugar, flour, and guar gum into a small bowl and set aside.

3. Combine egg whites, cream of tartar, salt, vanilla, and almond extract in large bowl of electric mixer. Start mixer at medium speed and beat until whites are foamy. Gradually increase speed to high. Add sugar 2 tablespoons at a time, beating until sugar dissolves and whites form stiff peaks. Do not scrape bowl while beating.

4. Fold flour mixture into egg whites in three additions, using a rubber spatula. Pour batter into ungreased 10-inch tube pan. Use the spatula to break any air bubbles and smooth the batter.

5. Place cake in oven and turn down oven temperature to 375°. Bake about 35 minutes or until top of cake springs back when lightly touched with finger and any cracks on surface look dry.

6. Invert cake in pan on funnel or narrow-necked bottle (an empty wine bottle is perfect); cool completely. Loosen cake with sharp knife and remove from pan onto a serving plate.

VANILLA SPONGE CAKE OR JELLY ROLL

Makes two 8- or 9-inch rounds or one 15-inch jelly roll. Recipe can be cut in half.

Light, delectable sponge cake is a classic dessert that you can use in many delicious ways. Make strawberry shortcake, jelly rolls, and cakes filled with lemon curd, flavored custards, or whipped cream. Follow the directions carefully and you will get a flavorful sponge with a perfect texture.

$\frac{3}{4}$ cup Brown Rice Flour Mix (see p. 6)

$\frac{1}{2}$ teaspoon baking powder

$\frac{1}{4}$ teaspoon guar gum *or* xanthan gum if guar gum is unavailable

$\frac{1}{8}$ teaspoon salt

6 large eggs, separated, at room temperature

$\frac{3}{4}$ cup granulated sugar, divided

2 teaspoons pure vanilla extract

$\frac{1}{4}$ teaspoon pure almond extract

1. Preheat oven to 350°F. Position rack in center of oven. Line two 8-inch round layer cake pans with parchment or wax paper and spray very lightly with cooking spray. If making a jelly roll cake, line a 10 $\frac{1}{2}$ x 15 $\frac{1}{2}$-inch jelly roll pan with parchment or wax paper and grease very lightly with cooking spray.

2. Whisk flour, baking powder, guar gum, and salt together in a small bowl. Set aside.

3. Beat egg whites in large bowl of electric mixer. Start mixer at medium speed and beat until whites are foamy. Gradually increase speed to high. Add $\frac{1}{4}$ cup of the sugar, 1 tablespoon at a time, beating until sugar dissolves and whites form medium soft peaks. Do not scrape bowl while beating. Set aside.

4. Beat egg yolks in large bowl of electric mix until thick and lemon colored. Add remaining $\frac{1}{2}$ cup sugar gradually, 1 tablespoon at a time, and continue to beat until light colored and fluffy. Add flour mixture, vanilla extract, and almond extract and mix until smooth. Batter will be thick.

5. Fold $\frac{1}{3}$ of the beaten egg whites into the batter to lighten it; gently fold in remaining egg whites. Pour batter into cake pans and place in center of preheated oven. Bake 20–22 minutes (8-inch round) or until cake springs back when touched lightly (bake 18–20 minutes for 9-inch rounds, and 16–18 minutes for 10 $\frac{1}{2}$ x 15 $\frac{1}{2}$-inch jelly roll).

Serve at room temperature or slightly chilled. Can be made a day ahead. Store frosted cake in refrigerator. Unfrosted cake layers can be covered tightly with plastic wrap and stored in refrigerator for one day. Unfrosted cake layers can also be covered with plastic wrap and then with foil and stored in freezer for up to three weeks. Best when eaten within three days of baking.

6. *For cake rounds:* Use a small knife to cut around pan sides to loosen cake. Invert pans onto a rack. Peel off paper. Cool completely before filling or frosting.

For jelly roll: Invert pan onto a clean dish towel. Peel off paper. Roll cake and towel together into a roll and place on rack to cool. Cool completely before filling or frosting.

CHOCOLATE SPONGE CAKE OR JELLY ROLL

Makes two 8- or 9-inch rounds or one 15-inch jelly roll. Recipe can be cut in half.

Chocolate sponge cake is one of those classic desserts that you will want in your baking repertoire. Use this light, flavorful sponge to make Yule Logs for the holidays or cakes filled with whipped cream and berries for special celebrations. It is easy to make; just follow the directions carefully and let your imagination go as you create your own special treats.

$1/3$ cup plus 1 tablespoon Brown Rice Flour Mix (see p. 6)

$1/3$ cup unsweetened cocoa powder

$1/2$ teaspoon baking powder

$1/4$ teaspoon guar gum *or* xanthan gum if guar gum is unavailable

$1/8$ teaspoon salt

6 large eggs, separated, at room temperature

$3/4$ cup granulated sugar, divided

2 teaspoons pure vanilla extract

1. Preheat oven to 350°F. Position rack in center of oven. Line two 8-inch round layer cake pans with parchment or wax paper and spray very lightly with cooking spray. If making a jelly roll cake, line a 10 $1/2$ x 15 $1/2$-inch jelly roll pan with parchment or wax paper and spray very lightly with cooking spray.

2. Whisk flour, cocoa powder, baking powder, guar gum, and salt together in a small bowl. Set aside.

3. Beat egg whites in large bowl of electric mixer. Start mixer at medium speed and beat until whites are foamy. Gradually increase speed to high. Add $1/4$ cup of the sugar, 1 tablespoon at a time, beating until sugar dissolves and whites form medium soft peaks. Do not scrape bowl while beating. Set aside.

4. Beat egg yolks in large bowl of electric mixer until thick and lemon colored. Add remaining $1/2$ cup sugar gradually, 1 tablespoon at a time, and continue to beat until light colored and fluffy. Add flour mixture and vanilla extract and mix until smooth. Batter will be thick.

5. Fold $1/3$ of the beaten egg whites into the batter to lighten it; gently fold in remaining egg whites. Pour batter into cake pans and place in center of preheated oven. Bake for 20–22 minutes (8-inch round) or until cake springs back when touched lightly (bake 18–20 minutes for 9-inch rounds, and 16–20 minutes for 10 $1/2$ x 15 $1/2$-inch jelly roll).

6. *For cake rounds:* Use a small knife to cut around pan sides to loosen cake. Invert the pans onto a rack. Peel off paper. Cool completely before filling or frosting.

For jelly roll: Invert the pans onto a clean dish towel. Peel off paper. Roll cake and towel together into a roll and place on rack to cool for 30 minutes. Unroll and cool completely before filling or frosting.

CARROT CAKE

Carrot cake is a traditional favorite that you can find in most cookbooks and magazines. My version is made with fresh shredded carrots, sweetened coconut, crunchy walnuts, and a bit of cinnamon and nutmeg. I recreated it in a delectable new gluten-free form that is so good my family and friends couldn't tell the difference. Give it a try; it could become a new favorite of yours.

Makes two 9-inch rounds. Recipe can be cut in half.

3 cups Brown Rice Flour Mix (see p. 6)

1 1/2 teaspoons xanthan gum

1 tablepoon baking powder

2 teaspoons baking soda

1 teaspoon salt

2 teaspoons cinnamon

1/2 teaspoon nutmeg

2 cups granulated sugar

1 1/2 cups canola oil

4 large eggs

2 teaspoons pure vanilla extract

2 cups grated, peeled carrots

1 cup chopped walnuts

1 cup shredded sweetened coconut

Cream Cheese Icing (recipe follows)

1/2 cup toasted sweetened flaked coconut for garnish*

* Spread sweetened flaked coconut in a thin layer on a small baking tray. Bake in preheated 350°F oven, stirring every few minutes until light golden brown. This will only take a few minutes. Don't leave the oven!

1. Preheat oven to 350°F. Position rack in center of oven. Line two 9-inch round layer cake pans with parchment or wax paper and spray lightly with cooking spray.

2. Place flour, xanthan gum, baking soda, baking powder, salt, cinnamon, and nutmeg in medium mixing bowl and whisk until thoroughly combined. Set aside.

3. Beat sugar, oil, and eggs in large bowl of electric mixer until smooth, about 1 minute. Add vanilla and mix well.

4. Pour flour mixture into the sugar and oil mixture and beat at medium-low speed for 1 minute. Fold in carrots, walnuts, and coconut.

5. Pour batter into prepared pans and bake in center of oven for 40 minutes or until a toothpick inserted in center of cake comes out clean.

Serve slightly chilled or at room temperature. Can be made a day ahead. Store frosted cake in refrigerator. Unfrosted cake layers can be covered tightly with plastic wrap and stored in refrigerator for one day. Unfrosted cake layers can be covered with plastic wrap and then with foil and stored in freezer for up to three weeks. Best when eaten within three days of baking.

6. Cool cake layers in the pans on a rack for 10 minutes. Use a small knife to cut around pan sides to loosen cake. Invert cake layers onto a rack, peel off paper, and cool completely.

7. Place one cake layer on platter. Spread 1 cup frosting over top and sides. Place second layer on top. Spread remaining frosting over entire cake. Sprinkle toasted coconut over the top or press onto sides.

CREAM CHEESE ICING

½ cup unsalted butter, room temperature

½ cup low-fat cream cheese, room temperature

3 cups confectioners' sugar, sifted if lumpy

1 teaspoon pure vanilla extract

1 lemon, grated and juiced

1. Beat butter and cream cheese in large bowl of electric mixer until light and fluffy.

2. Add confectioners' sugar and beat at low speed until well blended. Beat in vanilla, grated lemon rind, and lemon juice until smooth.

GINGERBREAD

On a cold winter day there is nothing more comforting than the sweet smell of gingerbread baking in the oven. My original recipe, converted to gluten-free, makes a traditional-style cake that features a delicate blend of ginger, cinnamon, and molasses. Dust it with a little powdered sugar and you've got a quick dessert. I like to serve this gingerbread with homemade applesauce on the side.

1²/₃ cups Brown Rice Flour Mix (see p. 6)

1¹/₄ teaspoons baking soda

³/₄ teaspoon xanthan gum

1¹/₂ teaspoons ground ginger

³/₄ teaspoon cinnamon

³/₄ teaspoon salt

1 large egg, lightly beaten

¹/₂ cup granulated sugar

¹/₂ cup molasses

¹/₂ cup canola oil

¹/₂ cup boiling water

Confectioners' sugar

1. Preheat oven to 350°F. Position rack in center of oven. Lightly grease a kugelhoph mold with cooking spray.

2. Place flour, baking soda, xanthan gum, ginger, cinnamon, and salt in large bowl of electric mixer and mix at low speed until thoroughly combined.

3. Add egg, sugar, and molasses and mix until smooth, about 1 minute. Pour oil and boiling water over batter and mix until smooth, about 30 seconds.

4. Pour batter into prepared pan and bake in center of oven for 40 minutes or until top springs back when touched and a toothpick inserted in center of cake comes out clean (bake 35 minutes for 8 x 8-inch square).

5. Cool cake in pan on a rack for 5 minutes. Use a small knife to cut around pan sides to loosen cake if necessary. Invert cake onto a rack and cool. Sift confectioners' sugar over cake and serve warm (or at room temperature) with applesauce.

Makes one 8 x 8-inch square cake or 9-inch kugelhoph crown-shaped mold (fluted ring mold).*

Can be made a day ahead. Store Gingerbread in refrigerator, covered tightly with plastic wrap. Gingerbread can be covered with plastic wrap and then with foil and stored in freezer for up to three weeks. Best when eaten within three days of baking.

* Use a 9-inch kugelhoph crown-shaped mold or a fluted ring mold that would hold 8 to 10 cups filled to the top rim. Do not use a flat-bottomed tube pan.

NEW YORK CHEESECAKE

Makes one 10-inch round cake.

There are countless recipes for cheesecakes of all kinds. But to New Yorkers, where cheesecake originated, there is only one kind, and it doesn't have chocolate or pecans or raspberry puree. And it certainly isn't made with fat-free cream cheese and evaporated milk. No, if you are going to have cheesecake, you should have the real thing. And here it is. Just be sure to share it with a lot of friends and family. Take note: This cake should be prepared one day before serving.

Crust

1¼ cups Brown Rice Flour Mix (see p. 6)

1 teaspoon xanthan gum

10 tablespoons unsalted butter, room temperature.

¼ cup granulated sugar

1 large egg yolk

Grated rind of 1 lemon

Remove from refrigerator one hour before serving. Store in refrigerator for up to five days. Whole cake or sections can be tightly covered with plastic wrap and then with foil and stored in freezer for up to one month.

* Philadelphia® Original Cream Cheese is best.

1. Preheat oven to 350°F. Position rack in center of oven. Grease bottom of 10-inch springform pan with cooking spray. Dust lightly with rice flour.

2. Mix all ingredients for crust in bowl of electric mixer and mix at low speed. Press about ⅓ of dough into detached bottom of springform pan and bake 12 minutes. Cool slightly on rack. While bottom is baking, roll the rest of dough out between two pieces of wax paper and refrigerate. Turn oven control to 475°F.

Cream Cheese Filling

5 8-oz. packages cream cheese*

1¾ cups granulated sugar

3 tablespoons Brown Rice Flour Mix (see p. 6)

¼ teaspoon salt

5 large eggs

2 large egg yolks

2 tablespoons half-and-half *or* whole milk *or* light cream

1 tablespoon grated orange rind

Grated rind of 1 lemon

1. To make filling, beat cream cheese until smooth in large bowl of electric mixer at medium speed. Reduce speed and slowly add

sugar, then flour, salt, eggs, egg yolks, half-and-half, and orange and lemon rind. Scrape bowl and beaters; beat at high speed for 5 more minutes.

2. Attach bottom of springform pan to sides. Press remaining dough around sides to within 1 inch of top of pan. Pour cream cheese filling into pan. Bake in center of oven for 12 minutes; turn oven control down to 300°F and bake 50 minutes more. Turn off oven, but do not open door; leave cake in oven another 15 minutes. Cool cake on wire rack and refrigerate. When cold, remove pan sides and slide cheesecake off bottom onto a platter. Serve with sliced fresh strawberries.

CLASSIC CHEESECAKE

Makes one 9-inch round cake.

This classic cheesecake is slightly less dense than New York style cheesecake but just as creamy and flavorful. Make it with the crust or without; it will be delicious either way. I like to serve slices topped with seasonal fresh fruit or fruit compote. It's easy and fast to make and sure to become a much requested favorite. Take note: Make cheesecake one day before serving.

Crust

 1 cup Brown Rice Flour Mix (see p. 6)

 1 teaspoon xanthan gum

 5 tablespoons unsalted butter

 $\frac{1}{4}$ cup granulated sugar

1. Preheat oven to 350°F. Position rack in center of oven. Grease bottom of 9-inch round springform pan with cooking spray. Dust lightly with rice flour.

2. Place flour, xanthan gum, butter, and sugar in bowl of electric mixer. Mix on low speed until crumbly. Press into detached bottom of springform pan.

3. Bake in center of oven for 12 minutes. Remove from oven and set aside. Turn oven control up to 475°F.

Remove from refrigerator one hour before serving. Store in refrigerator for up to five days. Whole cake or sections can be tightly covered with plastic wrap and then with foil and stored in freezer for up to one month.

* Philadelphia® Original Cream Cheese is best.

Cream Cheese Filling

 4 8-oz. packages cream cheese*

 $1\frac{1}{3}$ cups granulated sugar

 1 tablespoon pure vanilla extract

 4 large eggs

 8 ozs. sour cream (low-fat can be used)

 Juice and grated rind of 1 large lemon

1. Beat cream cheese until smooth in bowl of electric mixer at medium speed. Reduce speed and slowly add sugar and vanilla. Beat in eggs one at a time. Scrape bowl and beaters. Add sour cream, lemon juice, and grated lemon rind and mix until well blended.

2. Attach bottom of springform pan to sides. Pour cream cheese batter into pan. Bake in center of oven for 10 minutes; turn oven control down to 200°F and bake 1 hour more. Turn off oven, but do not open door; leave cake in oven for another 15 minutes. Cool cake on wire rack and refrigerate. When cold, remove sides and slide cheesecake off bottom onto a platter. Serve with fresh fruit.

CUSTARD CAKE WITH FRUIT

Custard cakes are common to a great many cuisines, but they go by a variety of names: Clafouti, Far Breton, Pasteis de Nata, Bougatsa—you might even have your own favorite. These cakes are homey comfort food made simple. Fresh fruit and a quickly made batter are baked until a golden, crusty, custardy cake emerges hot from the oven. Serve it warm sprinkled with powdered sugar and you'll have a delicious dessert you can serve after dinner or at a special brunch.

Makes one 9-inch cake.

1 large Granny Smith apple *or* 1 large Bosc pear

1 teaspoon unsalted butter

1 teaspoon brown sugar

2 tablespoons calvados *or* cognac

1/2 cup Brown Rice Flour Mix (see p. 6)

1/2 cup granulated sugar

1/8 teaspoon salt

4 large eggs

2 cups whole milk

1 1/2 teaspoons pure vanilla extract

confectioners' sugar for garnish

1. Peel and core apple; cut into eight slices. Cut each slice into four chunks. Melt 1 teaspoon butter in a small sauté pan over medium-high heat. Stir in 1 teaspoon brown sugar. Mix in apples and coat with butter mixture. Sauté until light golden brown, stirring constantly. Remove from heat. Pour calvados over apples and ignite; allow flames to burn off. Set aside to cool.

2. Preheat oven to 375°F. Position rack in center of oven. Lightly grease a 9-inch round glass (Pyrex) or ceramic deep-dish pie pan with cooking spray and dust lightly with rice flour.

3. Whisk flour, sugar, and salt in a large bowl.

4. Break eggs into center of flour mixture and whisk until just smooth. Add milk and vanilla extract and whisk until just smooth.

5. Pour batter into prepared pan. Drop sautéed apples into the batter. Put pan in center of oven; bake about 55 minutes (a knife inserted into center of cake should come out clean). Do not open oven for 45 minutes.

6. Cool cake in the pan on a rack for 1 hour. Sift confectioners' sugar over top.

*Serve warm, at
room temperature,
or slightly chilled.
Can be made a day
ahead. Store cake
covered tightly with
plastic wrap in
refrigerator. Best
when eaten within
three days of baking.*

CUSTARD CAKE WITH CHERRIES

Replacement Step 1: Melt 1 teaspoon butter in a small sauté pan over medium-high heat. Stir in 1 teaspoon brown sugar. Mix in 1½ cups pitted cherries and coat with butter mixture. Turn off heat. Pour cognac over cherries and ignite; allow flames to burn off. Proceed with Step 2 above.

SOUR CREAM COFFEE CAKE

Sour cream coffee cake is a traditional offering at holiday brunches and morning coffees. My friend Daria made this one for me years ago and I've never found another that I like better. It converted well to its new gluten-free form: It's still easy to make and yummy.

Take note: It may appear that there is not enough batter for two layers. Just be sure to make two very thin layers of batter, with the apple and nut mixture in between.

Makes one 9-inch tube cake.

- $\frac{1}{2}$ cup chopped walnuts
- 2 teaspoons cinnamon
- $1\frac{1}{2}$ cups granulated sugar, divided
- 1 medium apple
- 2 cups Brown Rice Flour Mix (see p. 6)
- $1\frac{1}{2}$ teaspoons baking powder
- 1 teaspoon baking soda
- $\frac{3}{4}$ teaspoon xanthan gum
- $\frac{1}{2}$ teaspoon salt
- 2 large eggs, room temperature
- 2 teaspoons pure vanilla extract
- 1 cup sour cream, room temperature
- $\frac{1}{3}$ cup canola oil

1. Preheat oven to 350°F. Position rack in center of oven. Grease a 9-inch tube pan with removable bottom with cooking spray.

2. Mix walnuts, cinnamon, and $\frac{1}{2}$ cup of sugar in a small bowl. Set aside.

3. Peel and core apple; cut into 8 slices. Cut each slice horizontally into 8 small pieces, not long thin slices. Set aside.

4. Whisk flour, baking powder, baking soda, xanthan gum, and salt together in a small bowl. Set aside.

5. Beat eggs in large bowl of electric mixer until well blended. Add remaining sugar, 1 tablespoon at a time, and beat until creamy-colored and light. Add vanilla, flour mixture, sour cream, and oil and beat at medium-low speed for 30 seconds.

6. Evenly spread $\frac{1}{2}$ of batter into prepared pan. Top with apple pieces and $\frac{1}{2}$ of nut mixture. Evenly spread remaining batter over the top;

Serve slightly chilled or at room temperature. Can be made a day ahead. Store cake covered tightly with plastic wrap in refrigerator. Best when eaten within three days of baking.

sprinkle with remaining nut mixture. There is not much batter, so do not be afraid to spread what will appear to be two very thin layers of batter, with the apples and nut mixture in between; spread with a cake spatula or butter knife. The batter will rise and give you a cake several inches high.

7. Place in center of oven and bake about 50 minutes or until a toothpick inserted in center of cake comes out clean. Do not open oven for 45 minutes.

8. Cool cake in pan on a rack for 20 minutes. Remove sides of pan and cool completely on rack. To remove cake from bottom, use two pancake turners to lift cake onto a cake plate.

CRUMB CAKE

Looking for a simple, classic crumb cake? This one is easy to make and everything a crumb cake needs to be: delicious, velvety cake flavored with vanilla and topped with delectable crumbs and a hint of cinnamon. It will soothe your longing for this old-time favorite. Take note: My cake is not the square yeast-based comfort food created by German bakers in New York so long ago. It is more traditional in shape and flavor and more "cakey" in texture. Make one to serve for brunch, coffee with friends, after-school snacks, or simple summer suppers with a side of fresh peaches and berries.

Makes one 9-inch tube cake.

Crumb Topping (recipe follows)
2 cups Brown Rice Flour Mix (see p. 6)
1 1/2 teaspoons baking powder
1 teaspoon baking soda
3/4 teaspoon xanthan gum
1/2 teaspoon salt
2 large eggs, room temperature
1 1/4 cups granulated sugar
2 teaspoons pure vanilla extract
1 cup sour cream, room temperature*
1/3 cup canola oil

Best with regular sour cream, not low-fat.

1. Prepare Crumb Topping (recipe follows).

2. Preheat oven to 350°F. Position rack in center of oven. Grease a 9-inch tube pan with removable bottom with cooking spray (do not use an angel food cake pan).

3. Whisk flour, baking powder, baking soda, xanthan gum, and salt in a small bowl. Set aside.

4. Beat eggs in large bowl of electric until well blended. Add sugar one tablespoon at a time, and beat until creamy colored and light. Add vanilla, flour mixture, sour cream, and oil and beat at medium-low speed for 30 seconds. Do not overbeat.

5. Spread batter into prepared pan. Top with Crumb Topping (recipe follows).

6. Place in center of oven and bake about 50 minutes or until a toothpick inserted in the center of cake comes out clean. Do not open oven for first 45 minutes.

7. Cool cake in the pan on a rack for 20 minutes. Remove sides of pan

Serve slightly chilled or at room temperature. Can be made a day ahead. Store cake covered tightly with plastic wrap in refrigerator. Best when eaten within three days of baking.

and cool completely on rack. To remove cake from bottom, use two pancake turners to lift cake onto a cake plate. It is easier to remove the cake from the pan if it is cold.

CRUMB TOPPING

 1 cup plus 2 tablespoons Brown Rice Flour Mix (see p. 6)
$\frac{1}{3}$ cup packed dark brown sugar
$\frac{1}{3}$ cup granulated sugar
 1 teaspoon cinnamon
$\frac{1}{2}$ teaspoon xanthan gum
 6 tablespoons unsalted butter, melted

1. Combine flour, brown sugar, granulated sugar, cinnamon, and xanthan gum in a small bowl; stir to blend. Pour in butter and stir until all dry ingredients are moistened. Gently break into medium and small (the size of M&Ms®) crumb pieces with spoon.

VANILLA POUND CAKE

Vanilla pound cake is a classic dessert traditionally made with equal parts of butter, sugar, and eggs. But when I started to test gluten-free versions, I quickly realized that using butter would not give me the result I wanted. My gluten-free pound cake uses canola oil and whole-milk yogurt with great effect. In fact, during pound-cake-testing week, I was making several pound cakes a day (to the delight of my kids and testers). I started sending large chunks of pound cake to school with my gluten-tolerant son, who passed big pieces around the lunch table to his friends. Late in the week, I received a call from a mother who said her son wanted my Chocolate Chip version (see below) for his birthday dinner. So here it is. You *can* make a great pound cake without butter.

1½ cups Brown Rice Flour Mix (see p. 6)

2½ teaspoons baking powder

½ teaspoon xanthan gum

¼ teaspoon salt

3 large eggs

1 cup granulated sugar

1 cup plain whole-milk yogurt

⅓ cup canola oil

2 teaspoons pure vanilla extract

Confectioners' sugar, for garnish

1. Preheat oven to 350°F. Position rack in center of oven. Grease a 9-inch bundt pan or kugelhoph mold with cooking spray.

2. Whisk flour, baking powder, xanthan gum, and salt in a small bowl. Set aside.

3. Beat eggs in large bowl of electric mixer at medium-high speed; gradually add sugar 1 tablespoon at a time and beat until light colored and thickened.

4. Add flour mixture, yogurt, oil, and vanilla extract and beat at medium-low speed for 30 seconds.

5. Evenly spread batter into prepared pan. Place in center of oven and bake about 50 minutes (a toothpick inserted in center of cake should come out clean). Do not open oven for 45 minutes.

Makes one 9-inch bundt-shaped cake* or three 5 x 3-inch loaves.

Serve slightly chilled or at room temperature. Can be made a day ahead. Store cake covered tightly with plastic wrap in refrigerator. Pound Cake can be covered with plastic wrap and then with foil and stored in freezer for up to three weeks. Best when eaten within four days of baking.

* Use a 9-inch (across top) kugelhoph crown-shaped mold or a fluted ring mold that holds 8 to 10 cups filled to the top rim. If you use a 9 x 5-inch loaf pan, cake will be dense and heavy. Do not use a 9-inch flat-bottomed tube pan or you will have a 1-inch-high cake. You can use mini bundt pans, but you will need to adjust baking time.

6. Cool cake in the pan on a rack for 10 minutes. Carefully remove cake from pan and cool completely on rack. Sift confectioners' sugar over top.

CHOCOLATE CHIP POUND CAKE

Stir in ⅔ to ¾ cup semisweet chocolate chips before spreading batter in pan.

LEMON POUND CAKE

This is the perfect little cake to serve with coffee and tea. It has a bright lemon flavor, a tender crumb, and a velvety texture. Dust it with powdered sugar or dribble a tangy lemon glaze over the top (recipe follows). I also like to make it with fresh blueberries when they are in season or poppy seeds (recipes follow). No matter which version you make, you'll have a simple, delicious cake that you'll want to make again and again.

1½ cups Brown Rice Flour Mix (see p. 6)

2½ teaspoons baking powder

½ teaspoon xanthan gum

¼ teaspoon salt

3 large eggs

1 cup granulated sugar

1 cup plain whole-milk yogurt

⅓ cup canola oil

1 teaspoon pure vanilla extract

1 teaspoon pure lemon extract

1 tablespoon grated lemon rind

Confectioners' sugar, for garnish (optional)

1. Preheat oven to 350°F. Position rack in center of oven. Grease a 9-inch bundt pan or kugelhoph mold with cooking spray.

2. Whisk flour, baking powder, xanthan gum, and salt together in a small bowl. Set aside.

3. Beat eggs in large bowl of electric mixer at medium-high speed; gradually add sugar, 1 tablespoon at a time, and beat until light colored and thickened.

4. Add flour mixture, yogurt, oil, vanilla extract, lemon extract, and lemon rind and beat at medium-low speed for 30 seconds.

5. Evenly spread batter into prepared pan. Place in center of oven and bake about 50 minutes (a toothpick inserted in center of cake should come out clean). Do not open oven for 45 minutes.

6. Cool cake in the pan on a rack for 10 minutes. Carefully remove cake from pan and cool completely on rack. Sift confectioners' sugar over top or brush on lemon glaze (recipe follows).

Makes one 9-inch bundt-shaped cake* or three 5 x 3-inch loaves.

Serve slightly chilled or at room temperature. Can be made a day ahead. Store cake covered tightly with plastic wrap in refrigerator. Pound Cake can be covered with plastic wrap and then with foil and stored in freezer for up to three weeks. Best when eaten within four days of baking.

* Use a 9-inch (across top) kugelhoph crown-shaped mold or a fluted ring mold that holds 8 to 10 cups filled to the top rim. If you use a 9 x 5-inch loaf pan, cake will be dense and heavy. Do not use a 9-inch flat-bottomed tube pan or you will have a 1-inch-high cake. You can use mini bundt pans, but you will need to adjust baking time.

LEMON BLUEBERRY POUND CAKE

Stir in ⅔ to ¾ cup fresh dry blueberries before spreading batter in pan.

LEMON POPPY SEED POUND CAKE

Stir in ⅓ cup poppy seeds before spreading batter in pan.

LEMON GLAZE

¼ cup granulated sugar

2 tablespoons fresh lemon juice

1. Put sugar and lemon juice in small saucepan and whisk over medium-high heat until sugar is dissolved.
2. Use pastry brush to brush glaze on cooled pound cake.

EUROPEAN-STYLE COFFEE CAKE (CHEESE-FILLED)

After many years of gluten-free baking, I finally felt hunger pangs for the simple elegance of a European-style yeast cake. These cakes are really enriched bread dough—tender, chewy, and slightly sweetened. I filled mine with cream cheese flavored with vanilla and a hint of lemon, but you can use the "dough" part of the recipe to make your own family favorites filled with poppy seed, nuts, raisins, and cinnamon, or cooked and thickened fruit.* The dough can't be rolled, but it can be divided into two layers. I recommend using a tube pan to enhance the rise. Serve this seemingly modest, but quietly addictive cake for Sunday brunch and then enjoy the leftovers (if there are any) for several days after.

Cheese Filling

    8 oz. cream cheese

    $\frac{1}{3}$ cup granulated sugar

    $\frac{1}{2}$ teaspoon xanthan gum

    1 teaspoon pure vanilla extract

    1 teaspoon lemon zest, optional

    1 large egg yolk

Dough

    1 cup skim or 2% milk, heated to 110°F

    1 packet (1/4 oz.) active dry yeast granules (not quick-rise)

    2 cups Brown Rice Flour Mix (see p. 6), separated

    $\frac{1}{4}$ cup granulated sugar, separated

    2 large eggs (room temperature is best)

    2 tablespoons canola oil

    1 teaspoon xanthan gum

    $\frac{3}{4}$ teaspoon ground cardamom

    $\frac{1}{2}$ teaspoon salt

    $1\frac{1}{2}$ teaspoons pure vanilla extract

Icing

    $\frac{1}{2}$ cup confectioners' sugar

    1 tablespoon milk

    $\frac{1}{2}$ teaspoon pure vanilla extract

    $\frac{1}{4}$ cup sliced almonds

1. Beat all ingredients for cheese filling in large bowl of electric mixer until fluffy. Set aside.

Use a touch (about $\frac{1}{4}$ to $\frac{1}{2}$ teaspoon) of xanthan gum or guar gum to keep the filling from separating and leaking into the cake batter. Make sure fruit is room temperature before layering into batter.

Cook's Note: Dry ingredients can be mixed ahead and stored in plastic containers for future use. Do not add yeast until ready to bake cake.

Cake is best when fresh but can be prepared in advance. Bake according to directions. Remove from oven and allow to cool on a rack. Wrap well in plastic wrap and store in refrigerator for up to three days. To reheat, freshen cake by sprinkling bottom with a bit of water, wrap in foil, and warm in preheated 350°F oven about 15 minutes. Icing may melt a bit when reheated. For best presentation when preparing ahead, ice after reheating. Individual pieces can be reheated briefly in microwave.

2. Lightly grease a 9-inch tube pan with removable bottom with cooking spray.

3. Combine warm milk (110°F), yeast, 1 tablespoon of the brown rice flour mix, and 1 tablespoon of the sugar in a measuring cup; stir until well blended. Cover with a towel and set aside for 5 to 10 minutes until mixture becomes foamy.

4. Mix eggs and canola oil together in a small bowl and set aside.

5. Mix remaining brown rice flour mix, remaining 3 tablespoons sugar, xanthan gum, cardamom, and salt in large bowl of electric mixer. Add vanilla, warm milk/yeast mixture, egg, and oil to the bowl; mix until just blended. Scrape bowl and beaters and then beat at high speed for 3 minutes.

6. Pour $\frac{1}{3}$ of dough into prepared pan. Drop cheese filling by soup spoonful onto top of dough and arrange in a ring around the surface of the entire cake. Top with remaining dough from mixing bowl. Smooth dough with a knife or spatula so it completely covers cheese filling. Cover with a light dish towel and let rise in a warm place until cake has doubled or more in size (80°F is ideal and almost essential for this very heavy dough to rise in 1 to $1\frac{1}{2}$ hours. It will be about 1 inch below the top of the pan).

7. Preheat oven to 375°F. Position rack in center of oven. Place cake in center of oven and bake about 35–45 minutes, until golden brown and cooked through. Do not open oven for first 30 minutes.

8. Cool cake in the pan on a rack for 10 minutes. Remove sides of pan and cool 20 minutes on rack. Cake will fall slightly. To remove cake from bottom, use two pancake turners to lift cake onto a cake plate.

9. Combine confectioners' sugar, milk, and vanilla in a small bowl and stir until smooth and creamy. Drizzle icing over top and sides of cake and sprinkle almonds over it.

CHAPTER 6

Pies and Tarts

TRADITIONAL PIE CRUST

TART SHELL CRUST

CHOCOLATE TART
SHELL CRUST

APPLE PIE with
CRUMB TOPPING

FRUIT PIES

RUSTIC APPLE TART
Rustic Plum Tart

PECAN PIE

KEY LIME PIE

CHOCOLATE CREAM PIE

COCONUT CREAM PIE

VANILLA CREAM PIE FILLING
Fresh Berry Fruit Tarts
Boston Cream Pie
Banana Cream Pie

I WAS WORRIED ABOUT making pie crust when I first started trying to convert my treasured recipes to gluten-free. But I worried needlessly. Gluten-free flours make fabulous pie crusts and tart shells. In fact, this is a job they were made for. Crusts made with gluten-free flours taste delicious and stay fresh long after those with wheat have withered into soggy messes. Even juicy fruit pies and lemon meringue pie hold up better with a gluten-free crust.

I have included recipes for several classic pies, all favorites of mine. But you can use the crusts with any of your own family favorites. Just be sure to replace any flour in the filling with corn starch.

The Traditional Pie Crust rolls out easily, and you will be able to place it into the pie pan without a problem—just follow the directions carefully. This crust is also easy to prepare ahead of time because you can wrap the dough in a flattened ball or roll it out and place it in the pan and then freeze it.

In addition, you won't need to make a cookie crumb crust ever again, and you won't want to once you've tasted my Tart Shell Crust and Chocolate Tart Shell Crust. Both of these crusts work well with cream pies and fruit tarts, and both can be used for the bottom of cheesecakes. Be sure to try the Chocolate Tart Shell Crust for ice cream pie.

This chapter uses the following pans:

- 8- or 9-inch pie pan
- 9- or 10-inch tart shell
- Large, heavy baking sheet (for Rustic Tart)

THE LAST WORD ON PIE CRUSTS

- Set up before starting the recipe: assemble all the ingredients
- *Use cold butter*
- Measure carefully (see Chapter 3)
- Use the right size pan or adjust baking time to compensate
- Preheat the oven to the proper temperature (make sure the oven is calibrated correctly)
- Do not open the oven door more than necessary
- Use a timer because you can get distracted

TRADITIONAL PIE CRUST

This really is a fabulous pie crust, perhaps even better than those made with wheat. It stands up well to fruit fillings, custards, and even lemon meringue. It is probably the only pie crust you will ever eat that is as good the second day as it is the first.

It is easy to make in a mixer—no messy hands or time-consuming pastry cutters. You will become a pie-crust-making phenomenon in your own home. When you make the Traditional Pie Crust, be sure to use the sweet rice flour called for in the recipe. It will help give you a great crust. (I recommend Authentic Foods® sweet rice flour.)

Take note: When you prebake this crust, do so at a lower temperature than is commonly used for pie crusts made with wheat (see directions below). This is to make sure the dough cooks before it browns. If you notice the crust rising in the middle while it is baking, open the oven quickly and prick it once with a small sharp knife. I also suggest that you partially bake this pie crust whenever you are making a fruit pie or quiche.

Makes one 8- or 9-inch pie crust or one 10-inch tart crust.

1 cup plus 2 tablespoons Brown Rice Flour Mix (see p. 6)

2 tablespoons sweet rice flour (see p. 7)

1 tablespoon granulated sugar (omit if using for a savory pie filling)

$\frac{1}{2}$ teaspoon xanthan gum

$\frac{1}{4}$ teaspoon salt

6 tablespoons cold unsalted butter (not margarine) cut into 6 pieces

1 large egg

2 teaspoons orange juice *or* lemon juice

1. Spray 9-inch pie pan or tart pan (with removable bottom) with cooking spray. Generously dust with rice flour.

2. Mix flours, sugar, xanthan gum, and salt in large bowl of electric mixer. Add butter and mix until crumbly and resembling coarse meal.

3. Add egg and orange juice. Mix on low speed until dough holds together; it should not be sticky. Form dough into a ball, using your hands, and place on a sheet of wax paper. Top with a second sheet of wax paper and flatten dough to 1 inch thickness. *Dough can be frozen at this point for up to 1 month; wrap in plastic wrap and then use foil as an outer wrap.*

4. Roll out dough between the 2 sheets of wax paper. If dough seems tacky, refrigerate for 15 minutes before proceeding. Remove top

sheet of wax paper and invert dough into pie pan. Remove remaining sheet of wax paper, and crimp edges for single-crust pie. *Dough can also be frozen at this point for up to 1 month; line pie shell with wax paper, wrap in plastic wrap, and use foil as an outer wrap.*

To prebake a bottom pie crust:

Preheat oven to 375°F. Gently prick pastry in 3 or 4 places with a fork. Bake pastry for about 25 minutes or until golden. Remove from oven and cool completely on a wire rack. *Prebaked pie shells can be stored in airtight plastic containers or plastic wrap in refrigerator for 3 days. For longer storage, wrap in plastic wrap and then in foil, and store in freezer for up to 2 weeks.*

To partially bake a bottom pie crust:

Preheat oven to 375°F. Bake pastry for 10 minutes. Remove from oven. Fill and bake as per recipe.

TART SHELL CRUST

Gluten-free flours make great tart shells. They are crunchy and delicious, and they stay that way for days. This crust is actually a little like the best cookie crumb crust you ever had—but better. You can make it in minutes and then let your imagination go: fruit tarts, key lime tart, lemon curd tart, chocolate cream tart, coconut cream tart, banana cream tart—just dream it up, and you can make it. You can also use this crust for the bottom of cheesecakes (prebake 12 minutes at 350°F); it doesn't get soggy like graham cracker crumbs—ever.

1 cup Brown Rice Flour Mix (see p. 6)

¼ cup granulated sugar

1 teaspoon xanthan gum

5 tablespoons cold unsalted butter

1 teaspoon pure vanilla extract

1. Preheat oven to 350°F. Position rack in center of oven. Grease 9-inch pie pan or tart pan (with removable bottom) with cooking spray. Generously dust with rice flour.

2. Combine flour, sugar, and xanthan gum in large bowl of electric mixer (or food processor). Add butter and mix (or pulse) on low speed until crumbly. Add vanilla and mix well. Press into bottom and up sides of pie or tart pan.

3. Bake in center of oven for about 18 minutes or until light golden. Cool on rack in pan. For a tart, place pan on top of a broad glass and carefully push down sides. For best results, remove pan sides and bottom once tart shell is filled and chilled.

Makes one 9-inch pie crust or one 9-inch tart crust.

Cover with plastic wrap and store in refrigerator. Best when eaten within three days of baking.

CHOCOLATE TART SHELL CRUST

Makes one 9-inch pie crust or one 9-inch tart crust.

This delicious pie crust has a rich chocolate flavor and crunchy texture. It stays crunchy and firm better than any chocolate cookie crumb pie crust you have ever eaten. I use it to make chocolate cream pie and ice cream pie, but you can come up with your own favorites. In addition, it is a great recipe to use when kids want to bake something themselves because it's so easy. Let them dream up the perfect ice cream pie for a family celebration.

$\frac{3}{4}$ cup plus 1 tablespoon Brown Rice Flour Mix (see p. 6)

$\frac{1}{3}$ cup granulated sugar

$\frac{1}{4}$ cup unsweetened cocoa powder

$\frac{1}{2}$ teaspoon xanthan gum

$\frac{1}{8}$ teaspoon salt

5 tablespoons cold unsalted butter

1 teaspoon pure vanilla extract

Cover with plastic wrap and store in refrigerator. Best when eaten within three days of baking.

1. Preheat oven to 350°F. Position rack in center of oven. Generously grease a 9-inch pie pan or tart pan (with removable bottom) with cooking spray. Generously dust with rice flour.

2. Combine flour, sugar, cocoa powder, xanthan gum, and salt in large bowl of electric mixer (or food processor). Add butter and mix (or pulse) on low speed until crumbly. Add vanilla and mix well. Press into bottom and up sides of pie or tart pan.

3. Bake in center of oven for about 18 minutes or until cooked through. Cool on rack in pan. For a tart, place pan on top of a broad glass and carefully push down sides. For best results, remove pan sides and bottom once tart shell is filled and chilled.

APPLE PIE WITH CRUMB TOPPING

Serves 10.

What could be more classic than apple pie? This is my favorite recipe for it, and the only one I ever make. I must say it is a better pie with its new gluten-free crust and crumb topping: They don't get soft the second and third day like they did when I made them with wheat. I use a variety of Granny Smith and Yellow Delicious apples, but you can use your own favorites.

1 9-inch Traditional Pie Crust (see p. 87), unbaked

Crumb Topping

¾ cup Brown Rice Flour Mix (see p. 6)

½ cup granulated sugar

½ teaspoon xanthan gum

⅓ cup unsalted butter, cold and diced

Filling

6 cups thinly sliced tart apples

½ cup granulated sugar

¼ cup brown sugar

1 tablespoon corn starch

1 teaspoon cinnamon

½ teaspoon nutmeg

1 tablespoon lemon juice

1 tablespoon butter

To prepare Pie Crust:

1. Preheat oven to 375°F. Position rack in center of oven. Grease 9-inch pie pan with cooking spray, and generously dust with rice flour. Place pie pastry into pie pan and flute edges. Partially bake crust in oven for 10 minutes. Cool on rack while preparing apples and crumb topping. Turn oven temperature up to 400°F.

To make Crumb Topping:

2. Combine flour, sugar, and xanthan gum in a medium mixing bowl and cut in butter. Topping should resemble cornmeal in texture. Set aside.

To make Filling:

3. Mix sliced apples with sugars, corn starch, cinnamon, nutmeg, and lemon juice in a large mixing bowl. Fill prepared pastry crust with apple mixture, mounding it slightly. Dot with cut-up pieces of butter.

4. Spoon Crumb Topping over apples and pat it down into place. Cover entire pie with foil. Place in center of oven and bake for 30 minutes.

5. Remove foil. Turn oven temperature down to 375°F and bake for 30–40 minutes more or until filling is bubbling and top is golden. If edges of crust are browning too quickly, cover them with more foil. Cool on a rack before serving. Can be made a day ahead.

FRUIT PIES

1 9-inch Traditional Pie Crust (see p. 87). For top crust, use Crumb Topping (see recipe p. 78) or a second 9-inch Traditional Pie Crust chilled and rolled out between 2 sheets of wax paper

6 cups of berries *or* peeled and sliced fruit.

¾–1 cup of sugar, depending on sweetness of fruit (use granulated sugar *or* a combination of granulated and brown sugar)

1–3 tablespoons corn starch, depending on moisture content of fruit (fresh berries and peaches will need more, for instance)

Cinnamon, nutmeg, *and/or* ginger (to taste)

1 tablespoon lemon juice

1 tablespoon unsalted butter

To prepare Pie Crust:

1. Preheat oven to 375°F. Position rack in center of oven. Grease 9-inch pie pan with cooking spray, and generously dust with rice flour. Place pie pastry into pie pan and flute edges. Partially bake crust in oven for 10 minutes. Cool on rack while preparing fruit filling and crumb topping (if using). Turn oven temperature up to 400°F.

To make Filling:

2. Mix fruit with sugar, corn starch, spices, and lemon juice in a large mixing bowl. Fill prepared pastry crust with fruit mixture, mounding it slightly. Dot with cut-up pieces of butter.

3. Spoon Crumb Topping (if using) over fruit and pat it down into place. Or cover with second prepared pie crust and crimp edges.

For pie with Crumb Topping:

Bake as instructed on p. 78, Steps 4 and 5, but once you turn the oven down to 375°F, adjust baking time based on fruit (fresh blueberries, peaches, and plums will take less time to bake than apples, etc.).

For pie topped with Traditional Pie Crust:

Bake at 375°F for 45–50 minutes or until crust is nicely browned and fruit juices in center of pie are bubbling.

Serves 10.

Store in refrigerator. Serve chilled or allow pie to come to room temperature. Best when eaten within four days of baking.

RUSTIC APPLE TART

Serves 8.

A trip to the local farmers' market inspired this beautiful, fragrant tart. I wanted to make an apple pie but wanted something that matched the rustic mood of the dinner I was about to make. The idea of throwing pie dough onto a baking sheet and filling it with some of the freshly picked Golden Delicious apples on my counter proved irresistible. I was concerned about how to avoid getting an undercooked, soggy crust because I knew I wouldn't be able to prebake a free-form tart (and I have always recommended prebaking pie crusts/tarts). However, by rolling the dough thin enough, making the sides thick enough, and baking it at a higher temperature in the bottom third of the oven, I was able to make a perfect tart with a crisp, delicate crust and tender apples. I used Golden Delicious, but Granny Smith or Stayman-Winesap would also work well.

Can be made a day ahead. Store in refrigerator. Serve chilled or allow tart to come to room temperature. Best when eaten within four days of baking

> Prepared Traditional Pie Crust (see p. 87) dough
> 5 cups firm apples cut into small chunks (see instructions below)
> 1/4 cup granulated sugar
> 1 tablespoon corn starch
> 1 teaspoon cinnamon
> 1/4 teaspoon nutmeg
> 1 tablespoon lemon juice
> 2 tablespoons unsalted butter
> 1 1/2 tablespoons apple or red currant jelly, optional

1. Preheat oven to 400°F. Position rack *in bottom third* of oven. Line a large baking sheet with parchment paper.

2. Roll pie dough into a 12-inch round between two sheets of wax paper. Remove the top sheet and use your fingers to push dough in from the edges to make a perfect 11-inch round: the dough around the edges should now be thicker than the 9 inches across the center (this will make it easier for you to bake the tart the necessary time without the edges getting overdone). Turn the round of dough over onto the parchment paper on baking sheet and remove other piece of wax paper.

3. Peel, core, and slice apples into eight equal slices. Cut each slice into three equal chunks to make 5 cups; put into a large bowl. Add sugar, corn starch, cinnamon, nutmeg, and lemon juice; stir until apples are well coated. Spoon apples over center of pie dough, leaving a 1-inch edge around the entire round. Carefully fold edges of dough over apples and push down slightly so the dough is well supported by the apples. Patch any holes in the dough so juices don't leak out. Dot tops of apples with thin slices of butter.

4. Place in center of rack and bake for 40–50 minutes, until crust is golden brown and apples are tender. Cool on a rack before serving.

5. Optional: Melt apple jelly (or red currant jelly) in a small saucepan. Brush melted jelly over top of apples with a pastry brush.

RUSTIC PLUM TART

Replace apples with 5 cups fresh, ripe, and pitted plums (cut each plum into four slices and cut each slice into two chunks). Use 3 tablespoons corn starch instead of one tablespoon.

PECAN PIE

Serves 10–12.

Pecan pie is a holiday classic. My favorite recipe came from family friend Miriam Sursa, and it never fails to please. It is not too sweet and it's chock full of luscious pecans. But why wait for a holiday to make it? Get baking, and treat yourself and your friends to this delicious pie today.

1 9-inch Traditional Pie Crust (see p. 87), unbaked
1 cup granulated sugar
¾ cup light corn syrup
¼ cup maple syrup
½ cup unsalted butter
½ teaspoon salt
3 large eggs
2 teaspoons pure vanilla extract
2 cups pecans (chopped and whole)

Store in refrigerator. Serve chilled or allow pie to come to room temperature. Best when eaten within four days of baking.

1. Preheat oven to 375°F. Position rack in center of oven. Grease 9-inch pie pan with cooking spray, and generously dust with rice flour. Place pie pastry into pie pan and flute edges. Partially bake crust in oven for 8 minutes while you prepare filling. Remove crust from oven and lower oven temperature to 350°F.

2. Combine sugar, corn syrup, maple syrup, butter, and salt in heavy saucepan over medium heat; stir frequently until sugar is dissolved. Remove from heat.

3. Beat the eggs in a small bowl and quickly whisk into saucepan. Add vanilla and pecans; mix well. Pour into partially baked prepared 9-inch pie shell.

4. Bake in center of oven for 45–50 minutes until center is set. If edges of crust are browning too quickly, cover them with foil. Cool on a rack before serving. Can be made a day ahead.

KEY LIME PIE

Key Lime Pie is one of those special desserts that makes people smile. I like to serve it in the summer after a spicy barbecue. But in warm weather, I don't want to turn the oven on twice to make one dessert, so I bake my Tart Shell Crust and then cook the filling on the stove, the way you would make any lemon curd.

Take note: This pie does not have a deep filling if you follow the directions as given. Key Lime Pie is somewhat rich, so I tend to keep it small. If you double the filling, as I sometimes do, you may have slightly more than you need, but it makes a nice deep pie.

1 prebaked Tart Shell Crust (see p. 89), baked in a 9-inch pie pan or 9-inch tart pan

Filling

½ cup Nellie & Joe's Key West Lime Juice (or other brand of key lime juice; regular lime juice is not the same)

3 large egg yolks

1 14-oz. can sweetened condensed milk

Topping

¾ cup heavy cream

2 tablespoons confectioners' sugar

1½ teaspoons pure vanilla extract

To make Filling:

1. Combine lime juice and egg yolks in small saucepan. Cook over medium-low heat until thickened and liquid thickly coats back of wooden spoon. Stir constantly. Liquid should simmer but not boil. This should take 5–6 minutes.

2. Remove from heat and stir in sweetened condensed milk. Pour filling into small bowl and press plastic wrap directly onto surface to prevent hardening. Refrigerate until cool.

3. Pour cooled filling into prebaked Tart Shell Crust. If using a tart pan, place pan on top of a broad glass and carefully push down sides of shell. For best results, remove pan bottom once tart shell is filled and chilled.

To make Topping:

4. Combine heavy cream, confectioners' sugar, and vanilla in large bowl of electric mixer; beat until stiff peaks form. Use pastry bag to pipe sweetened heavy cream around edges of pie. Refrigerate pie until well chilled. Serve cold.

Serves 8–10.

Store in refrigerator. Best when eaten within three days of baking.

CHOCOLATE CREAM PIE

Serves 8–10.

I have always loved chocolate cream pie. It is the kind of dessert you get to enjoy after special family dinners. I passed my love for it onto my children, and it has become a favorite in our house. Now, when I make it, it doesn't last long and the leftovers disappear from the refrigerator at an alarming rate. The crunchy chocolate tart shell and the rich, creamy chocolate custard are a winning combination.

1 prebaked Chocolate Tart Shell Crust (see p. 90), baked in a 9-inch pie pan or 9-inch tart pan; *or* one prebaked Traditional Pie Crust (see p. 87), baked in a 9-inch pie pan

Filling

4 ozs. semisweet chocolate

4 large egg yolks

$\frac{2}{3}$ cup granulated sugar

$\frac{1}{4}$ cup corn starch

$\frac{1}{4}$ teaspoon salt

2 cups whole milk

1 tablespoon unsalted butter

1 tablespoon pure vanilla extract

Topping

$\frac{3}{4}$ cup heavy cream

2 tablespoons confectioners' sugar

1 $\frac{1}{2}$ teaspoons pure vanilla extract

3 tablespoons shaved semisweet chocolate*

* Use a potato peeler to shave sides of a bar of semisweet chocolate.

To make Filling:

1. Melt chocolate in small, heavy saucepan over low heat, stirring constantly. Remove from heat and cool until lukewarm.

2. Beat egg yolks in large bowl of electric mixer at medium-high speed until foamy. Gradually add sugar a little at a time and continue beating until the mixture is pale yellow and thick. Add the corn starch and salt and beat until well blended.

3. Bring milk to a boil in a large, heavy saucepan over medium-high heat while you are beating the egg yolks.

4. With the mixer on low, gradually add hot milk to egg mixture in a thin stream. Quickly scrape sides and bottom of bowl and mix at medium speed until well blended.

5. Pour the custard mixture back into the saucepan and cook it over medium-high heat, stirring constantly with a wire whip, until it comes to a boil and thickens. Lower heat and cook for 1 minute more. Remove from heat and beat in melted chocolate, butter, and vanilla.

6. Place custard in medium bowl or plastic container to cool. Cover with plastic wrap to prevent a skin from forming over the surface and chill in the refrigerator. *Can be stored in refrigerator for up to 5 days or in freezer for up to 1 month in a tightly sealed container. Keep plastic wrap on surface.*

7. Pour cooled chocolate custard into cooled prebaked Chocolate Tart Shell Crust or Traditional Pie Crust.

To make Topping:
8. Combine heavy cream, confectioners' sugar, and vanilla in large bowl of electric mixer; beat until stiff peaks form. Use pastry bag to pipe sweetened heavy cream around edges of pie. Sprinkle shaved chocolate over whipped cream. Refrigerate until well chilled. Serve cold.

Store in refrigerator. Best when eaten within three days of baking.

COCONUT CREAM PIE

Serves 10.

The best Coconut Cream Pies are usually found in little out-of-the-way restaurants and old inns. In reality, I found them hard to come by even in cookbooks, so I created this recipe years ago. It's full of rich coconut flavor but not too sweet. I like to make it in the crunchy Tart Shell Crust, but traditionalists might prefer the Traditional Pie Crust. No matter which you choose, you'll have a great pie and lots of requests for second helpings.

> 1 prebaked Tart Shell Crust (see p. 89), baked in a 9-inch pie pan or 9-inch tart pan; *or* 1 prebaked Traditional Pie Crust (see p. 87), baked in a 9-inch pie pan

Filling

> 2 large eggs
>
> $\frac{1}{2}$ cup granulated sugar
>
> $\frac{1}{4}$ cup corn starch
>
> $\frac{1}{4}$ teaspoon salt
>
> 1 13.5-oz. can coconut milk
>
> Whole milk to make 2 cups of liquid with coconut milk
>
> 1 tablespoon unsalted butter
>
> 1 teaspoon pure vanilla extract
>
> 1 teaspoon pure coconut extract

Topping

> $\frac{3}{4}$ cup heavy cream
>
> 2 tablespoons confectioners' sugar
>
> 1$\frac{1}{2}$ teaspoons pure vanilla extract
>
> $\frac{1}{4}$ cup toasted sweetened flaked coconut*

* Spread sweetened flaked coconut in a thin layer on a small baking tray. Bake in preheated 350°F oven, stirring every few minutes until light golden brown. This will only take a few minutes. Don't leave the oven!

To make Filling:

1. Beat eggs in large bowl of electric mixer at medium-high speed until foamy. Gradually add sugar a little at a time and continue beating until the mixture is pale yellow and thick. Add corn starch and salt and beat until well blended.

2. Bring coconut milk and whole milk (total 2 cups liquid) to a boil in a large, heavy saucepan over medium-high heat while you are beating the eggs.

3. With the mixer on low, gradually add hot milk mixture to egg mixture in a thin stream. Quickly scrape sides and bottom of bowl and mix at medium speed until well blended.

4. Pour the custard mixture back into the saucepan and cook it over medium-high heat, stirring constantly with a wire whip, until it comes to a boil and thickens. Lower heat and cook for 1 minute more. Remove from heat and beat in butter, vanilla, and coconut extract.

5. Put custard into medium bowl or plastic container to cool. Cover with plastic wrap to prevent skin from forming over the surface and chill in refrigerator. *Can be stored in refrigerator for up to 5 days or in freezer for up to 1 month in a tightly sealed container. Keep plastic wrap on surface.*

6. Pour cooled coconut custard into cooled prebaked Tart Shell Crust or Traditional Pie Crust.

To make Topping:

7. Combine heavy cream, confectioners' sugar, and vanilla in large bowl of electric mixer; beat until stiff peaks form. Use pastry bag to pipe sweetened heavy cream around edges of pie. Sprinkle toasted coconut over top of whipped cream. Refrigerate until well chilled. Serve cold.

Store in refrigerator. Best when eaten within three days of baking.

VANILLA CREAM PIE FILLING

Makes about 2½ cups.

You can use this simple, delicious vanilla custard in a wide variety of desserts. It has a dense, creamy texture and a rich vanilla flavor. The recipe is relatively simply: Just follow the step-by-step instructions and you'll have excellent results each time you make it. This custard is my filling of choice for Fresh Berry Fruit Tarts, Boston Cream Pie, and Banana Cream Pie (see recipes below).

- 4 large egg yolks
- ⅔ cup granulated sugar
- ¼ cup corn starch
- ¼ teaspoon salt
- 2 cups whole milk
- 1 tablespoon unsalted butter
- 2 tablespoons vanilla extract

Can be stored in refrigerator for up to five days or in freezer for up to one month in a tightly sealed container. Keep plastic wrap directly on surface of custard.

1. Beat egg yolks in large bowl of electric mixer at medium-high speed until foamy. Gradually add sugar a little at a time and continue beating until the mixture is pale yellow and thick. Add corn starch and salt and beat until well blended.

2. Bring milk to a boil in a large, heavy saucepan over medium-high heat while you are beating the egg yolks.

3. With the mixer on low, gradually add hot milk to egg mixture in a thin stream. Quickly scrape sides and bottom of bowl and mix at medium speed until well blended.

4. Pour the custard mixture back into the saucepan and cook it over a medium-high heat, stirring constantly with a wire whip, until it comes to a boil and thickens. Lower heat and cook for 1 minute more. Remove from heat and beat in butter and vanilla.

5. Put custard in medium bowl or plastic container to cool. Cover with plastic wrap to prevent a skim from forming over surface and chill in refrigerator.

FRESH BERRY FRUIT TARTS

Spread cooled Vanilla Cream Pie Filling into cooled prebaked Traditional Pie Crust (see p. 87) or Tart Shell Crust (see p. 89). Arrange 1 1/2–2 cups fresh strawberries, blueberries, and/or raspberries (rinsed and completely dry) on top of custard.

Place 1/2 cup strawberry jelly and 1 tablespoon brandy or cognac in small saucepan and simmer until jelly is dissolved and liquefied but thickened slightly. Carefully brush onto berries. Refrigerate until ready to serve.

Store in refrigerator. Best when eaten within three days of baking.

BOSTON CREAM PIE

Use a long, thin knife to slice a cooled 8- or 9-inch round of vanilla layer cake horizontally in half (use Vanilla Cupcakes recipe, p. 46, and follow instructions to make 8- or 9-inch cake round). Spread about half the cooled Vanilla Cream Pie Filling across bottom cake half (consider making only half the recipe unless you want some leftover). Replace top half of cake.

Spread Chocolate Glaze (recipe follows) evenly across top layer of cake. Chill until chocolate has set.

Take note: Cake is easiest to cut before glaze becomes too hard.

Store in refrigerator. Best when eaten within three days of baking.

Chocolate Glaze
Melt 6 ounces semisweet chocolate and 4 tablespoons unsalted butter in a small, heavy saucepan over medium-low heat; stir constantly until smooth. Immediately remove from heat.

BANANA CREAM PIE

Cut two large ripe bananas into 1/4-inch-thick slices and mix into cooled Vanilla Cream Pie Filling. Spread into cooled prebaked Traditional Pie Crust (see p. 87) or Tart Shell Crust (see p. 89). Pipe Whipped Cream Topping (recipe follows) around outer rim of pie and chill until very cold.

Store in refrigerator. Best when eaten within three days of baking.

Whipped Cream Topping
Combine 3/4 cup heavy cream, 2 tablespoons confectioners' sugar, and 1 1/2 teaspoons vanilla in large bowl of electric mixer; beat until stiff peaks form. Use pastry bag to pipe sweetened heavy cream around edges of pie.

CHAPTER 7

Cookies

CHOCOLATE CHIP COOKIES

CREAM-FILLED CHOCOLATE
COOKIES

BUTTER COOKIES
Cream-Filled Butter Cookies
Chocolate-Filled Butter Cookies

SUGAR COOKIES

SHORTBREAD COOKIES
Coconut
Lemon
Lemon Cornmeal

CHOCOLATE SHORTBREAD
COOKIES

LINZERTORTE COOKIES

ALMOND BUTTER COOKIES

PECAN BUTTER COOKIES

COCONUT MACAROONS

GINGERSNAPS

GINGERBREAD MEN

OATMEAL COOKIES
Almond Crisps

ALMOND BISCOTTI

HAZELNUT BISCOTTI

MANDELBROT
Walnut Mandelbrot

BLACK and WHITE COOKIES

CHOCOLATE PEANUT
BUTTER BALLS

WE ALL HAVE FAVORITE COOKIES that we can't resist. They make our mouths water, remind us of holidays or special family members, and bring comfort and happiness. Fortunately for the gluten-intolerant, cookies are relatively easy to make gluten-free. In fact, many are actually better without wheat. You will find easy success in this chapter. The recipes are very basic and simple to master. In fact, if you are a baking novice, I suggest you start with a cookie recipe. It's hard to go wrong.

If you have a well-stocked pantry (see Chapter 3), you'll be able to make any of these recipes at a moment's notice. You'll also find suggestions for freezing dough because I think having easy access to premade cookie dough is a luxury worth having. You can bake a fresh batch of cookies for after-school snacks or a special after-dinner treat without starting from scratch.

During the holidays, I usually have at least three cookie doughs in my freezer, fewer during the rest of the year. The only trick you may want to fine-tune is making a smooth log of cookie dough to slice. Many of the recipes here call for shaping the dough into a log so that you can easily slice the cookies. After you put the dough in the refrigerator or freezer to chill, take it out and reshape the log after about 15 minutes to make sure it does not flatten out.

Have you ever noticed that sometimes when you make a cookie recipe, the cookies turn out crisp and high, and the next time you make the same cookie recipe with exactly the same ingredients, the cookies are flat and chewy? The difference is due to the temperature of the ingredients—particularly the fats. If you use cold butter or shortening, your cookies will not spread as much, will take longer to bake, and will be crisper (though not necessarily crisp). In fact, we purposely chill the dough when we make shortbreads. If you use room-temperature butter or shortening, especially if the room is warm, your cookies will spread more, take less time to bake, and be chewier.

This chapter uses the following pans:
- Large, heavy baking sheets or cookie trays

THE LAST WORD ON COOKIES

- Set up before starting the recipe: assemble all the ingredients
- Measure carefully (see Chapter 3)
- Preheat the oven to the proper temperature (make sure the oven is calibrated correctly)
- Do not open the oven door more than necessary
- Use a timer because you can get distracted. Test for doneness at the first time given in the recipe, then continue baking, if necessary, until the cookie is fully cooked. Make a note of the total baking time for the next time you make the recipe

CHOCOLATE CHIP COOKIES

This is the very first recipe I converted to gluten-free. I was hungry for these cookies for more than a year before I tried to make them without wheat. Six months later, when we found out one of my sons could no longer eat gluten, making them became a necessity: these had been his favorite cookies.

Take note: The recipe calls for vegetable shortening (yes, you can use the new shortenings made without trans fats); if you use butter, the dough will spread all over the cookie sheet.

I usually make up a batch of dough, bake one sheet, and then freeze the rest of the dough in two small, tightly sealed containers. If you want to make chocolate chip cookie dough ice cream, make a half recipe, using a pasteurized egg substitute to make the dough. Then roll it into tiny pieces, freeze it, and add it to your ice cream maker as instructed.

1 cup vegetable shortening (not butter or margarine)

1 cup granulated sugar

½ cup dark brown sugar

2 large eggs

1 tablespoon pure vanilla extract

2 cups plus 2 tablespoons Brown Rice Flour Mix (see p. 6)

1½ teaspoons baking soda

1 teaspoon xanthan gum

½ teaspoon salt

12 ozs. chocolate chips (optional: plus ¼ cup)

1 cup chopped nuts, optional

1. Preheat oven to 375° F. Position rack in center of oven. Lightly grease cookie sheet with cooking spray.

2. Beat shortening and both sugars at medium speed in large bowl of electric mixer. Add eggs and vanilla; beat until fluffy.

3. Add flour, baking soda, xanthan gum, and salt; mix at medium speed until well blended. Mix in chocolate chips and nuts.

4. Drop heaping teaspoons of dough onto cookie sheet 2 inches apart. Bake in center of oven for 8–10 minutes until light golden brown. (For convection ovens, bake at 350°F using no more than 3 trays at a time.) Transfer to a wire rack and cool. Store in an airtight container.

Makes about 70 cookies. Recipe can be cut in half.

Best when eaten within three days of baking. After three days, store in refrigerator. Can be kept in refrigerator for two weeks or frozen for up to one month.

Unbaked dough can be kept in refrigerator for up to three days in tightly sealed plastic container or frozen for up to one month. To freeze, cover top of dough with plastic wrap and place inside tightly sealed plastic container so no air touches dough.

CREAM-FILLED CHOCOLATE COOKIES

Makes about 40 filled cookies or 80 single cookies.

This cookie does not really try to replace the store-bought version we all know and remember. It has more real chocolate flavor and tastes fresher. The cream filling does, however, try to give the kids on my cookie-testing panels what they want and expect in a cream-filled cookie: the sweet, shortening-based filling that kids everywhere seem to love (you can use the new shortenings made without trans fats). I tried fancy real cream fillings and buttercreams, but no, the cream filling below was the winner. Of course, you *could* use a more grown-up filling, but then the little kid in *you* might squawk.

Unbaked dough can be stored in refrigerator for up to 3 days or frozen for up to 2 months. To freeze, wrap plastic-wrapped log of dough in foil.

$\frac{3}{4}$ cup unsalted butter

1 cup granulated sugar

1 large egg

1 teaspoon pure vanilla extract

1$\frac{3}{4}$ cups Brown Rice Flour Mix (see p. 6)

$\frac{1}{4}$ cup sweet rice flour (see p. 7)

$\frac{1}{2}$ cup baking cocoa

1 teaspoon baking powder

1 teaspoon baking soda

1 teaspoon xanthan gum

$\frac{1}{4}$ teaspoon salt

Cream Filling

3 tablespoons vegetable shortening

2 cups confectioners' sugar

$\frac{3}{4}$ teaspoon pure vanilla extract

2 tablespoons hot water

1. Beat butter and sugar at medium speed in large bowl of electric mixer until light and creamy. Add egg and vanilla and beat well.

2. Add flours, baking cocoa, baking powder, baking soda, xanthan gum, and salt; mix until a soft, smooth dough is formed.

3. Divide dough into two equal halves. Drop first half in small mounds across a large sheet of plastic wrap. Fold the plastic over the dough and shape into a long, 1-inch-diameter log, leaving plastic open at the ends. Twist ends and flatten dough at each end. Try to smooth log by rolling back and forth on counter. Repeat with second half of dough. Refrigerate both rolls until well chilled.

4. Preheat oven to 350°F. Position rack in center of oven. Lightly grease cookie sheet with cooking spray.

5. Using a thin, sharp knife, slice chilled dough into $\frac{1}{8}$-inch slices and place 1 inch apart on cookie sheet. Bake in center of oven for about 9 minutes or until cooked through. Cool slightly on cookie sheet and transfer to wire rack to cool completely.

To make Cream Filling:

6. Combine shortening, confectioners' sugar, vanilla, and hot water in large bowl of electric mixer. Beat until light and creamy. Spread filling on one side of a cookie and cover with another cookie. Store in airtight container.

After three days, store cookies in refrigerator. Can be kept in refrigerator for two weeks or frozen for up to one month.

BUTTER COOKIES

Makes about
40 cookies. Recipe can
be doubled.

One day I started to crave the kind of tender, flavorful butter cookies they sell at good bakeries. Recreating them proved to be a bit of a challenge, but the end result is this classic butter cookie with an excellent melt-in-your-mouth texture and taste. Dress them up with candied cherries, dip them in chocolate and sprinkles, or make sandwich cookies by spreading the Cream Filling or Chocolate Filling (recipes follow) between two cookies and pressing them together. For effortless variety, try jam, lemon curd, or prepared frostings. You can also use this recipe to make cut-out or spritz butter cookies to decorate for holidays.

Unbaked dough can be stored in refrigerator for up to one week or frozen for up to two months. To freeze, wrap logs in plastic wrap and then wrap in foil.

After three days, store cookies in refrigerator. Can be kept in refrigerator for two weeks or frozen for up to one month.

$1/2$ cup unsalted butter

$1/3$ cup granulated sugar

1 large egg

$1 1/2$ teaspoons pure vanilla extract

1 cup Brown Rice Flour Mix (see p. 6)

$1/4$ teaspoon baking powder

$1/4$ teaspoon xanthan gum

$1/8$ teaspoon salt

1. Preheat oven to 325°F. Position rack in center of oven. Lightly grease cookie sheet with cooking spray.

2. Beat butter and sugar together in large bowl of electric mixer until light and creamy. Add egg and vanilla and mix until smooth.

3. Add flour, baking powder, xanthan gum, and salt; beat at medium-high speed until a soft, smooth dough is formed.

4. Shape dough into a flat square and wrap in wax paper; refrigerate for 30 minutes. Drop half of dough in small mounds across a large sheet of plastic wrap. Fold the plastic over the dough and shape into a long, 1-inch-diameter log, leaving plastic open at the ends. Twist ends and flatten dough at each end. Try to smooth log by rolling back and forth on counter. Repeat with second half of dough. Refrigerate both rolls until well chilled. *For spritz cookies: Chill until cold.*

5. Using a thin, sharp knife, slice chilled dough into $1/4$-inch slices and place 1 inch apart on cookie sheet. Top with granulated sugar, colored sprinkles, candied cherries, or mini chocolate morsels, if desired. Bake in center of oven for 12–15 minutes or until a very light golden color. Bottom should be light golden brown. Transfer to a wire rack and cool. Store in an airtight container.

CREAM-FILLED BUTTER COOKIES

Cream Filling

    3 tablespoons vegetable shortening

    2 cups confectioners' sugar

    $\frac{3}{4}$ teaspoon vanilla

    2 tablespoons hot water

1. Combine shortening, confectioners' sugar, vanilla, and hot water in large bowl of electric mixer. Beat until light and creamy. Spread filling on one side of a cookie and cover with another cookie. Store in airtight container.

After three days, store cookies in refrigerator. Can be kept in refrigerator for two weeks or frozen for up to one month.

CHOCOLATE-FILLED BUTTER COOKIES

Chocolate Filling

    3 ozs. semisweet chocolate, chopped

    1 teaspoon canola oil

1. Combine chopped chocolate and canola oil in a small, heavy saucepan. Melt chocolate over a low heat, stirring constantly. Remove from heat. Spread filling on one side of a cookie and cover with another cookie. Store in airtight container.

After three days, store cookies in refrigerator. Can be kept in refrigerator for two weeks or frozen for up to one month.

SUGAR COOKIES

Makes about
80 cookies.

These sugar cookies are light, crunchy, sweet, and delicious—just like sugar cookies are supposed to be. In fact, they passed the kid testing panel with flying colors. They are perfect just the way they are, or you can dress them up with sprinkles or colored icings for the holidays. The sweet rice flour is necessary to help give them the body they need to pass the sugar cookie-criterion test set by my panel of experts: crunchy yet chewy. The dough freezes well and is ideal to keep on hand for snacks or school lunches.

$^3/_4$ cup unsalted butter

1 cup granulated sugar

1 large egg

1 tablespoon pure vanilla extract

1$^3/_4$ cups Brown Rice Flour Mix (see p. 6)

$^1/_4$ cup sweet rice flour (see p. 7)

1 teaspoon baking powder

1 teaspoon xanthan gum

$^1/_4$ teaspoon salt

Unbaked dough can be stored in refrigerator for up to one week or frozen for up to two months. To freeze, wrap logs in plastic wrap and then wrap in foil.

After three days, store cookies in refrigerator. Can be kept in refrigerator for two weeks or frozen for up to one month.

1. Beat butter and sugar in large bowl of electric mixer until light and creamy. Add egg and vanilla and mix until smooth.

2. Add flours, baking powder, xanthan gum, and salt; beat until a thick, smooth dough is formed.

3. Shape dough into a flat square and wrap in wax paper; refrigerate for 30 minutes. Drop half of dough in small mounds across a large sheet of plastic wrap. Fold the plastic over the dough and shape into a long, 1-inch-diameter log, leaving plastic open at the ends. Twist ends and flatten dough at each end. Try to smooth log by rolling back and forth on counter. Repeat with second half of dough. Refrigerate both rolls until well chilled.

4. Preheat oven to 350°F. Position rack in center of oven. Lightly grease cookie sheet with cooking spray.

5. Using a thin, sharp knife, slice chilled dough into $^1/_4$-inch slices and place 1 inch apart on cookie sheet. Bake in center of oven for 12–15 minutes or until a very light golden color. Transfer to a wire rack and cool. Store in an airtight container.

For cutout cookies: Roll out dough between 2 large sheets of wax paper. Chill until very cold. Cut into desired shapes with cookie cutters, and chill again on cookie sheet before baking.

SHORTBREAD COOKIES

The original recipe for these shortbreads was a family favorite. I often used the dough to make cut-out cookies for holidays: little Christmas trees with red or green sprinkles in December, colorful Easter eggs in the spring, tiny orange pumpkins in the fall, delicate hearts with red sprinkles for Valentine's Day. I made them year 'round even when there were no holidays because my children loved them. Fortunately, they are still a favorite in their new gluten-free version.

You can make these shortbreads in my easy roll-and-slice version, pat them into traditional rounds and cut them into pie-shaped wedges, or use a cookie cutter to cut them into special shapes. No matter which method you choose, you'll have a great-tasting classic shortbread that will keep you coming back for more. Try the coconut, lemon, and lemon cornmeal versions, too, for a really special treat (recipes follow).

$\frac{1}{2}$ cup unsalted butter

$\frac{1}{4}$ cup granulated sugar

$1\frac{1}{2}$ teaspoons pure vanilla extract

$\frac{3}{4}$ cup Brown Rice Flour Mix (see p. 6)

$\frac{1}{4}$ cup sweet rice flour (see p. 7)

$\frac{1}{4}$ teaspoon xanthan gum

$\frac{1}{8}$ teaspoon salt

Granulated sugar

1. Beat butter and sugar in large bowl of electric mixer until light and creamy. Add vanilla and mix well.

2. Add flours, xanthan gum, and salt; mix until a soft dough is formed.

3. Drop dough in small mounds across a large sheet of plastic wrap. Fold the plastic over the dough and shape into a long, 1-inch-diameter log, leaving plastic open at the ends. Twist ends and flatten dough at each end. Try to smooth log by rolling back and forth on counter. Refrigerate until well chilled.

4. Preheat oven to 350°F. Position rack in center of oven. Lightly grease cookie sheet with cooking spray.

5. Using a thin, sharp knife, slice chilled dough into $\frac{5}{8}$-inch slices and place on greased cookie sheet 1 inch apart. Sprinkle with granulated sugar. Chill cookies (on cookie sheet) until cold before baking. Bake in center of oven for 12–14 minutes or until light golden. Cookies should not brown. Cool slightly on cookie sheet and transfer to wire rack to cool completely. Store in an airtight container.

Alternate shape: Pat dough into two 6-inch rounds, about $\frac{1}{2}$ inch thick,

Makes about 30 cookies. Recipe can be doubled.

Unbaked dough can be stored in refrigerator for up to one week or frozen for up to two months. To freeze, wrap plastic-wrapped log of dough in foil.

After three days, store cookies in refrigerator. Can be kept in refrigerator for two weeks or frozen for up to one month.

on cookie sheet. Sprinkle with granulated sugar. Crimp edges decoratively and prick top of dough with tines of fork. Lightly score circle of dough into six triangles; do not push knife completely through dough. Bake about 15 minutes until light golden and centers are cooked. Cookies should not brown. Cut out triangles with a sharp knife while still warm.

For cutout cookies: Roll out dough between 2 large sheets of wax paper. Chill until very cold. Cut into desired shapes with cookie cutters, and chill again on cookie sheet before baking.

COCONUT SHORTBREAD COOKIES

In Step 2 add ¼ cup shredded sweetened coconut that was pulverized in a food processor or blender, and ½ teaspoon coconut extract.

LEMON SHORTBREAD COOKIES

In Step 2, add 1 teaspoon (packed) grated lemon rind, and ½ teaspoon lemon extract.

LEMON CORNMEAL SHORTBREAD COOKIES

In Step 2, add 1 teaspoon (packed) grated lemon rind, and ½ teaspoon lemon extract, and substitute ¼ cup cornmeal for ¼ cup of the Brown Rice Flour Mix.

CHOCOLATE SHORTBREAD COOKIES

Makes about
40 cookies.
Recipe can be doubled.

This is an exquisite, melt-in-your-mouth shortbread cookie that children of all ages will love. The rich chocolate flavor is perfect with milk or special after-dinner coffees. The dough mixes up quickly and freezes well. I usually make a double batch and freeze several small rolls to use in later weeks.

 ½ cup unsalted butter

 ¼ cup granulated sugar

   1 teaspoon pure vanilla extract

 ¾ cup Brown Rice Flour Mix (see p. 6)

   2 tablespoons sweet rice flour (see p. 7)

 ¼ cup cocoa powder

 ¼ teaspoon xanthan gum

 ⅛ teaspoon salt

 ½ cup semisweet mini chocolate chips

   Granulated sugar

1. Beat butter and sugar in large bowl of electric mixer until light and creamy. Add vanilla and mix well.

2. Add flours, cocoa powder, xanthan gum, and salt; mix until a soft dough is formed. Mix in chocolate chips.

3. Shape dough into a flat square and wrap in wax paper; refrigerate for 30 minutes. Drop dough in small mounds across a large sheet of plastic wrap. Fold the plastic over the dough and shape into a long, 1-inch-diameter log, leaving plastic open at the ends. Twist ends and flatten dough at each end. Try to smooth log by rolling back and forth on counter. Refrigerate until well chilled.

4. Preheat oven to 350°F. Position rack in center of oven. Lightly grease cookie sheet with cooking spray.

5. Using a thin, sharp knife, slice chilled dough into ⅝-inch slices and place on greased cookie sheet 1 inch apart. Sprinkle with granulated sugar. Chill cookies (on cookie sheet) until cold before baking. Bake in center of oven for 8–10 minutes or until centers are cooked. Cool slightly on cookie sheet and transfer to wire rack to cool completely. Store in an airtight container.

Unbaked dough can be stored in refrigerator for up to one week or frozen for up to two months. To freeze, wrap plastic-wrapped log of dough in foil.

After three days, store cookies in refrigerator. Can be kept in refrigerator for two weeks or frozen for up to one month.

Alternate shape: Pat dough into two 6-inch rounds, about ½ inch thick, on cookie sheet. Sprinkle with granulated sugar. Crimp edges decoratively and prick top of dough with tines of fork. Lightly score circle of dough into six triangles, but do not push knife through dough. Bake 12–14 minutes or until centers are cooked. Cut triangles out with a sharp knife while still warm.

LINZERTORTE COOKIES

These were the most difficult of all the cookies to convert to gluten-free. I tried unsuccessfully for two Christmases to get Linzertorte connoisseur Carl Scariati to give me his seal of approval. I had made them for decades in their fabulous original form, and that was a hard act to follow. The texture is supposed to be light yet rich, crumbly but firm, delicate enough to melt in your mouth yet with enough staying power to blend with the raspberry preserves. Finally, I developed a gluten-free version that made Carl smile, and I am proud to include it in this book.

Makes about
40 filled cookies
or 80 single cookies.

- 1 cup unsalted butter
- $^2/_3$ cup confectioners' sugar
- 3 tablespoons well-beaten large egg
- 1 $^1/_2$ cups Brown Rice Flour Mix (see p. 6)
- $^1/_2$ cup sweet rice flour (see p. 7)
- $^1/_2$ teaspoon xanthan gum
- 1 $^1/_3$ cups finely ground walnuts
- $^1/_2$ cup seedless red raspberry preserves
- Confectioners' sugar, for garnish

1. Beat butter and sugar in large bowl of electric mixer until light and fluffy. Add egg and mix until smooth.

2. Add flours and xanthan gum; beat until a smooth dough is formed. Mix in walnuts.

3. Roll dough $^1/_4$ inch thick between two large sheets of wax paper. Chill until very cold. Cut into desired shapes with 1 $^1/_2$-inch cookie cutters. Chill cookies (on cookie sheet) until cold before baking.

4. Preheat oven to 325°F. Position rack in center of oven. Lightly grease cookie sheet with cooking spray.

5. Bake in center of oven for 12–14 minutes or until a very light golden color. Test for doneness. Bottom should be golden. Transfer to a wire rack and cool. Store unfilled cookies in an airtight container.

6. Within 4 hours of serving, spread half of the cookies you plan to use with $^1/_2$ teaspoon of raspberry preserves. Top with remaining cookies. Sift confectioners' sugar over all completed cookies. Store any uneaten filled cookies in refrigerator. *For best texture, it is best to fill them within 4 hours of serving.*

Unbaked dough can be stored in refrigerator for up to one week or frozen for up to two months. To freeze, shape dough into a flattened round; wrap in plastic wrap and then wrap in foil.

After three days, store cookies in refrigerator. Can be kept in refrigerator for two weeks or frozen for up to one month.

ALMOND BUTTER COOKIES

Makes about
60 cookies.
Recipe can be
cut in half.

These luscious butter cookies have a rich almond flavor and a firm texture. I made the original recipe for years at Christmastime because they reminded me of a cookie made with almond paste that my grandparents would bring me when I was a child. Now in their gluten-free form, they are great for the holidays or any time you yearn for something a little special. Both the dough and the cookies freeze exceptionally well.

3½ ozs. almond paste

½ cup granulated sugar

2 large egg yolks

½ teaspoon almond extract

¾ cup unsalted butter

2 cups Brown Rice Flour Mix (see p. 6)

½ teaspoon xanthan gum

⅔ cup finely chopped almonds

Confectioners' sugar

Unbaked dough can be kept in refrigerator for up to three days in tightly sealed plastic container or frozen for up to one month. To freeze, cover top of dough with plastic wrap and place inside tightly sealed plastic container so no air touches dough.

After three days, store cookies in refrigerator. Can be kept in refrigerator for two weeks or frozen for up to one month.

1. Preheat oven to 350°F. Position rack in center of oven. Lightly grease cookie sheet with cooking spray.

2. Beat almond paste, sugar, egg yolks, and almond extract in large bowl of electric mixer for 3 minutes or until almond paste is thoroughly incorporated and smooth. Add butter and beat until light and fluffy.

3. Add flour and xanthan gum; beat until a smooth dough is formed. Mix in almonds.

4. Use your hands to shape dough into ¾-inch balls, crescents, or ovals and place on cookie sheet.

5. Bake in center of oven for 12–14 minutes or until a very light golden color. Test for doneness. Bottom should be light golden brown. Transfer to a wire rack and cool. Sprinkle with confectioners' sugar. Store in an airtight container.

PECAN BUTTER COOKIES

Perhaps you have missed the taste and texture of those delicate pecan-based cookies called Mexican Wedding Cakes. The cookie has other names as well, including pecan sandies and pecan meltaways. But no matter what you call it, it is a recipe that converts well to gluten-free. This buttery cookie is chock full of sweet nutty pecans. It's great for holiday cookie trays, afternoon snacks with iced tea and lemonade, or anytime you want a tender, delicious cookie.

> 1 cup unsalted butter
>
> 6 tablespoons confectioners' sugar
>
> 2 teaspoons pure vanilla extract
>
> 2 cups Brown Rice Flour Mix (see p. 6)
>
> 1 teaspoon xanthan gum
>
> 1 cup pecans, toasted and chopped*
>
> Confectioners' sugar

1. Preheat oven to 350°F. Position rack in center of oven. Lightly grease cookie sheet with cooking spray.

2. Beat butter and sugar in large bowl of electric mixer until light and creamy. Add vanilla and mix until smooth.

3. Add flour and xanthan gum; beat until a smooth dough is formed. Mix in pecans.

4. Use your hands to shape dough into 1-inch balls. Roll balls in confectioners' sugar and place on cookie sheet.

5. Bake in center of oven for 12–15 minutes or until a very light golden color. Test for doneness. Bottom should be light golden brown. Transfer to a wire rack and cool. Store in an airtight container.

Makes about 50 cookies. Recipe can be cut in half.

Unbaked dough can be kept in refrigerator for up to three days in tightly sealed plastic container or frozen for up to one month. To freeze, cover top of dough with plastic wrap and place inside tightly sealed plastic container so no air touches dough.

After three days, store cookies in refrigerator. Can be kept in refrigerator for two weeks or frozen for up to one month.

* Bake pecans about 5 minutes in preheated 350°F oven.

COCONUT MACAROONS

*Makes about
20 cookies.
Recipe can be doubled.*

Everyone who loves macaroons seems to have a favorite recipe. My family had been making this one in its original form for years, and it was a treasured Christmas cookie. Fortunately, it was really easy to convert to gluten-free. In fact, no one was able to tell the first year I made the switch. Be sure you mix the cream of coconut well before you measure it (you can freeze the rest to use another time).

    2 7-oz. packages sweetened flaked coconut
    $\frac{2}{3}$ cup confectioners' sugar
    $\frac{1}{4}$ cup canned cream of coconut
    1 oz. cream cheese
    3 tablespoons Brown Rice Flour Mix (see p. 6)
    1 large egg white
    1 teaspoon pure vanilla extract
    Pinch of salt

After three days, store cookies in refrigerator. Can be kept in refrigerator for two weeks or frozen for up to one month.

1. Preheat oven to 325°F. Position rack in center of oven. Line cookie sheet with heavy foil and spray lightly with cooking spray.

2. Chop contents of one 7-ounce bag of coconut with confectioners' sugar in food processor for 1 minute.

3. Add cream of coconut, cream cheese, flour, egg white, vanilla, and salt; process until a soft dough is formed.

4. Place balance of coconut in a soup bowl. Drop rounded teaspoons of dough into coconut and roll to coat completely; drop onto cookie sheet 2 inches apart. Bake in center of oven for about 20 minutes or until golden. Transfer to wire rack and cool. Store in airtight container.

GINGERSNAPS

There's something about a spicy gingersnap cookie and a cup of fragrant, hot mulled cider that shouts Christmas. Come the beginning of December and the first sightings of Santa hats in the stores, visions of sugar and spice blend with distant strains of *The Nutcracker Suite* to get me in the mood for the holidays. But, of course, these gingersnaps are good any time you'd like to add a little spice to your day. Fast and easy to make, they are a great cookie to keep in the refrigerator or freezer because they stay fresh for a long time. The dough also freezes well, so you can bake a fresh batch anytime you want.

Makes about 56 cookies.

$\frac{3}{4}$ cup vegetable shortening

1 cup granulated sugar

1 large egg

$\frac{1}{4}$ cup molasses

1$\frac{3}{4}$ cups Brown Rice Flour Mix (see p. 6)

$\frac{1}{4}$ cup sweet rice flour (see p. 7)

2 teaspoons baking soda

$\frac{1}{2}$ teaspoon xanthan gum

1 teaspoon cinnamon

$\frac{3}{4}$ teaspoon ground ginger

$\frac{1}{4}$ teaspoon ground cloves

$\frac{1}{4}$ teaspoon salt

Confectioners' sugar

1. Beat shortening and sugar in large bowl of electric mixer until light and creamy. Beat in egg and molasses and mix until smooth.

2. Add flours, baking soda, xanthan gum, cinnamon, ginger, cloves, and salt; mix to form a soft dough. Shape dough into a flat square and wrap in plastic wrap. Refrigerate for 30 minutes.

3. Preheat oven to 375°F. Position rack in center of oven. Lightly grease cookie sheet with cooking spray.

4. Use your hands to shape dough into 1-inch balls. Roll balls in confectioners' sugar and place on cookie sheet.

5. Bake 8–10 minutes or until cooked through. Transfer to a wire rack and cool. Store in an airtight container.

Unbaked dough can be kept in refrigerator for up to three days in tightly sealed plastic container or frozen for up to one month. To freeze, cover top of dough with plastic wrap and place inside tightly sealed plastic container so no air touches dough.

After three days, store cookies in refrigerator. Can be kept in refrigerator for two weeks or frozen for up to one month.

GINGERBREAD MEN

*Makes about 24
2-inch cookies.*

Gingerbread Men are a classic holiday cookie. Just say the words, and memories of flour, cookie cutters, and the sweet smell of cinnamon come rushing back to even the littlest bakers. Mine are delicately spiced and a tad crisp with the tiniest bit of chew. If you desire, roll them a little thicker than $\frac{1}{4}$ inch and bake them a little less; they will be slightly softer. You can also cut them with larger (or smaller) cookie cutters, depending on your family tradition, but you will have to adjust the baking time. The cookies keep well in the refrigerator and can be successfully frozen so you can enjoy these special treats all through the holiday season.

$\frac{1}{4}$ cup vegetable shortening

$\frac{1}{4}$ cup granulated sugar

1 egg yolk (from a large egg)

2 tablespoons molasses

$\frac{3}{4}$ cup Brown Rice Flour Mix (see p. 6)

$\frac{1}{4}$ cup sweet rice flour (see p. 7)

$\frac{1}{2}$ teaspoon baking soda

$\frac{1}{4}$ teaspoon xanthan gum

$\frac{1}{2}$ teaspoon cinnamon

1 teaspoon powdered ginger

$\frac{1}{8}$ teaspoon ground cloves

$\frac{1}{8}$ teaspoon salt

Unbaked dough can be kept in refrigerator for up to three days in tightly sealed plastic container or frozen for up to one month. To freeze, cover top of dough with plastic wrap inside the tightly sealed plastic container so no air touches dough.

After three days, store cookies in refrigerator. Can be kept in refrigerator for two weeks or frozen for up to one month.

1. Beat shortening and sugar in large bowl of electric mixer until light and creamy. Beat in egg yolk and molasses and mix until smooth.

2. Add flours, baking soda, xanthan gum, cinnamon, ginger, cloves, and salt; mix to form a soft dough. Roll dough between two sheets of wax paper to about $\frac{1}{4}$-inch thick. Refrigerate until well chilled (at least an hour).

3. Preheat oven to 350°F. Position rack in center of oven. Lightly grease cookie sheet with cooking spray.

4. Use a 2" cookie cutter to cut out gingerbread men; place on cookie sheet $\frac{1}{2}$ inch apart. Chill cutout cookies on cookie sheet until very cold before baking.

5. Bake 6–9 minutes until cooked through; check cookies after 6 minutes (baking time depends on how thick your baking sheet is and on how thick you rolled dough). Transfer to a wire rack and cool. Decorate as desired or sprinkle with powdered confectioners' sugar. Store in an airtight container.

OATMEAL COOKIES

These delicious cookies are full of the warm flavors we associate with autumn: cinnamon, nutmeg, and ginger. If you use butter, they will be somewhat chewy; shortening makes a crisper version. You can use the same recipe, but add sliced slivered almonds in place of the oatmeal and raisins to make Almond Crisps (recipe follows). They are perfect for an afternoon snack, but special enough to serve for dessert after dinner with a fruit sorbet or homemade applesauce.

Makes about 60 cookies. Recipe can be cut in half.

> 1 cup unsalted butter *or* vegetable shortening
>
> 1 cup dark brown sugar
>
> 1 cup granulated sugar
>
> 2 large eggs
>
> 1 tablespoon pure vanilla extract
>
> 2 cups Brown Rice Flour Mix (see p. 6)
>
> 2 teaspoons baking powder
>
> 1 teaspoon baking soda
>
> $3/4$ teaspoon xanthan gum
>
> $1/2$ teaspoon salt
>
> $1/2$ teaspoon cinnamon
>
> $1/2$ teaspoon nutmeg
>
> $1/2$ teaspoon ground ginger
>
> 2 cups gluten-free quick-cooking or rolled oats*
>
> 1 cup raisins

1. Preheat oven to 350°F. Position rack in center of oven. Lightly grease cookie sheet with cooking spray.

2. Beat butter (or shortening) and sugars in large bowl of electric mixer until light and creamy. Add eggs and vanilla and mix until smooth.

3. Add flour, baking powder, baking soda, xanthan gum, salt, cinnamon, nutmeg, and ginger; beat until a smooth dough is formed. Mix in oats and raisins.

4. Drop heaping teaspoons of dough onto cookie sheet. Bake in center of oven for about 10 minutes. Transfer to a wire rack and cool. Store in an airtight container.

ALMOND CRISPS

In Step 3, replace oatmeal and raisins with 4 cups sliced or slivered almonds.

Unbaked dough can be kept in refrigerator for up to three days in tightly sealed plastic container or frozen for up to one month. To freeze, cover top of dough with plastic wrap and place inside tightly sealed plastic container so no air touches dough.

After three days, store cookies in refrigerator. Can be kept in refrigerator for two weeks.

* Although there is concern in the gluten-free community about our ability to buy uncontaminated oats, it appears that McCanns® Irish Oatmeal is a product we can trust. In addition, Bob's Red Mill® and several other companies also package and sell "gluten-free" oatmeal.

ALMOND BISCOTTI

*Makes about
36 cookies.*

You will find different versions of this classic biscotti everywhere you go. I had a much-loved recipe and was worried I would never be able to make it again. Luckily, gluten-free flours make fabulous biscotti, and my recipe is even better now in its new gluten-free form. These biscotti are simple to make and keep amazingly well in the refrigerator or freezer. Make a batch once and you'll never want to be without them again.

After three days, store cookies in refrigerator. Can be kept in refrigerator for three weeks or frozen for up to six weeks.

* Bake almonds about 6 minutes in pre-heated 350°F oven.

2 cups Brown Rice Flour Mix (see p. 6)
1 cup granulated sugar
1 teaspoon baking powder
1 teaspoon xanthan gum
$\frac{1}{8}$ teaspoon salt
2 large eggs
1 tablespoon Amaretto
2 teaspoons pure almond extract
$1\frac{1}{2}$ teaspoons pure vanilla extract
1 teaspoon unsalted butter, room temperature
$\frac{3}{4}$ cup whole almonds, lightly toasted and coarsely chopped*

1. Preheat oven to 300°F. Lightly grease and flour a large cookie sheet with cooking spray and rice flour.

2. Combine flour, sugar, baking powder, xanthan gum, and salt in large bowl of electric mixer. Add eggs, Amaretto, almond extract, vanilla, and butter; beat at medium speed until well combined. Mix in almonds. Dough will be very sticky and crumbly.

3. Use your hands to shape dough into two slightly flattened logs, each 8 inches long, 2 inches wide, and 1 inch high. Place logs 2 $\frac{1}{2}$ inches apart on cookie sheet.

4. Place in center of oven and bake 40–45 minutes or until light golden brown. Logs will spread and flatten. Remove to a cutting board and cool 8 minutes.

5. Using a cutting board and serrated knife, slice logs diagonally into $\frac{1}{2}$-inch-wide biscotti. Place biscotti back on cookie sheet with the cut surfaces down and return to oven. Bake another 15–20 minutes or until golden brown. Turn biscotti over and bake another 12–15 minutes until golden brown on second side. Remove from oven and cool completely on a rack. Store in airtight container.

HAZELNUT BISCOTTI

These crunchy biscotti are flavored with hazelnut liqueur and anise. They can be addictive, so you might find yourself keeping a small stash in your refrigerator or freezer. Grab one in the morning to go with your coffee, or serve them after dinner with a luscious dessert wine. They are easy to make; just follow the directions. And keep a bottle of Frangelico and some hazelnuts in your pantry so you can make them whenever your supply runs out.

2 cups Brown Rice Flour Mix (see p. 6)

1 cup granulated sugar

1 1/4 teaspoons baking powder

1 teaspoon xanthan gum

2 large eggs

3 tablespoons Frangelico liqueur

1 1/2 teaspoons pure vanilla extract

1 1/2 teaspoons pure anise extract

1 cup whole hazelnuts, lightly toasted, skins removed, and coarsely chopped*

1. Preheat oven to 300°F. Position rack in center of oven. Lightly grease a large cookie sheet with cooking spray and dust with rice flour.

2. Combine flour, sugar, baking powder, and xanthan gum in large bowl of electric mixer. Add eggs, Frangelico, vanilla, and anise extract; beat at medium speed until well combined. Mix in hazelnuts. Dough will be thick.

3. Use your hands to shape dough into two slightly flattened logs, each 10 inches long, 3 inches wide, and 1/2 inch high. Place logs 2 1/2 inches apart on cookie sheet.

4. Place in center of oven and bake 40 minutes or until light, firm, and dry. Logs will spread slightly. Remove from oven and cool 8 minutes.

5. Using a cutting board and serrated knife, slice logs diagonally into 1/2-inch-wide biscotti. Place biscotti back on cookie sheet with the cut surfaces down and return to oven. Bake another 15–20 minutes or until golden brown. Turn biscotti over and bake another 15–20 minutes. Remove from oven and cool completely on rack. Store in airtight container.

Makes about 36 cookies.

After three days, store cookies in refrigerator. Can be kept in refrigerator for three weeks or frozen for up to six weeks.

* Bake hazelnuts about 6 minutes in preheated 350°F oven. Skins are more easily removed after baking.

MANDELBROT

My mother made the wheat version of this recipe with walnuts (see recipe that follows) in large batches to give as gifts at Christmas. I always looked forward to receiving her precious little gift bag, and I'd always hide it away to enjoy it with my morning coffee. Mandelbrot is a Jewish nut-filled biscotti-like cookie, but it is enriched with more oil and eggs than its Italian cousin. This delicate, crunchy cookie is easy to make and more than a bit addictive. When I converted the recipe to gluten-free, I found that many of the traditional versions contained almonds (and lemon zest, which I choose to leave out, but you can add back in). I make both versions now, but the walnut version always brings back special memories.

*After three days, store
in refrigerator. Can be
kept in refrigerator for
three weeks or frozen
for up to six weeks.*

   2 cups plus 1 tablespoon Brown Rice Flour Mix (see p. 6)
   1 cup granulated sugar
   1 teaspoon baking powder
   $\frac{3}{4}$ teaspoon xanthan gum
   2 large eggs
   $\frac{1}{3}$ cup canola oil
   2 teaspoons pure almond extract
   1 teaspoon pure vanilla extract
   $1\frac{1}{4}$ cups whole almonds, coarsely chopped

1. Preheat oven to 325°F. Lightly grease a large cookie sheet with cooking spray and dust with rice flour.
2. Combine flour, sugar, baking powder, and xanthan gum in large bowl of electric mixer. Add eggs, oil, almond extract, and vanilla; beat at medium speed until well combined. Mix in almonds. Dough will be very sticky.
3. Use a spatula and floured hands to shape dough into three logs, each measuring 8 x 2 inches and 1 inch high, on prepared cookie sheet. Place logs $2\frac{1}{2}$ inches apart on cookie sheet.
4. Place in center of oven and bake 40–45 minutes, until light golden brown. Logs will spread and flatten. Remove to a cutting board and cool 8 minutes.
5. Using a serrated knife, slice logs on diagonal into $\frac{1}{2}$-inch wide mandelbrot. Place mandelbrot back on cookie sheet, standing up, and return to oven. Bake another 10–15 minutes until light golden brown. Remove from oven and cool completely on a rack. Store in an airtight container.

WALNUT MANDELBROT

In Step 2, replace almonds with $1\frac{1}{4}$ cups coarsely chopped walnuts. Add 1 tablespoon pure vanilla extract. Omit almond extract.

BLACK AND WHITE COOKIES

Black and White Cookies are really flat little cakes covered with a thin icing. Although they are rarely found outside of the New York metropolitan area, this regional treat can be found on almost every block in New York City. They are delicious in their new gluten-free form, and even if you've never had one before, you will find this cookie a welcome addition to your gluten-free repertoire. If the somewhat labor-intensive task of frosting one half of the cookie with vanilla icing and the other half with chocolate fails to hold any allure, feel free to make them all vanilla or all chocolate. In addition, one creative kid tester asked to create a "sandwich cookie" using regular vanilla cake icing more along the lines of a Whoopie Pie. But no matter how you frost your Black and White Cookies, they'll bring big smiles when you serve them with a glass of milk or a cup of coffee for an afternoon snack.

1 1/4 cups Brown Rice Flour Mix (see p. 6)

1 tablespoon buttermilk powder

1/2 teaspoon baking soda

1/4 teaspoon baking powder

1/4 teaspoon xanthan gum

1/4 teaspoon salt

7 tablespoons unsalted butter, softened

1/2 cup granulated sugar

1 large egg

1 teaspoon vanilla

1/4 cup water

1. Preheat oven to 350°F. Position rack in center of oven. Lightly grease cookie sheet with cooking spray.

2. Combine brown rice flour mix, buttermilk powder, baking soda, baking powder, xanthan gum, and salt in a small bowl and set aside.

3. Beat butter and sugar at medium speed in large bowl of electric mixer until light and fluffy. Add egg and vanilla and beat well.

4. Reduce speed to low and add flour mixture and water in two additions; mix until just smooth.

5. Drop rounded tablespoons of batter 1 inch apart onto cookie sheets and flatten *very slightly*. Bake in center of oven for about 12 minutes until tops are puffed and cookies are very pale golden and cooked through (tops should spring back when touched). Cool slightly on cookie sheet and transfer to wire rack to cool completely.

Makes about 24 cookies.

Best when eaten within three days of baking. After three days, store in refrigerator. Can be kept in refrigerator for two weeks or frozen for up to three weeks.

6. Using a small spatula or butter knife, spread Vanilla Icing (recipe follows) over flat side of each cookie. As Vanilla Icing dries, spread Chocolate Icing (recipe follows) over other half. Once icing is dry, store cookies in an airtight container. Place sheets of wax paper between layers of cookies.

VANILLA ICING

$1\frac{1}{3}$ cups confectioners' sugar

1 or 2 teaspoons light corn syrup

1 teaspoon fresh lemon juice

$\frac{1}{2}$ teaspoon pure vanilla extract

1-2 tablespoons water

1. In a small bowl, stir together confectioners' sugar, light corn syrup, fresh lemon juice, vanilla extract, and 1 tablespoon water. Add more water, $\frac{1}{2}$ teaspoon at a time, until smooth, spreadable consistency is reached.

CHOCOLATE ICING

$1\frac{1}{3}$ cups confectioners' sugar

$\frac{1}{4}$ cup unsweetened cocoa powder

1 or 2 teaspoons light corn syrup

1 teaspoon fresh lemon juice

$\frac{1}{4}$ or $\frac{1}{2}$ teaspoon pure vanilla extract

2-3 tablespoons water

1. In a small bowl, stir together confectioners' sugar, cocoa powder, light corn syrup, fresh lemon juice, vanilla extract, and 1 tablespoon water. Add more water, $\frac{1}{2}$ teaspoon at a time, until smooth, spreadable consistency is reached.

CHOCOLATE PEANUT BUTTER BALLS

If you like chocolate and peanut butter, these are probably the most addictive cookies on the planet. Family friend Diane Gillooly brought them each year to our annual Christmas caroling party. People would actually wait for her to arrive and then descend on her offering like locusts. I finally asked for the recipe so I could make it gluten-free for my family. I still only make Chocolate Peanut Butter Balls for the holidays, but we think about them throughout the year. Try them and you'll see why.

> $^{1}/_{2}$ cup unsalted butter
>
> 18 ozs. smooth peanut butter
>
> $3^{1}/_{2}$ cups confectioners' sugar
>
> $2^{1}/_{2}$ cups gluten-free crispy rice cereal*
>
> 16 ozs. semisweet chocolate, chopped

1. Mix butter, peanut butter, and sugar together in large mixing bowl of electric mixer. Beat until creamy.

2. Add crispy rice cereal and mix until cereal is incorporated into dough. Chill until cold.

3. Form into 1-inch balls and refrigerate 12 hours. (It is easier to form balls if dough is chilled first.)

4. In a double boiler or microwave, melt chocolate and keep warm.

5. Dip balls in warm chocolate. Place on wax paper to cool. Refrigerate until chocolate hardens. Store in refrigerator in airtight container. Serve at room temperature or slightly chilled. Best when eaten within 1 week.

Makes about 72 cookies. Recipe can be cut in half.

* There are currently very few gluten-free rice cereals, but Erewhon® Gluten Free Crispy Brown Rice Whole Grain Cereal is very good. Contact U.S. Mills, Inc., Erewhon, 200 Reservoir Street, Needham, MA 02494 (www.usmillsinc.com) to find a supplier.

CHAPTER 8

Other Sweet Treats

BROWNIES

LEMON SQUARES
Key Lime Squares

ICE CREAM SANDWICHES

APPLE CRISP
Pear Crisp

SUMMER FRUIT CRISP
Peaches, Apricots, Plums, Cherries,
or Berries

PUMPKIN BREAD PUDDING
with Caramel Sauce

COCONUT BREAD PUDDING

CREAM PUFFS
Profiteroles

VANILLA FILLING
for Cream Puffs and Eclairs

ECLAIRS

OLD-FASHIONED BUTTERMILK
DOUGHNUTS

CHOCOLATE DOUGHNUTS

APPLE CIDER DOUGHNUTS

THIS CHAPTER IS FILLED with a broad assortment of delectable treats. Some, like the brownies and fruit crisps, are so basic and simple that they might become a regular part of your baking routine. Others, like the eclairs and cream puffs, are a little more involved and might be saved for more special occasions. But no matter which recipe you choose, detailed, step-by-step instructions will allow you to try making things you might never have tried before.

Interestingly enough, many of the recipes here are actually better without wheat. The toppings on the fruit crisps and the crust of the lemon squares will stay firm and crunchy for days. No one will ever believe the brownies are gluten-free. And the ice cream sandwiches are so good, no one will care. Work your way through this chapter and try them all. The luscious bread puddings and fancy pastry cream puffs and eclairs will turn heads and become favorites.

This chapter uses the following pans:
- 9-inch deep-dish pie plate
- 9-inch round cake pan
- 8-inch square baking pan
- glass or ceramic 13 x 9 x 2-inch baking dish
- glass or ceramic 11 x 7 x 2-inch baking dish
- large, heavy baking sheet

THE LAST WORD ON SWEET TREATS

- Set up before starting the recipe: assemble all the ingredients

- Measure carefully (see Chapter 3)

- Use an instant-read thermometer to check temperature of the puff paste dough for the cream puffs and eclairs

- Preheat the oven to the proper temperature (make sure the oven is calibrated correctly)

- Do not open the oven door more than necessary

- Use a timer because you can get distracted

BROWNIES

Once you make this recipe, it will surely become a part of your gluten-free baking repertoire. My simple-to-make brownie is slightly chewy, slightly cake-like, and has a rich chocolate flavor. It keeps well in the refrigerator and freezes exceptionally well. It is perfect à la mode for dessert or by itself for school lunches and afternoon snacks.

$2/3$ cup Brown Rice Flour Mix (see p. 6)

$1/2$ teaspoon salt

$1/2$ teaspoon baking powder

$1/2$ teaspoon xanthan gum

2 ozs. unsweetened chocolate

4 ozs. semisweet chocolate

$1/2$ cup unsalted butter

$1\frac{1}{4}$ cups granulated sugar

2 teaspoons pure vanilla extract

3 large eggs

$3/4$ cup chopped toasted walnuts, optional*

1. Preheat oven to 325°F. Position rack in lower-middle oven. Line bottom and sides of 8-inch square baking pan with foil and grease with cooking spray.

2. Combine flour, salt, baking powder, and xanthan gum in a small bowl. Set aside.

3. Melt chocolate and butter in a heavy, medium-size saucepan over low heat. Remove from heat; whisk in sugar and vanilla. Whisk in eggs, one at a time, and continue to whisk until mixture is completely smooth and glossy. Add flour mixture and whisk until just incorporated. Stir in nuts.

4. Pour batter into prepared pan and place in center of oven. Bake about 45 minutes or until a tester inserted into the center comes out with wet crumbs. Cool in pan on rack for 5 minutes. Remove brownies from pan by lifting out foil, and cool completely on rack. Cut into squares or triangles.

Makes 16 brownies.

Brownies can be stored in refrigerator for up to five days or in freezer for four weeks; wrap in plastic wrap and then in foil.

* Bake walnuts about 5 minutes in preheated 350°F oven.

LEMON SQUARES

Light, luscious lemon squares are a favorite classic dessert. My gluten-free version has a melt-in-your-mouth crumbly crust and a tangy, not too sweet lemon filling. They are easy to make and disappear way too fast. Bake the lemon squares several hours ahead or the day before you plan on serving them in order to give them time to cool. They are perfect for a springtime picnic, dessert after a special dinner, or enjoy them with a cup of afternoon tea. No matter when you eat them, they are always a delicious treat.

Crust

   1 cup Brown Rice Flour Mix (see p. 6)
   1/4 cup granulated sugar
   1 teaspoon xanthan gum
   5 tablespoons cold unsalted butter

1. Preheat oven to 350°F. Position rack in center of oven. Grease bottom of 8-inch square baking pan with cooking spray and generously dust with rice flour.

2. Put flour, sugar, and xanthan gum in large bowl of electric mixer; mix to blend. Add butter and mix on low speed until crumbly. Press dough into bottom of baking pan.

3. Bake in center of oven for 15 minutes or until very light golden.

Lemon Filling

   3 large eggs
   3/4 cup granulated sugar
   2 tablespoons Brown Rice Flour Mix (see p. 6)
   1/2 teaspoon baking powder
   1/8 teaspoon salt
   1/3 cup fresh lemon juice
   2 teaspoons lemon rind
   1/2 teaspoon pure lemon extract
      confectioners' sugar

1. Beat eggs in large bowl of electric mixer at high speed until foamy. Add sugar, flour, baking powder, salt, lemon juice, lemon rind, and lemon extract. Beat until well blended. Pour onto partially baked crust.

2. Bake in center of oven for 20 minutes or until set. Cool on wire rack. Cut into 16 squares or triangles; remove from baking pan onto serving plate. Sift confectioners' sugar over tops. Serve at room temperature or slightly chilled.

KEY LIME SQUARES

Substitute ⅓ cup Nellie & Joe's Key West Lime Juice (or other brand of key lime juice if this is not available; regular lime juice is not the same) for lemon juice, and 2 teaspoons lime rind for lemon rind. Use lime extract, if available, instead of lemon extract.

Store any leftover lemon squares in a tightly sealed container in refrigerator. Do not freeze. Best when eaten within four days of baking.

ICE CREAM SANDWICHES

Makes approximately 12 filled sandwiches.

Summer is the perfect season for ice cream sandwiches. But you have to admit, they are hard to find gluten-free. Now you can indulge in this old-fashioned favorite once again. They are easy to make and delicious. The cookie is full of rich chocolate flavor, with none of the chemical taste or preservatives of the store-bought variety. You get to choose the ice cream filling, so let your imagination soar with all the possibilities—mint chocolate chip, coffee, strawberry, toffee crunch, checkerboard of vanilla and chocolate. Cant wait? You won't miss those stale old ice cream sandwiches from the corner store ever again. Get baking!

$^3/_4$ cup unsalted butter

1 cup granulated sugar

1 large egg

1 teaspoon pure vanilla extract

1$^1/_2$ cups Brown Rice Flour Mix (see p. 6)

$^1/_2$ cup sweet rice flour (see p. 7)

$^1/_2$ cup baking cocoa

1 teaspoon xanthan gum

1 teaspoon baking powder

1 teaspoon baking soda

$^1/_4$ teaspoon salt

Filling

Your favorite ice cream

Unbaked dough can be kept in refrigerator for up to three days or frozen for up to two months. To freeze, wrap plastic-wrapped log of dough in foil.

1. Preheat oven to 350°F. Position rack in center of oven. Lightly grease cookie sheet with cooking spray.

2. Beat butter and sugar at medium speed in large bowl of electric mixer until well blended. Add egg and vanilla and beat well.

2. Add flours, baking cocoa, xanthan gum, baking powder, baking soda, and salt and mix until a soft dough is formed.

3. To shape into a square (for traditionally shaped ice cream sandwiches), drop dough in a mound on large sheet of plastic wrap. Fold the plastic over the dough and shape into a long rectangle 6 inches long, 2$^1/_2$ inches wide, and 2$^1/_2$ inches high, using plastic to flatten ends. Try to smooth dough with your fingers. Refrigerate until well chilled.

4. Using a thin, sharp knife, slice chilled dough into $^1/_4$-inch-thick

squares ($2\frac{1}{2}$ x $2\frac{1}{2}$ inches) and place 1 inch apart on cookie sheet. Bake in center of oven for 11–12 minutes or until cooked through. (Cook 1–2 minutes extra for a crisper cookie.) Cool slightly on cookie sheet and transfer to wire rack to cool completely.

5. Cut ice cream into squares 1 to $1\frac{1}{2}$ inches thick. Place each ice cream square on a cookie and cover each with another cookie. Wrap each sandwich in plastic wrap and store in airtight container in freezer. Cookies and ice cream can also be kept separately and assembled just before serving.

For round ice cream sandwiches: Mound dough on plastic wrap, fold the plastic over the dough, and shape it into a round log 3 inches in diameter and 6 inches long.

The edges of each ice cream sandwich can be dipped into tiny chocolate morsels, M&Ms, or other crushed candies for an extra added treat!

Store cookies in airtight container. After three days, store in refrigerator. Can be kept in refrigerator for two weeks or frozen for up to one month.

APPLE CRISP

Serves 6.

If you find yourself yearning to use those apples you picked last weekend, consider making this delicious apple crisp. It is easy to prepare and keeps well in the refrigerator. I like to serve it warm for dessert with ice cream or frozen yogurt, but I also look forward to eating the leftovers cold for breakfast. I use a combination of apples—usually Granny Smith and Golden Delicious, but you can use any combination of cooking apples.

> 1 cup Brown Rice Flour Mix (see p. 6)
> ¾ cup granulated sugar
> 1¼ teaspoons baking powder
> 1 teaspoon cinnamon
> ½ teaspoon xanthan gum
> ½ teaspoon salt
> 1 large egg
> 6 cups thinly sliced peeled apples
> ⅓ cup butter, melted

Store any leftovers tightly covered in refrigerator. Can be rewarmed in microwave.

1. Preheat oven to 350°F. Position rack in center of oven. Lightly grease 9-inch round cake pan with cooking spray.

2. Combine flour, sugar, baking powder, cinnamon, xanthan gum, and salt in small bowl. Add egg and stir to mix well (mixture will be crumbly).

3. Place apples in cake pan and sprinkle top with flour mixture. Drizzle with melted butter.

4. Place cake pan in center of oven and bake about 40 minutes or until apples are tender and topping is a golden color. Serve warm.

PEAR CRISP

Substitute 6 cups thickly sliced peeled pears for apples.

SUMMER FRUIT CRISP
(PEACHES, APRICOTS, PLUMS, CHERRIES, OR BERRIES)

Serves 6.

This is one of those desserts you can pull together in minutes, but it tastes like you spent hours. Try it when you have fresh ripe fruit from summer farm stands. In the winter, you can use the new flash-frozen fruits available in grocery stores. Take note: Defrost frozen fruit in a colander so any liquid drains away before putting it in the pan.

 5 heaping cups thinly sliced peeled fresh peaches
   (or other fruit)
 $1/3$–$1/2$ cup granulated sugar
 2 tablespoons corn starch
 $1/2$ teaspoon cinnamon
 $1/4$ teaspoon nutmeg
 3 tablespoons lemon juice

Topping Mixture

 1 cup Brown Rice Flour Mix (see p. 6)
 $1/2$ cup brown sugar
 $1/2$ teaspoon cinnamon
 $1/2$ teaspoon xanthan gum
 $1/4$ teaspoon salt
 $1/3$ cup unsalted butter, melted

Store any leftovers tightly covered in refrigerator for up to three days. Can be rewarmed in microwave.

1. Preheat oven to 375°F. Position rack in center of oven. Grease 9-inch deep-dish pie plate with cooking spray.

2. In large mixing bowl, toss peaches with sugar, corn starch, and spices until evenly coated. Stir in lemon juice. Pour peach mixture into prepared pie plate. Set aside.

3. Prepare topping mixture by combining flour, brown sugar, cinnamon, xanthan gum, and salt in a small bowl; stir to blend. Pour in butter, and stir until all dry ingredients are moistened. Break into small pieces with spoon. Apply topping mixture evenly over peaches and pat it firmly into place.

4. Bake in center of oven for about 40 minutes or until bubbly and brown. Serve warm with vanilla ice cream or yogurt.

PUMPKIN BREAD PUDDING WITH CARAMEL SAUCE

Serves 10.

This bread pudding is delicious comfort food with a twist. The aroma of pumpkin and spices will fill your home and keep everyone glued to the table, ready for dessert. Needless to say, the leftovers are also good for breakfast. The trick for making a good gluten-free bread pudding is to use *good bread* and to toast it slightly in the oven. Don't waste good ingredients trying to make the best of those dense, hard, flavorless loaves of bread available in the freezer sections of food stores.

8 cups gluten-free "plain white" bread* (about 1¼ to 1½ lbs.)

2 cups half-and-half

1 15-oz. can pumpkin puree

1 cup dark brown sugar

4 large eggs

1½ teaspoons cinnamon

½ teaspoon nutmeg

½ teaspoon ginger

½ teaspoon allspice

2 teaspoons pure vanilla extract

½ cup golden raisins

confectioners' sugar

Caramel Sauce

⅔ cup dark brown sugar

¼ cup unsalted butter

⅓ cup heavy cream

1. Preheat oven to 325°F. Position rack in center of oven. Remove crusts from bread and cut into ½-inch squares. Spread bread cubes on a large baking sheet and bake until cubes are dried out and light golden. Allow to cool thoroughly.

2. Preheat oven to 350°F. Lightly grease a glass or ceramic 11 x 7 x 2-inch baking dish with cooking spray.

3. Whisk half-and-half, pumpkin, brown sugar, eggs, spices, and vanilla extract in large bowl until smooth. Fold in bread cubes and raisins. Let sit for 30 minutes.

* You can make your own bread (see p. 158) using Bread Flour Mix A or Bread Flour Mix B, or you can use a fresh, top-quality rice bread that is not purchased frozen (such as Whole Foods' Sandwich Bread). The small, hard-frozen rice breads will not make a good bread pudding.

4. Pour mixture into prepared baking dish and place in center of oven. Bake about 40 minutes or until tester inserted into center of bread pudding comes out clean.

5. Prepare Caramel Sauce while bread pudding bakes. Whisk brown sugar and butter in heavy saucepan over medium-high heat until butter melts. Whisk in cream and stir until sugar dissolves and sauce is smooth, about 3 minutes. Keep warm.

6. Sift confectioners' sugar over finished bread pudding. Serve warm with Caramel Sauce.

Store any leftovers tightly covered in refrigerator. Can be rewarmed in microwave.

COCONUT BREAD PUDDING

Serves 10.

Sweet coconut and crunchy pecans blend with a bit of pineapple to make this dessert something special. If you like coconut, this is one of those recipes you will make again and again. Serve it after spicy jambalayas and gumbos or tangy barbecues. Be sure to use a good-quality gluten-free bread, and toast it slightly as instructed in the directions for the best results.

6½ cups gluten-free "plain white" bread* (about 1 lb.)
½ cup sweetened shredded coconut
1 cup pecans, chopped and lightly toasted**
1 cup crushed (canned) pineapple, drained
1 15-oz. can cream of coconut (Coco Lopez® or Goya®)
2½ cups whole milk
½ cup granulated sugar
6 large eggs
1 tablespoon pure vanilla extract
confectioners' sugar

Store any leftovers tightly covered in refrigerator. Can be rewarmed in microwave.

*You can make your own bread (see p. 158) using Bread Flour Mix A or Bread Flour Mix B, or you can use a fresh, top-quality rice bread that is not purchased frozen (such as Whole Foods' Sandwich Bread). The small, hard-frozen rice breads will not make a good bread pudding.

** Bake pecans about 5 minutes in pre-heated 350°F oven.

1. Preheat oven to 325°F. Position rack in center of oven. Remove crusts from bread and cut into 1-inch squares. Spread bread cubes on a large baking sheet, and bake until cubes are dried out and light golden. Allow to cool thoroughly.

2. Preheat oven to 350°F. Lightly grease glass or ceramic 13 x 9 x 2-inch baking dish with cooking spray.

3. Mix bread, sweetened shredded coconut, toasted pecans, and crushed pineapple together in a large bowl and set aside.

4. Combine cream of coconut, whole milk, and sugar in heavy medium-size saucepan. Stir over medium heat until sugar dissolves and mixture is warm. Remove from heat.

5. Whisk eggs in large bowl to blend. Whisk in warm milk mixture and vanilla. Pour mixture over breadcrumbs and mix in VERY gently. Let sit for 30 minutes.

6. Pour mixture into prepared baking dish. Gently push bread mixture into milk mixture. Bake in center of oven until pudding is set and golden brown, about 45 minutes. Cool slightly.

7. Sift confectioners' sugar over pudding. Serve warm.

CREAM PUFFS

Cream Puffs are an old-fashioned treat. You can fill them with sweetened whipped cream or creamy puddings such as Vanilla Filling (see p. 145), or you can make Profiteroles by filling them with a scoop of ice cream and resting them in a pool of chocolate sauce (recipes follow). Cream Puffs really aren't hard to make; just follow the detailed instructions below and in no time you will have a plate full of luscious cream puffs to share with family and friends.

Take note: The baked puff paste dough freezes well, so double the recipe and make extra for the freezer. You'll have cream puff shells available to fill for fabulous last-minute desserts.

Make 8 puffs, 2 ½ to 3 inches diameter. Recipe can be doubled.

 ½ cup Brown Rice Flour Mix (see p. 6)

 1 teaspoon granulated sugar

 ⅛ teaspoon xanthan gum

 ⅛ teaspoon salt

 ¼ cup unsalted butter, cut into 4 pieces

 ½ cup fat-free milk

 ½ teaspoon pure vanilla extract

 2 large eggs

 Vanilla Filling (see p. 145)

Cook's Note: Soak saucepan in ice cold water for easy cleanup.

1. Preheat oven to 400°F. Position rack in center of oven. Line a large, heavy baking sheet with parchment paper.

2. Combine flour, sugar, xanthan gum, and salt in small bowl and set aside.

3. Bring butter and milk to a boil in a 1-quart saucepan over medium heat. Try not to allow too much of the milk to evaporate. As soon as the milk mixture boils, remove saucepan from heat and add flour mixture all at once. Use a soup spoon, and stir vigorously to combine. The dough should come together in a tight ball.

4. Return saucepan to a medium heat and cook, stirring constantly, until dough has a smooth appearance and oil from the butter begins to glisten on the surface (about 1 minute). The bottom of the pan will be coated with a thin film of dough, and the temperature of the inside of the dough taken with an instant-read thermometer should be 140°–150°F. (Use a thermometer; don't guess until you've done it many times!)

5. Transfer the dough to the large bowl of an electric mixer. Begin to beat dough at medium speed and add the vanilla and then the eggs one at a time; allow the first egg to be fully absorbed and the dough

to become smooth and shiny before adding the second. After each addition, the dough will separate into slippery little lumps before coming back together. Beat until dough is very smooth in consistency and is a very pale yellow color, about 2–3 minutes.

6. Use a pastry bag with a $\frac{1}{2}$-inch smooth, round opening at the tip. Fill the pastry bag with warm dough. Squeeze the dough onto the prepared baking sheet, making circular mounds 2 inches in diameter and 1 inch high at the highest point. Space the mounds 2 inches apart. Be sure to tap down any pointy dough tips that result from pulling away the pastry bag from each mound.

7. Put baking sheet on center rack in oven and bake about 25 minutes or *until dough rises and puffs are double or triple in size and dough turns golden brown.* Turn oven temperature down to 300°F but do not open door. Bake another 8–10 minutes or until puffs are firm and crusty to the touch. Remove baking sheet from oven; turn oven off.

8. Quickly and carefully slice each puff in half horizontally with a thin, pointy knife; leave one side connected, if desired. Put the puffs back on the baking sheet with the two halves open. Put baking sheet back in oven with door ajar for about 10 minutes or until the interiors have dried out. Take note: If the puffs are moist inside, they will shrink. Cool completely on a rack before filling and serving.

To use immediately:
Spoon desired filling into bottom half of puff and cover with top half. Sift confectioners' sugar over top if desired.

To use within 24 hours:
Store in an airtight container at room temperature. Recrisp in preheated 350°F oven. Allow to cool completely on a rack and fill as above.

To freeze for use within 2 weeks:
Store in an airtight container and freeze for up 2 weeks. Defrost, recrisp, cool, and fill as above.

PROFITEROLES

Fill cooled puffs with a scoop of vanilla or chocolate ice cream. To serve, spread warm chocolate sauce (recipe follows) on dessert plate and place profiteroles on top of sauce.

Chocolate Sauce
Combine $\frac{1}{2}$ cup heavy cream, 1 tablespoon unsalted butter, and 2 tablespoons light corn syrup in a small, heavy saucepan. Bring to a boil, whisking constantly. Remove from heat. Add 4 ounces chopped semisweet chocolate and whisk until smooth. Makes 1 cup.

Store in refrigerator until ready to serve. Best when eaten within three days of baking.

Chocolate sauce can be stored tightly covered in refrigerator for up to 3 weeks. Rewarm on stove or in microwave.

VANILLA FILLING
FOR CREAM PUFFS AND ECLAIRS

Makes about 2½ cups

     4 large egg yolks
  ⅔ cup granulated sugar
  ¼ cup corn starch
  ¼ teaspoon salt
     2 cups whole milk
     1 tablespoon unsalted butter
  1–2 tablespoons pure vanilla extract*

1. Beat egg yolks in large bowl of electric mixer at medium-high speed until foamy. Gradually add sugar a little at a time, and continue beating until the mixture is pale yellow and thick. Add the corn starch and salt and beat until well blended.

2. Bring milk to a boil in a large, heavy saucepan over medium-high heat while you are beating the egg yolks.

3. With the mixer on low, gradually add hot milk to egg mixture in a thin stream. Quickly scrape sides and bottom of bowl and mix at medium speed until well blended.

4. Pour the custard mixture back into the saucepan and cook it over medium-high heat, stirring constantly with a wire whip, until it comes to a boil and thickens. Lower heat and cook for 1 minute more. Remove from heat and beat in butter and vanilla.

5. Put custard in medium bowl or plastic container to cool. Cover top with plastic wrap to prevent a skin from forming over the surface, and chill in refrigerator.

LIGHTER VANILLA CREAM FILLING FOR CREAM PUFFS

Make half of Vanilla Filling recipe above. Beat 1 cup heavy cream in large bowl of electric mixer until stiff peaks form. Fold into prepared Vanilla Filling above.

Can be stored in refrigerator for up to five days or in freezer for up to one month in a tightly sealed container. Keep plastic wrap on surface.

* Optional flavoring for Cream Puffs: 1 tablespoon pure vanilla extract and 1–2 tablespoons rum, cognac, orange liqueur, or coffee-flavored liqueur.

* Optional flavoring for Eclairs: 1 tablespoon pure vanilla extract and 1 teaspoon (or to taste) pure almond extract.

ECLAIRS

Makes 8 eclairs, 5 inches long. Recipe can be doubled.

Eclairs are a special pastry dessert that convert well to gluten-free. You can double the recipe and make extra for the freezer because the baked puff paste dough actually freezes well. You can also make the eclairs larger than the directions detail below, but you will have to bake them longer. Before you do this, though, I suggest you make the recipe a few times following the directions exactly to get a feel for what the eclair should look like before you lower the temperature.

If you miss eating cannoli—those delicious crisp Italian pastries filled with a creamy ricotta mixture—this recipe might help you out a bit. Make the pastry below but fill it with your favorite cannoli filling. It won't be exactly what you remember, but it will help soothe the craving.

Cook's Note: Soak saucepan in ice cold water for easy cleanup.

$^1\!/_2$ cup Brown Rice Flour Mix (see p. 6)

1 teaspoon granulated sugar

$^1\!/_8$ teaspoon xanthan gum

$^1\!/_8$ teaspoon salt

$^1\!/_4$ cup unsalted butter, cut into 4 pieces

$^1\!/_2$ cup fat-free milk

$^1\!/_2$ teaspoon pure vanilla extract

2 large eggs

Chocolate Glaze (recipe follows)

Vanilla Filling (see p. 145)

1. Preheat oven to 400°F. Position rack in center of oven. Line a large, heavy baking sheet with parchment paper.

2. Combine flour, sugar, xanthan gum, and salt in small bowl and set aside.

3. Bring butter and milk to a boil in a 1-quart saucepan over medium heat. Try not to allow too much of the milk to evaporate. As soon as the milk mixture boils, remove pan from heat and add flour mixture all at once. Use a soup spoon, and stir vigorously to combine. The dough should come together in a tight ball.

4. Return the pan to medium heat and cook, stirring constantly, until dough has a smooth appearance and oil from the butter begins to glisten on the surface (about 1 minute). The bottom of the pan will be coated with a thin film of dough, and the temperature of the inside of the dough taken with an instant-read thermometer should be 140°–150°F. (Use a thermometer—don't guess until you've done the recipe many times.)

5. Transfer the dough to the large bowl of an electric mixer. Begin to mix dough at medium speed and add the vanilla and then the eggs one at a time; allow the first egg to be fully absorbed and the dough to become smooth and shiny before adding the second. After each addition, the dough will separate into slippery little lumps before coming back together. Beat until dough is very smooth in consistency and is a very pale color (2–3 minutes.)

6. Use a pastry bag with a $\frac{1}{2}$-inch smooth, round opening at the tip. Fill the pastry bag with warm dough. Squeeze the dough onto the prepared baking sheet, making strips 4 inches long by 1 inch wide. Space the strips 2 inches apart. Be sure to tap down any pointy dough tips that result from pulling away the pastry bag from each mound.

7. Put baking sheet on center rack in oven and bake about 25 minutes *or until dough rises and eclairs are double or triple in size and dough turns rich golden brown*. Turn oven temperature down to 300°F but do not open door. Bake another 8–10 minutes or until eclairs are firm and crusty to the touch. Remove baking sheet from oven; turn oven off.

8. Quickly and carefully slice each eclair in half horizontally with a thin, pointy knife; leave one side connected, if desired. Put the eclairs back on the baking sheet with the two halves open. Put baking sheet back in oven with door ajar for about 10 minutes or until interiors have dried out. Take note: If the eclairs are moist inside, they will shrink. Cool completely on a rack before filling and serving.

To use immediately:
Spoon filling onto bottom half of eclair and cover with top half.

To use within 24 hours:
Store in an airtight container at room temperature. Recrisp in preheated 350°F oven. Allow to cool completely on a rack and fill as above.

To freeze for use within 2 weeks:
Store in an airtight container and freeze for up to 2 weeks. Defrost, recrisp, cool, and fill as above.

9. Spread a thick strip of Chocolate Glaze (recipe follows) down length of each eclair. Refrigerate until ready to serve. Best when eaten within 3 days of baking.

Glaze can be made ahead and rewarmed in microwave. Store tightly covered in refrigerator for up to three weeks.

Chocolate Glaze

2 ozs. semisweet chocolate

1 1/2 tablespoons unsalted butter

1. Melt semisweet chocolate and butter in a small, heavy saucepan over medium-low heat; stir constantly until smooth. Immediately remove from heat and cool slightly. Makes about 1/3 cup.

OLD-FASHIONED BUTTERMILK DOUGHNUTS

*Makes 9
3-inch doughnuts
and 9 holes.*

There is an art to making a good gluten-free doughnut, and it starts with not being afraid to get a bit messy. When I first started testing recipes, it was apparent that the easier it was to roll and cut the dough, the firmer and denser the doughnut. The more flour I took out of the recipe, the better the doughnut tasted, but each time, the dough became softer to work with. So, if you can finesse a relatively soft uncooked dough into the hot oil, you can make a crisp on the outside, tender and light on the inside, Old-Fashioned Buttermilk Doughnut. It doesn't take much time, and they are surprisingly simple to make. Brew a big pot of coffee and make up a batch of doughnuts so good, no one will be able to tell they are gluten-free.

1¾ cups plus 1 tablespoon Brown Rice Flour Mix (see p. 6)

½ cup granulated sugar

½ teaspoon xanthan gum

1 tablespoon baking powder

1 teaspoon baking soda

½ teaspoon salt

¼ teaspoon nutmeg (or more, if desired)

Canola oil for frying

2 large eggs

7 tablespoons buttermilk

2 tablespoons canola oil

2 teaspoons pure vanilla extract

Rice flour (about 2 tablespoons used to flour boards)

Granulated sugar or confectioners' sugar

Serve doughnuts and holes warm or at room temperature. Best when eaten the day they are made. Wrap any left-over doughnuts (is that possible?) in plastic wrap and then foil to store in freezer for up to two weeks. Rewarm briefly in microwave.

Cook's Note: You can also save oil by frying the doughnuts in a heavy 3-quart saucepan filled with 2 inches of oil. Fry only two dough-nuts at a time.

1. Mix brown rice flour mix, sugar, xanthan gum, baking powder, baking soda and salt in a small bowl and set aside.

2. In large 5-quart saucepan (see Cook's Note at left), heat two inches of canola oil to 350°F. (Use a candy thermometer to maintain temperature. Temperatures higher than 350°F will brown doughnuts before they are fully cooked and prevent them from fully rising.)

3. In large bowl of electric mixer, beat eggs until light and foamy (this will take several minutes). Add brown rice flour mixture, buttermilk, oil, and vanilla; mix one minute at medium-low speed.

4. Liberally spread rice flour over surface of a wooden board (or marble

slab) and lightly flour hands. Use a spatula to move dough onto the wooden board in a ball shape. Dough will be sticky. Roll dough around in the rice flour until it is lightly covered. Gently press dough into a ½-inch round. Use a 3-inch round doughnut cutter (or a 3-inch round cookie cutter and 1-inch round cookie cutter) to cut nine doughnuts and nine doughnut holes. (After you press the dough into shape the first time, you should be able to cut six doughnuts.)

5. Use a pancake turner to gently lift three doughnuts and three holes into the hot oil. The doughnuts should rise slowly to the surface and puff. Cook one minute; turn with a slotted spoon. Cook other side for one minute (doughnuts should be brown in color); remove with slotted spoon to a paper towel-lined plate. Blot any residual oil off doughnuts. Cool slightly.

6. Repeat with remaining doughnuts and holes, making sure oil is heated to 350°F before proceeding.

7. Gently coat warm doughnuts with granulated sugar or confectioners' sugar (place sugar in a flat bottom bowl and use a spoon to help coat doughnuts).

VANILLA ICING FOR OLD-FASHIONED BUTTERMILK DOUGHNUTS

¾ cup confectioners' sugar

1 teaspoon pure vanilla extract

2 tablespoons half-and-half *or* milk

1. In a small bowl, stir together confectioners' sugar, vanilla, and half-and-half. Mix until smooth.

2. Gently spread tops of warm doughnuts with vanilla icing. Top with sprinkles, if desired.

CHOCOLATE DOUGHNUTS

What could be better than a chocolate doughnut and a cold glass of milk? Perhaps a chocolate doughnut with chocolate icing and sprinkles? If you have been yearning for a delicate, flavorful, melt-in-your-mouth chocolate doughnut, try this one. Follow the directions, expect to get a bit messy when you are cutting out the doughnuts, and then watch the happy, hungry faces appear from all over your home to watch you pull them from the hot oil.

Makes 9
3-inch doughnuts
and 9 holes.

Chocolate Icing (recipe follows)

1½ cups plus 2 tablespoons Brown Rice Flour Mix (see p. 6)

⅓ cup unsweetened cocoa powder

½ cup granulated sugar

½ teaspoon xanthan gum

1 tablespoon baking powder

1 teaspoon baking soda

½ teaspoon salt

Canola oil for frying

2 large eggs

7 tablespoons milk

2 tablespoons canola oil

½ teaspoon pure vanilla extract

1 tablespoon chocolate extract*

Rice flour (about 2 tablespoons used to flour boards)

Sprinkles, optional

1. Prepare Chocolate Icing (recipe follows) and set aside in a covered bowl.

2. Mix brown rice flour mix, cocoa powder, sugar, xanthan gum, baking powder, baking soda, and salt in a small bowl and set aside.

3. In large 5-quart saucepan (see Cook's Note at left), heat two inches of canola oil to 350°F. (Use a candy thermometer to maintain temperature. Temperatures higher than 350°F will brown doughnuts before they are fully cooked and prevent them from fully rising.)

4. In large bowl of electric mixer, beat eggs until light and foamy (this will take several minutes). Add brown rice flour mixture, milk, oil, vanilla, and chocolate extract; mix one minute at medium-low speed.

5. Liberally spread rice flour over surface of a wooden board (or marble slab) and lightly flour hands. Use a spatula to move dough onto

Serve doughnuts and holes warm or at room temperature. Best when eaten the day they are made. Wrap any left-over doughnuts (is that possible?) in plastic wrap and then foil to store in freezer for up to two weeks. Rewarm briefly in microwave.

Cook's Note: You can also save oil by frying the doughnuts in a heavy 3-quart saucepan filled with 2 inches of oil. Fry only two doughnuts at a time.

* Available at fine food stores and The Baker's Catalogue from King Arthur Flour (1-800-827-6836 or bakerscatalogue.com).

the wooden board in a ball shape. Dough will be sticky. Roll dough around in the rice flour until it is lightly covered. Gently press dough into a ½-inch round. Use a 3-inch round doughnut cutter (or a 3-inch round cookie cutter and 1-inch round cookie cutter) to cut nine doughnuts and nine doughnut holes. (After you press the dough into shape the first time, you should be able to cut six doughnuts.)

6. Use a pancake turner to gently lift three doughnuts and three holes into the hot oil. The doughnuts should rise slowly to the surface and puff. Cook one minute; turn with a slotted spoon. Cook other side for one minute (doughnuts should be brown in color); remove with slotted spoon to a paper towel-lined plate. Blot any residual oil off doughnuts. Cool slightly.

7. Repeat with remaining doughnuts and holes, but make sure oil is heated to 350°F before proceeding.

8. Gently spread tops of warm doughnuts with chocolate icing. Top with sprinkles, if desired. Coat doughnut holes with granulated sugar or confectioners' sugar.

CHOCOLATE ICING FOR CHOCOLATE DOUGHNUTS

½ cup confectioners' sugar

¼ unsweetened cocoa powder

1 teaspoon pure vanilla extract

3 tablespoons half-and-half *or* milk

1. In a small bowl, stir together confectioners' sugar, cocoa powder, vanilla, and half-and-half. Mix until smooth.

APPLE CIDER DOUGHNUTS

In the fall, you can find half-gallon jugs of delicious caramel-hued cider propped up on farmstand tables and grocery-store display cases everywhere. You'll also see apple cider doughnuts. But don't feel deprived: I've created a delicious gluten-free version of this autumn favorite. These tender apple cider doughnuts are flavored with a delicate hint of cinnamon and nutmeg, and topped off with a bit of cinnamon sugar. They are irresistible and simple to make—no deep fryers or 6 cups of oil. All you need is a large 5-quart saucepan (no messy stove top to clean) filled with two inches of canola oil. You will also need a candy thermometer to make sure the oil is the proper temperature. Mix up the doughnuts, cut them on a floured board, carefully lift them into the oil with a spatula, and you'll be biting into this special treat in no time.

Makes 9
3-inch doughnuts
and 9 holes.

1¾ cups plus 1 tablespoon Brown Rice Flour Mix (see p. 6)

¼ cup granulated sugar

½ teaspoon xanthan gum

1 tablespoon baking powder

1 teaspoon baking soda

½ teaspoon salt

¾–1 teaspoon cinnamon

¼ teaspoon nutmeg

Canola oil for frying

2 large eggs

7 tablespoons apple cider

2 tablespoons canola oil

Cinnamon sugar*

Rice flour (about 2 tablespoons used to flour boards)

Serve doughnuts and holes warm or at room temperature. Best when eaten the day they are made. Wrap any left-over doughnuts (is that possible?) in plastic wrap and then foil to store in freezer for up to two weeks. Rewarm briefly in microwave.

Cook's Note: You can also save oil by frying the doughnuts in a heavy 3-quart saucepan filled with 2 inches of oil. Fry only two dough-nuts at a time.

* To make cinnamon sugar, combine ⅓ cup granulated sugar with 1 teaspoon cinnamon.

1. Mix brown rice flour mix, sugar, xanthan gum, baking powder, baking soda, salt, cinnamon, and nutmeg in a small bowl and set aside.

2. In large 5-quart saucepan (see Cook's Note at left), heat two inches of canola oil to 350°F. (Use a candy thermometer to maintain temperature. Temperatures higher than 350°F will brown doughnuts before they are fully cooked and prevent them from fully rising.)

3. In large bowl of electric mixer, beat eggs until light and foamy (this will take several minutes). Add brown rice flour mixture, apple cider, and 2 tablespoons of oil; mix one minute at medium-low speed.

4. Liberally spread rice flour over surface of a wooden board (or marble

slab) and lightly flour hands. Use a spatula to move dough onto the wooden board in a ball shape. Dough will be sticky. Roll dough around in the rice flour until it is lightly covered. Gently press dough into a $\frac{1}{2}$-inch round. Use a 3-inch round doughnut cutter (or a 3-inch round cookie cutter and 1-inch round cookie cutter) to cut nine doughnuts and nine doughnut holes. (After you press the dough into shape the first time, you should be able to cut six doughnuts.)

5. Use a pancake turner to gently lift three doughnuts and three holes into the hot oil. The doughnuts should rise slowly to the surface and puff. Cook one minute; turn with a slotted spoon. Cook other side for one minute (doughnuts should be golden brown in color); remove with slotted spoon to a paper towel-lined plate. Blot any residual oil off doughnuts. Cool slightly.

6. Repeat with remaining doughnuts and holes, but make sure oil is heated to 350°F before proceeding.

7. Gently coat warm doughnuts with cinnamon sugar (place cinnamon sugar in a flat-bottom bowl and use a spoon to coat doughnuts).

CHAPTER 9

Breads, Bread Crumbs, Pizza, and More

YOU PROBABLY ALREADY realize that you can no longer take bread for granted. Good gluten-free sandwich bread is hard to find. And finding a great loaf of gluten-free Italian or French bread, well, it's a journey filled with heartbreak. But you may find solace here. Although the wheat breads we are familiar with are clearly difficult to reproduce gluten-free, you can still make delicious bread. The recipes in this chapter do not compromise on tenderness for sandwich breads or crusty crusts and chewy interiors for European-style breads. Follow the directions carefully, and you will be able to find a new favorite or two.

And now a word about pizza. Even though you may have thought of pizza as a fast food, it never really was. The pizza maker in a *good* pizza parlor had been hard at work making the dough, cooking the sauce, and grating the cheese long before you got there. In fact, it would be safe to say that it took him longer to make that crust than it took you to drive over and pick up your pizza (or for them to deliver it to you). Good gluten-free pizza is definitely not fast food; it will take some thought and some prep time. But the pizza recipe in this book makes a fabulous pizza, and you will be happy when you eat it. In spite of my warning, it really doesn't take long to make.

BASIC SANDWICH BREAD
Buttermilk Sandwich Bread

MULTIGRAIN SANDWICH BREAD

CINNAMON BREAD
Cinnamon Raisin Bread

"RYE" BREAD

TRADITIONAL DINNER ROLLS
Multigrain Dinner Rolls

HAMBURGER/HOT DOG BUNS

ENGLISH MUFFINS
Cinnamon-Raisin English Muffins

FRENCH-ITALIAN BREAD

MULTIGRAIN ARTISAN BREAD

PECAN RAISIN ARTISAN BREAD

GOLDEN ITALIAN BREAD WITH RAISINS AND FENNEL

SUBMARINE SANDWICH BREAD

RUSTIC FLAT BREAD (Focaccia)

CHALLAH
Challah Bread with Raisins

BABKA (UKRAINIAN STYLE)

IRISH SODA BREAD

PIZZA CRUST

SOFT PRETZELS

EGG BAGELS

WALNUT BREAD

BUTTERMILK BISCUITS

BREAD CRUMBS

Even better, you can prebake the crust; then when you are ready to eat, simply put on the sauce and cheese and finish baking the pizza in the oven.

There are several other tempting nontraditional bread recipes in this book for you to try, including a few special favorites from my house: Buttermilk Biscuits and Walnut Bread.

This chapter uses the following pans:

- $8\frac{1}{2}$ x $4\frac{1}{2}$-inch loaf pan (not nonstick!)
- 9 x 5-inch loaf pan
- French bread pan, 4 inches wide, for Submarine Sandwich Bread*
- French bread pan, $2\frac{1}{2}$ inches wide, for French–Italian Bread*
- 9-inch round cake pan
- 12-inch round pizza pan (with ridged bottom, not smooth) *or* 12-inch bottom of springform pan (with ridged bottom, not smooth)**
- 9-inch round pizza pan (with ridged bottom, not smooth) *or* 9-inch bottom of springform pan (with ridged bottom, not smooth)**
- Large, heavy baking sheets
- 12-cup square muffin pan (see Traditional Dinner Rolls recipe for details)

THE LAST WORD ON BREADS

- Set up before starting the recipe: assemble all ingredients.
- Measure carefully (see Chapter 3).
- **Check the date on your yeast to make sure it is fresh**. The recipes in this book use dependable $\frac{1}{4}$ ounce packets of active dry yeast granules readily available in grocery stores.
- When making bread, heat water to 110°F; lower temperatures will inhibit the rise and higher temperatures could kill the yeast. Are your eggs at room temperature? (If not, put them in a bowl of warm water.)
- To create a warm place for your breads and pizza to rise, you can preheat your oven to 80°F, turn the oven off, put the bread or pizza dough inside. If you can only preheat your oven to a temperature higher than 80°F, open it up and air it out before you put in the dough, or don't let it preheat all the way. **If the oven is too warm, your bread will not rise correctly when you bake it!**
- Preheat the oven to the proper temperature before baking (make sure the oven is calibrated correctly).
- Do not open the oven door more than necessary.
- Use an instant-read thermometer to check temperatures of liquids for breads and interiors of finished baked breads.
- Use a timer because you can get distracted.
- **Double checking: Why doesn't my bread rise? Why doesn't my bread rise well? Why does my bread rise, and then fall?**

Are you measuring the liquid correctly? Too much liquid can cause your bread to fall. If everything else on this list is correct, try reducing the liquid by 1 tablespoon. If you make bread when it's raining and the house is humid, your bread flour may absorb more moisture than it needs. The extra water in the dough will weigh it down. As in wheat baking, the amount of moisture in the air will affect the rise.

Or perhaps you were so careful about spooning the flour into the measuring cups that you ended up a little short of flour (either when you made the bread flour mix, or when you measured it for the recipe). If you think this might be the case, try adding a tablespoon or two of flour to the dough. If that works, try not to spoon the flour into the cup as lightly next time you're mixing and measuring flours.

Or perhaps you didn't wait until the bread had risen to the proper level because you figured enough time had elapsed, or you waited too long and let it over-proof.

* Available from The Baker's Catalogue from King Arthur Flour (1-800-827-6836 or bakerscatalogue.com), Amazon.com, Sur La Table, other online sellers, and local kitchen supply stores.

** I use inexpensive foil pizza pans from the grocery store for 12" pies. When I make 9" pies, I use two 9–10" bottoms from inexpensive springform cake pans (I use Kaiser springform pans). They have ridged, quilt-like bumps, just like the foil pizza pans. The bumps make the crust a little more crisp and make it easier to spread the dough. If you can't find pans with ridges or bumps, use flat-bottom ones. Your pizza will still be delicious.

BASIC SANDWICH BREAD

Makes one 1-lb. loaf.

Looking for a delicious sandwich bread? This loaf has the consistency of home-made white bread: It's not squishy like mass-produced bread, and it won't harden like a rock or become crumbly. You can make kid-friendly peanut butter and jelly sandwiches for a school lunch or scrumptious grilled cheese and Philly cheese steak sandwiches when you're near a stove. You can also make a yummy piece of buttered toast.

Take note: Allow the bread to rise slowly. Don't put it in a place that is too warm—the ideal temperature is about 80°F. A fast rise will contribute to an unstable bread that is likely to fall. The xanthan gum needs time to set in gluten-free breads. Also, try not to let the bread rise above the pan before you bake it because this will also contribute to instability.

Wrap bread well in plastic wrap and then foil. Store in refrigerator for up to three days or freezer for up to three weeks.

Cook's Notes: Dry ingredients can be mixed ahead and stored in plastic containers for future use. Do not add yeast until just ready to bake bread.

For sandwiches kids will like, use $\frac{1}{4}$ cup sweet rice flour and 1 $\frac{3}{4}$ cups Bread Flour Mix to get a "softer" bread.

> 2 large eggs (room temperature is best)
> 3 tablespoons canola oil
> 2 cups Bread Flour Mix A or B (see pp. 8 and 9)
> 1 $\frac{1}{2}$ teaspoons xanthan gum
> $\frac{1}{2}$ teaspoon salt
> 1 teaspoon unflavored gelatin
> 2 tablespoons granulated sugar
> 1 packet ($\frac{1}{4}$ oz.) of active dry yeast granules (not quick-rise)
> $\frac{3}{4}$ cup plus 2 tablespoons milk, heated to 110°F

1. Lightly grease an 8$\frac{1}{2}$ x 4$\frac{1}{2}$-inch loaf pan (not nonstick!) with cooking spray and dust with rice flour.

2. Mix eggs and canola oil together in a small bowl and set aside.

3. Mix all dry ingredients in large bowl of electric mixer. Quickly add warm milk and egg and oil mixture to the bowl; mix until just blended. Scrape bowl and beaters, and then beat at high speed for 3 minutes. Spoon dough into prepared pan; cover with a light cloth and let rise in a warm place for 30–40 minutes or until dough just reaches $\frac{1}{2}$ inch below top of pan. If you use a warm 80°F oven to help the bread rise, and you have only one oven, you will have to pull the bread out before it is finished rising in order to preheat the oven to bake it.

4. Place rack in center of oven. Preheat oven to 400°F while bread is rising (do not use a convection oven; bread will brown too quickly).

5. Bake bread in center of preheated oven for 10 minutes; cover with aluminum foil and bake another 40–45 minutes. Your bread should have a hollow sound when tapped on the sides and bottom, and your instant-read thermometer should register about 195°F–200°F. Remove bread from oven and turn onto a rack to cool.

BUTTERMILK SANDWICH BREAD

Old-fashioned buttermilk bread makes a great sandwich or a golden piece of toast. The buttermilk keeps the bread softer and more tender (i.e., fresher) than loaves made with regular milk.

Substitute ¾ cup plus 2 tablespoons fresh buttermilk (heated to 110°F) for regular milk in Basic Sandwich Bread recipe above (or ¾ cup plus 2 tablespoons water [110°F] and 3 tablespoons buttermilk powder).

Bake an extra 5–10 minutes longer than the Basic Sandwich Bread recipe above (bake another 45–55 minutes after you cover bread with foil). Your bread should have a hollow sound when tapped on the sides and bottom, and your instant-read thermometer should register about 205° F.

MULTIGRAIN SANDWICH BREAD

Makes one 1-lb. loaf.

You can bake a rich variety of multigrain gluten-free sandwich breads simply by substituting ¼ cup of a whole-grain flour for the Bread Flour Mix below. I like teff flour, which makes a delicious, hearty bread reminiscent of whole-wheat bread, but you could use coarsely ground oatmeal, amaranth, or Montina. I add sesame seeds, sunflower seeds, and golden flax seeds, but you can add your own favorites in whatever proportions you want (but don't add more than 6 tablespoons overall, or your bread will be too dense).

Take note: Allow the bread to rise slowly. Don't put it in a place that is too warm; the ideal temperature is about 80°F. A fast rise will contribute to an unstable bread that is likely to fall. The xanthan gum needs time to "set" in gluten-free breads. Also, try not to let the bread rise above the pan before you bake it, because this will also contribute to instability.

Wrap bread well in plastic wrap and then foil. Store in refrigerator for up to three days or freezer for up to three weeks.

Cook's Note: Dry ingredients can be mixed ahead and stored in plastic containers for future use. Do not add yeast until just ready to bake bread.

White corn meal

2 large eggs (room temperature is best)

3 tablespoons canola oil

1¾ cups Bread Flour Mix A (see p. 8)

¼ cup teff flour

1½ teaspoons xanthan gum

½ teaspoon salt

1 teaspoon unflavored gelatin

2 tablespoons granulated sugar

1 packet (¼ oz.) of active dry yeast granules (not quick-rise)

¾ cup plus 2 tablespoons milk, heated to 110°F

2 tablespoons sesame seeds

2 tablespoons sunflower seeds

2 tablespoons golden flax seeds

1. Lightly grease an 8½ x 4½-inch loaf pan (not nonstick!) with cooking spray and dust with white corn meal.

2. Mix eggs and canola oil together in a small bowl and set aside.

3. Mix all dry ingredients in large bowl of electric mixer. Quickly add warm milk and egg and oil mixture to the bowl; mix until just blended. Scrape bowl and beaters, and then beat at high speed for 3 minutes. Add seeds and mix well. Spoon dough into prepared pan;

cover with a light cloth and let rise in a warm place for 30–40 minutes or until dough just reaches top of pan. Lightly dust top of loaf with white corn meal.

4. Place rack in center of oven. Preheat oven to 400°F while bread is rising (do not use a convection oven; bread will brown too quickly).

5. Bake bread in center of preheated oven for 10 minutes; cover bread with aluminum foil and bake another 45–50 minutes. Your bread should have a hollow sound when tapped on the sides and bottom. Your instant-read thermometer should register about 205°F. Remove bread from oven and turn onto a rack to cool.

CINNAMON BREAD

Makes one 1-lb. loaf.

Wake up to the warm scent of cinnamon toast floating through the air. In order to make cinnamon bread, bakers typically roll bread dough into a large rectangle, sprinkle cinnamon sugar over it, and then roll it into a log before putting it into a loaf pan. Gluten-free bread dough is too soft for this process, but I found that I could lightly fold the cinnamon sugar into my dough and then pour it into the loaf pan. Thus, this recipe is a nontraditional version of an old classic. Any cinnamon sugar that gets onto the crust of the bread will over-brown (and maybe even burn a bit), so be careful not to let too much of it reach the top, sides, or bottom.

Take note: Allow the bread to rise slowly. Don't put it in a place that is too warm; the ideal temperature is about 80°F. A fast rise will contribute to an unstable bread that is likely to fall. The xanthan gum needs time to "set" in gluten-free breads. Also, try not to let the bread rise above the pan before you bake it, because this will also contribute to instability.

Wrap bread well in plastic wrap and then foil. Store in refrigerator for up to three days or freezer for up to three weeks.

Cook's Note: Dry ingredients can be mixed ahead and stored in plastic containers for future use. Do not add yeast until just ready to bake bread.

$\frac{1}{3}$ cup granulated sugar

1 $\frac{1}{2}$ teaspoons cinnamon

2 large eggs (room temperature is best)

3 tablespoons canola oil

2 cups Bread Flour Mix A or B (see pp. 8 and 9)

1 $\frac{1}{2}$ teaspoons xanthan gum

$\frac{1}{2}$ teaspoon salt

1 teaspoon unflavored gelatin

2 tablespoons granulated sugar

1 packet ($\frac{1}{4}$ oz.) of active dry yeast granules (not quick-rise)

$\frac{3}{4}$ cup plus 2 tablespoons milk, heated to 110°F

1. Lightly grease an 8 $\frac{1}{2}$ x 4 $\frac{1}{2}$-inch loaf pan (not nonstick!) with cooking spray and dust with rice flour.

2. Combine $\frac{1}{3}$ cup granulated sugar and cinnamon in a small bowl and set aside.

3. Mix eggs and canola oil together in a small bowl and set aside.

4. Mix all dry ingredients in large bowl of electric mixer. Quickly add warm milk and egg and oil mixture to the bowl; mix until just blended. Scrape bowl and beaters and then beat at high speed for 3 minutes. Scrape bowl and beaters again.

5. Sprinkle cinnamon sugar over the entire top of the dough while it is in the mixing bowl and lightly fold it in with a rubber spatula (about

six turns). It should not be completely mixed in. Spoon dough into prepared pan; cover with a light cloth and let rise in a warm place for about 30–40 minutes (until dough just reaches ½" below top of pan).

6. Place shelf in center of oven. Preheat oven to 400°F while bread is rising (do not use a convection oven because it will brown the bread too quickly).

7. Bake bread in center of preheated oven for 10 minutes; cover bread with aluminum foil and bake another 45–55 minutes. Your bread should have a hollow sound when tapped on the sides and bottom, and your instant-read thermometer should register about 200–205°F. Remove bread from oven and turn onto a rack to cool.

CINNAMON RAISIN BREAD

After completing Step 4 and before Step 5, add ½ to ¾ cup raisins to dough and mix on low speed until completely distributed.

"RYE" BREAD

Makes one 1-lb. loaf.

It took a long time, but I began to miss the uniquely satisfying flavor of rye bread. But how could I make it without rye flour, which has gluten? The trick is to use teff flour to provide the hearty richness and color this bread is known for. A touch of rye flavoring, now available in a gluten-free form, provides the necessary finishing touch. Rye bread is delicious and makes incredible grilled cheese sandwiches, patty melts, and—when you're in the mood for something different—savory bread crumbs for chicken cutlets that you can top with a bit of Gruyere cheese.

Take note: Allow the bread to rise slowly. Don't put it in a place that is too warm; the ideal temperature is about 80°F. A fast rise will contribute to an unstable bread that is likely to fall. The xanthan gum needs time to "set" in gluten-free breads. Also, try not to let the bread rise above the pan before you bake it, because this will also contribute to instability.

Wrap bread well in plastic wrap and then foil. Store in refrigerator for up to three days or freezer for up to three weeks.

Cook's Note: Dry ingredients can be mixed ahead and stored in plastic containers for future use. Do not add yeast until just ready to bake bread.

* An excellent gluten-free rye flavor is available from Authentic Foods (see page 17 for details).

    White corn meal

2 large eggs (room temperature is best)

3 tablespoons canola oil

1¾ cups Bread Flour Mix A (see p. 8)

¼ cup teff flour

1½ teaspoons xanthan gum

½ teaspoon salt

1 teaspoon unflavored gelatin

1 teaspoon rye flavor*

2 tablespoons granulated sugar

1 packet (¼ oz.) of active dry yeast granules (not quick-rise)

¾ cup plus 2 tablespoons milk, heated to 110°F

2 tablespoons caraway seeds

1. Lightly grease an 8½ x 4½-inch loaf pan (not nonstick!) with cooking spray and dust with white corn meal.

2. Mix eggs and canola oil together in a small bowl and set aside.

3. Mix all dry ingredients in large bowl of electric mixer. Quickly add warm milk and egg and oil mixture to the bowl; mix until just blended. Scrape bowl and beaters and then beat at high speed for 3 minutes. Add seeds and mix well. Spoon dough into prepared pan; sprinkle top of loaf with additional caraway seeds if desired (gently pat seeds into dough). Cover with a light cloth and let rise in a warm place for about 40–50 minutes (until dough just reaches 1 inch from top of pan).

4. Place rack in center of oven. Preheat oven to 400°F while bread is rising (do not use a convection oven because it will brown the bread too quickly).

5. Bake bread in center of preheated oven for 10 minutes; cover bread with aluminum foil and bake another 45–50 minutes. Your bread should have a hollow sound when tapped on the sides and bottom, and your instant-read thermometer should register about 200–205°F. Remove bread from oven and turn onto a rack to cool.

TRADITIONAL DINNER ROLLS

Makes 8 rolls.

Wrap rolls well in plastic wrap and then foil. Store in refrigerator for up to three days or freezer for up to three weeks.

Cook's Note: A square muffin pan is a square cupcake pan with 12 individual square forms. Size: 16" x11". It is available at fine cookware stores and online retailers. Dry ingredients can be mixed ahead and stored in plastic containers for future use, but do not add yeast until just ready to bake rolls.

* Or ¾ cup plus 2 tablespoons water (110° F) and 3 tablespoons buttermilk powder.

Think about it: warm, tender dinner rolls wrapped in a linen napkin and brought to the table in a breadbasket. Are you dreaming? No. Try this simple recipe and you'll be biting into a soft, buttery roll in no time. The key to making this old-fashioned favorite is the buttermilk, which enhances the texture. In addition, melted butter, which is traditionally added to the dough, gives these rolls a rich taste.

Take note: Allow the bread to rise slowly. Don't put it in a place that is too warm; the ideal temperature is about 80°F. A fast rise will contribute to an unstable bread that is likely to fall. The xanthan gum needs time to "set" in gluten-free breads. Also, try not to let the bread rise above the pan before you bake it, because this will also contribute to instability.

2 cups Bread Flour Mix A or B (see pp. 8 and 9)
1½ teaspoons xanthan gum
½ teaspoon salt
1 teaspoon unflavored gelatin
2 tablespoons granulated sugar
1 packet (¼ oz.) of active dry yeast granules (not quick-rise)
2 large eggs (room temperature is best)
3 tablespoons unsalted butter, melted and cooled slightly
¾ cup plus 2 tablespoons buttermillk, heated to 110°F
White corn meal, sesame seeds, or poppy seeds for top of rolls (optional)

1. Lightly grease 8 cups of a 12-cup square muffin pan (your Dinner Rolls will be square like wheat ones—see Cook's Note at left) or a 12-cup cupcake pan with cooking spray. If you use a cupcake pan, this recipe will make 10–12 rolls; be sure to fill each cupcake form no more than half way. Dust with rice flour or white corn meal (if using flour, it is easier to sift the flour over the top of the pan through a fine sieve).

2. Mix all dry ingredients in large bowl of electric mixer. Quickly add warm buttermilk, egg, and melted butter to the bowl; mix until just blended. Scrape bowl and beaters and then beat at high speed for 3 minutes. Spoon dough into prepared pan and smooth tops with a table knife or off-set spatula; sprinkle seeds or white corn meal over tops of rolls, if desired (lightly pat seeds into dough). Cover with a light cloth and let rise in a warm place for about 30–40 minutes (until dough just reaches about ½ inch from top of pan).

3. Place shelf in center of oven. Preheat oven to 400°F while rolls are rising (do not use a convection oven because it will brown the rolls too quickly).

4. Bake rolls in center of preheated oven for about 20 minutes; rolls should have a hollow sound when tapped on the sides and bottom. Your instant-read thermometer should register about 205°F. Remove rolls from oven and turn onto a rack to cool. Brush tops with more melted butter, if desired, before serving.

MULTIGRAIN DINNER ROLLS

Teff flour makes a delicious, hearty roll reminiscent of whole wheat, but you could use coarsely ground oatmeal, amaranth, or Montina instead. I add sesame seeds, sunflower seeds, and golden flax seeds, but you can add your own favorites in whatever proportions you want (don't add more than 6 tablespoons overall, or your rolls will be dense).

Use $1\frac{3}{4}$ cups Bread Flour Mix A and $\frac{1}{4}$ cup teff flour instead of 2 cups Bread Flour Mix A. Add 2 tablespoons sesame seeds, 2 tablespoons sunflower seeds, and 2 tablespoons golden flax seeds to dough after you beat it for 3 minutes. Dust pan with white cornmeal and dust tops of rolls with white corn meal before baking.

HAMBURGER AND HOT DOG BUNS

*Makes 6 or 7
hamburger buns
or 8 hot dog buns.*

Hamburger and hot dog buns are easy to make and delicious with gluten-free flours. These look like homemade buns made with wheat; they have the same shape and golden brown color. They also have a soft texture and a tender crust that will safely hold the juiciest burger, a relish-laden hot dog, or savory pulled pork barbecue. In order to create a gluten-free version of this all-American favorite, I've simply taken my basic sandwich bread dough and molded it into a new shape. However, the buns still have to rise slowly. Don't put them in a place that is too warm; the ideal temperature is about 80°F. Follow the directions and you'll be lighting up the grill in no time.

Wrap buns well in plastic wrap and then foil. Store in refrigerator for up to three days or freezer for up to three weeks. To reheat, freshen buns by sprinkling with a bit of water, wrap in foil, and warm in preheated 350°F oven.

Cook's Notes: Dry ingredients can be mixed ahead and stored in plastic containers for future use. Do not add yeast until just ready to bake buns.

* Available in fine cookware stores, The Baker's Catalogue from King Arthur Flour (1-800-827-6836, or bakerscatalogue.com), or other online sellers.

> 2 large eggs (room temperature is best)
> 3 tablespoons canola oil
> 2 cups Bread Flour Mix A or B (see pp. 8 and 9)
> $1\frac{1}{2}$ teaspoons xanthan gum
> $\frac{1}{2}$ teaspoon salt
> 1 teaspoon unflavored gelatin
> 2 tablespoons granulated sugar
> 1 packet ($\frac{1}{4}$ oz.) of active dry yeast granules (not quick-rise)
> $\frac{3}{4}$ cup plus 2 tablespoons milk, heated to 110°F

1. *To make hamburger buns*: Lightly grease a six-bun hamburger bun pan* (each bun form is about $4\frac{1}{2}$ inches in diameter) or six $4\frac{1}{2}$-inch pie pans with cooking spray. Dust with rice flour. If you want slightly smaller and thinner buns, use a six-bun hamburger pan and one $4\frac{1}{2}$-inch pie pan.
   To make hot dog buns: Lightly grease a triple-loaf French bread pan (the form for each loaf is $2\frac{1}{2}$ inches wide) with cooking spray and dust with rice flour.

2. Mix eggs and canola oil together in a small bowl and set aside.

3. Mix all dry ingredients in large bowl of electric mixer. Quickly add warm milk, egg, and oil to the bowl; mix until just blended. Scrape bowl and beaters and then beat at high speed for 3 minutes.

   For hamburger buns: Spoon dough into each of the six (or seven) prepared bun forms (or pie pans). Carefully smooth and flatten tops of buns with a table knife. Cover with a light cloth and let rise in a warm place for about 30–40 minutes (or until doubled in size).

For hot dog buns: Spoon dough into prepared French bread pan and form eight mini loaves 5 inches in length each (three buns in two of the three loaf forms, and two loaves in the third—the loaves can touch each other lightly). Carefully smooth dough with a butter knife. Cover and let rise in a warm place for about 30–40 minutes (or until doubled in size).

4. Place rack in center of oven. Preheat oven to 375°F while buns are rising (do not use a convection oven because it will brown the buns too quickly).

5. Place buns in center of preheated oven for about 15–20 minutes, until buns have a hollow sound when tapped on top. (After 15 minutes, cover with foil if browning too quickly). Remove buns from oven and turn onto a rack to cool.

ENGLISH MUFFINS

Makes 6 muffins.

Have you been yearning for a "real" English muffin? These muffins look and taste as good as the "real" ones. They toast up crisp around the edges and are filled with all the nooks and crannies the wheat versions are famous for. Split them with a fork by pricking the edges all the way around and then pull them apart. Spread each half with a bit of sweet butter or preserves, sit back, and enjoy the taste and crunch of this familiar comfort food.

White corn meal, optional

1½ cups Bread Flour Mix A (see p. 8)

1 teaspoon xanthan gum

½ teaspoon salt

1 tablespoon granulated sugar

1 packet (¼ oz.) of active dry yeast granules (not quick-rise)

¾ cup plus 1 tablespoon water, heated to 110°F

1 teaspoon canola oil

Muffins can be prepared in advance: cook according to directions. Remove from oven and allow to cool on a rack. Wrap well in plastic wrap and then foil. Store in refrigerator for up to three days or freezer for up to three weeks.

1. Lightly grease a six-bun hamburger bun pan* (each bun form is about 4½ inches in diameter) or six 4½-inch pie pans with cooking spray. Dust with white corn meal (or rice flour).

2. Mix all dry ingredients in large bowl of electric mixer. Pour warm water and canola oil into mixing bowl; mix until just blended. Scrape bowl and beaters and then beat at high speed for 2 minutes.

3. Spoon dough into prepared pan and spread it out to the edges with a table knife or off-set spatula. Carefully smooth and flatten top of buns with a table knife. Cover with a light cloth and let rise in a warm place (about 80°F) for about 20 minutes. Muffins should approximately double in height.

Cook's Note: Dry ingredients can be mixed ahead and stored in plastic containers for future use. Do not add yeast until just ready to bake muffins.

4. Place rack in center of oven. Preheat oven to 375°F while muffins are rising.

5. Bake muffins for about 15 minutes. Muffins should be very light in color and cooked through. Remove from pan and cool on a rack for 15 minutes. Open each muffin by piercing it with a fork around the edges. Carefully pull them apart and toast to desired crispness. Serve with butter or jam.

CINNAMON RAISIN ENGLISH MUFFINS

* Available in fine cookware stores, The Baker's Catalogue from King Arthur Flour (1-800-827-6836, or bakerscatalogue.com), or other online retailers.

Add 1¼–1½ teaspoons cinnamon to dry ingredients in Step 2. After beating dough for 2 minutes, add ⅓ cup raisins to dough and mix on low speed until completely distributed.

FRENCH–ITALIAN BREAD

I never thought I would be able to eat a piece of French or Italian bread again. But I was hungry for the fragrant loaves I had to leave behind. Although this one is missing the flavor of wheat, it has a great crunchy crust and a chewy interior that comes closer than any store-bought gluten-free loaf or recipe I've tried. If you want to darken the crust color, spray the loaf with a *light mist* of canola oil (or canola baking spray) before you put it in the oven. You can sprinkle it with sesame seeds to add a little extra flavor, or you can come to depend on the delicious nuttiness of the millet flour to stand in for the lack of wheat. Not a bad option either way. Grab a hunk of fabulous cheese and a bottle of wine and make a loaf today.

2 cups Bread Flour Mix A* (see p. 8)

1¼ teaspoons xanthan gum

¾–1 teaspoon salt (to taste)

4 teaspoons granulated sugar

1 packet (¼ oz.) of active dry yeast granules (not quick-rise)

2 teaspoons olive oil

1 cup water, heated to 110°F

1. Lightly grease a 2½-inch-wide French bread loaf pan and dust lightly with rice flour (spray and dust it over a paper towel if the pan has little holes in it).

2. Mix all dry ingredients in large bowl of electric mixer. Quickly add olive oil and warm water (110°F) to the bowl; mix until just blended. Scrape bowl and beaters, and then beat at high speed for 3 minutes. Spoon dough into prepared pan and use a table knife or off-set spatula to shape into a baguette-shaped loaf (tube shape) about 13 x 2 inches or two loaf-shaped loaves about 7 x 2 inches (do not flatten dough). Cover with a light cloth and let rise in a warm place (80°F is ideal) for 40–50 minutes or until dough has slightly more than doubled in size.

3. Place rack in center of oven. Preheat oven to 400°F while bread is rising (do not use a convection oven because it will brown the bread too quickly).

4. Bake bread in center of preheated oven for 40–50 minutes (35–45 minutes for two smaller loaves). When done, bread should have a hollow sound when tapped on the sides. Your instant-read thermometer should register 205–215°F. You can bake it longer to make a thicker crust; the color will deepen and the internal temperature will continue to rise. Remove bread from pan and cool on a rack at least 15 minutes before slicing. The crust will soften a bit after the bread cools, but you can easily recrisp it in the oven.

Makes one 14 x 3-inch loaf or two 8 x 3-inch loaves. Recipe can be doubled.

Loaves can be stored in refrigerator for up to three days or freezer for up to three weeks; wrap well in plastic wrap and then foil. Defrost in plastic wrap. Rewarm in 350°F preheated oven for 10–15 minutes; sprinkle bread with a bit of water and wrap in foil, but open the foil for the last five minutes.

Cook's Note: Dry ingredients can be mixed ahead and stored in plastic containers for future use. But do not add yeast until just ready to bake bread.

* The recipe specifies Bread Flour Mix A, but you can also use Bread Flour Mix B, in which case the bread will be blander in flavor and lighter in color.

MULTIGRAIN ARTISAN BREAD

Makes two 8 x 3-inch loaves. Recipe can be doubled.

I love to linger in the bakeries of master bread bakers and study their breads. The myriad of specialty artisan loaves created to tempt bread lovers has grown, and with it, my appreciation for how much you can do with so few ingredients. With my gluten-free flours, I've practiced making a variety of what I call multi-grain artisan breads. I usually use teff flour because I like the rich, nutty flavor and the darker, hearty color and texture it gives to my breads, but sometimes I use coarsely ground oatmeal for the sweet chewiness it imparts. I've tried other flours, but I always come back to teff and oatmeal because I think they make the most delicious multigrain breads with the best character. The recipe below is for my basic multigrain artisan bread with $\frac{1}{4}$ cup teff flour and 6 tablespoons combined of sesame, sunflower, and flax seeds. You can use this recipe as it is, or use another flour in place of the teff and whatever seed combinations you like to create artisan breads of your own design (do not use more than 6 table-spoons of seeds altogether, or your bread will be too dense).

Loaves can be stored in refrigerator for up to three days or freezer for up to three weeks; wrap well in plastic wrap and then foil. Defrost in plastic wrap. Rewarm in preheated 350°F oven for 10–15 minutes; sprinkle bread with a bit of water and wrap in foil, but open the foil for the last five minutes.

Cook's Note: Dry ingredients can be mixed ahead and stored in plastic containers for future use. Do not add yeast until just ready to bake bread.

White corn meal
$1\frac{3}{4}$ cups Bread Flour Mix A (see p. 8)
$\frac{1}{4}$ cup teff flour
$1\frac{1}{4}$ teaspoons xanthan gum
$\frac{3}{4}$ teaspoon salt
4 teaspoons granulated sugar
1 packet ($\frac{1}{4}$ oz.) of active dry yeast granules (not quick-rise)
2 teaspoons olive oil
1 cup water, heated to 110°F
2 tablespoons sesame seeds
2 tablespoons sunflower seeds
2 tablespoons golden flax seeds

1. Lightly grease a 4-inch-wide French bread loaf pan with cooking spray and dust with white corn meal (spray and dust it over a paper towel if the pan has little holes in it).

2. Mix flours, xanthan gum, salt, sugar, and yeast in large bowl of electric mixer. Quickly add olive oil and warm water (110°F) to the bowl; mix until just blended. Scrape bowl and beaters, and then beat at high speed for 3 minutes. Add seeds and mix well. Spoon dough into prepared pan and use a table knife or off-set spatula to shape into two baguette-shaped loaves (tube shape) about 7 x 2 inches (do not flatten dough). Cover with a light cloth and let rise in a warm place (80°F is ideal) for 40–50 minutes or until dough has slightly

more than doubled in size. Sprinkle tops and sides of loaves with additional corn meal.

3. Place rack in center of oven. Preheat oven to 400°F while bread is rising (do not use a convection oven because it will brown the bread too quickly).

4. Spray bread very lightly with canola oil baking spray (this will darken the crust). Bake in center of preheated oven for 35–45 minutes. When done, bread should have a hollow sound when tapped on the sides. Your instant-read thermometer should register 205–215°F. You can bake it longer to make a thicker crust; the color will deepen and the internal temperature will continue to rise. Remove bread from pan and cool on a rack at least 15 minutes before slicing. The crust will soften a bit after the bread cools, but you can easily recrisp it in the oven.

PECAN RAISIN ARTISAN BREAD

Makes two 8 x 3-inch loaves. Recipe can be doubled.

Pecan raisin bread can be found in fine restaurants and bread bakeries all across the country. It is delicious alongside a tossed green salad, perfect with a cheese plate, and it can turn a simple plate of roast chicken into something to be slowly savored with a glass of wine. I was able to create a flavorful gluten-free version that looks, tastes, and feels like it was made with wheat. You can serve it at your next dinner party and no one will know the difference. The recipe incorporates finely ground pecans into the dough for a rich, nutty taste. If you need more convincing, bite into a chewy, crusty hunk and let yourself be swayed by the chopped pecans and plump sweet raisins. No doubt about it: This bread is sure to become a part of your gluten-free baking repertoire.

Loaves can be stored in refrigerator for up to three days or freezer for up to three weeks; wrap well in plastic wrap and then foil. Defrost in plastic wrap. Rewarm in preheated 350°F oven for 10–15 minutes; sprinkle bread with a bit of water and wrap in foil, but open the foil for the last five minutes.

Cook's Note: Dry ingredients can be mixed ahead and stored in plastic containers for future use. Do not add yeast until just ready to bake bread.

Rice flour

2 cups Bread Flour Mix A (see p. 8)

2 tablespoons finely ground pecans

1¼ teaspoons xanthan gum

¾ teaspoon salt

4 teaspoons granulated sugar

1 packet (¼ oz.) of active dry yeast granules (not quick-rise)

2 teaspoons olive oil

1 cup water, heated to 110°F

¾ cup raisins

¾ cup pecans

1. Lightly grease a 2½-inch-wide French bread loaf pan with cooking spray and dust with rice flour (spray and dust it over a paper towel if the pan has little holes in it).

2. Mix flour, ground pecans, xanthan gum, salt, sugar, and yeast in large bowl of electric mixer. Quickly add olive oil and warm water (110°F) to the bowl; mix until just blended. Scrape bowl and beaters, and then beat at high speed for 3 minutes. Add raisins and pecans and mix well. Spoon dough into prepared pan and use a table knife or off-set spatula to shape into two baguette-shaped loaves (tube shape) about 7 x 2 inches (do not flatten dough). Cover with a light cloth and let rise in a warm place (80°F is ideal) for 40–50 minutes or until dough has slightly more than doubled in size. Use a sieve to dust tops and sides of loaves very lightly with plain rice flour. Spray breads very lightly with canola oil baking spray (this will help darken the crust).

3. Place rack in center of oven. Preheat oven to 400°F while bread is rising (do not use a convection oven because it will brown the bread too quickly).

4. Bake bread in center of preheated oven for 35–45 minutes. When done, bread should have a hollow sound when tapped on the sides. Your instant-read thermometer should register 205–215°F. You can bake it longer to make a thicker crust; the color will deepen and the internal temperature will continue to rise. Remove bread from pan and cool on a rack at least 15 minutes before slicing. The crust will soften a bit after the bread cools, but you can easily recrisp it in the oven.

GOLDEN ITALIAN BREAD WITH RAISINS AND FENNEL

Makes two 8 x 3-inch loaves. Recipe can be doubled.

Loaves can be stored in refrigerator for up to three days or freezer for up to three weeks; wrap well in plastic wrap and then foil. Defrost in plastic wrap. Rewarm in 350°F preheated oven for 10–15 minutes; sprinkle bread with a bit of water and wrap in foil, but open the foil for the last five minutes.

Cook's Note: Dry ingredients can be mixed ahead and stored in plastic containers for future use. Do not add yeast until just ready to bake bread.

After I moved out of New York City, I would make special trips back just to buy the wheat version of this incredible bread. It was called "Semolina with Golden Raisins and Fennel," the signature bread of Amy's Bread, a bakery started in 1992 by the very talented Amy Scherber. I had just about given up on ever tasting it again, but then I unlocked the key to making a good gluten-free French-Italian bread. It was just a matter of time before I added the golden raisins and fennel seeds I longed for. In order to create the same golden glow without semolina flour, I dusted the entire loaf with yellow corn meal (Amy dusts her bread with cornmeal as well). I don't spray this bread with cooking spray, as I do with many of my other breads, so it will stay light and colorful. Try it. Even if you weren't fortunate enough to taste the original, you may come to crave this delicious gluten-free copy.

Yellow corn meal
2 cups Bread Flour Mix A* (see p. 8)
1 1/4 teaspoons xanthan gum
3/4 teaspoon salt
4 teaspoons granulated sugar
1 packet (1/4 oz.) of active dry yeast granules (not quick-rise)
2 teaspoons olive oil
1 cup water, heated to 110°F
3/4 cup golden raisins
1 1/2 teaspoons fennel seeds

1. Lightly grease a 4-inch-wide French bread loaf pan with cooking spray and dust with yellow corn meal (spray and dust it over a paper towel if the pan has little holes in it).

2. Mix all dry ingredients in large bowl of electric mixer. Quickly add olive oil and warm water (110°F) to the bowl; mix until just blended. Scrape bowl and beaters, and then beat at high speed for 3 minutes. Add raisins and fennel and mix well. Spoon dough into prepared pan and use a table knife or off-set spatula to shape into two baguette-shaped loaves (tube shape) about 7 x 2 inches (do not flatten dough). Cover with a light cloth and let rise in a warm place (80°F is ideal) for 40–50 minutes or until dough has slightly more than doubled in size. Sprinkle tops and sides of loaves with more yellow corn meal.

3. Place rack in center of oven. Preheat oven to 400°F while bread is rising (do not use a convection oven because it will brown the bread too quickly).

4. Bake bread in center of preheated oven for 35–45 minutes. When done, bread should have a hollow sound when tapped on the sides. Your instant-read thermometer should register 205–215°F. Bread should be a light golden color. Remove bread from pan and cool on a rack at least 15 minutes before slicing. The crust will soften a bit after the bread cools, but you can easily recrisp it in the oven.

SUBMARINE SANDWICH BREAD

Makes one 12 x 3-inch loaf, two 8 x 3½-inch loaves, or three 5½ x 3-inch loaves. Recipe can be doubled.

Perhaps you've been craving the sort of chewy, crusty sandwich bread used to make a meatball hero, roast beef sub, or muffuletta. Hero, wedge, sub, hoagie, grinder—you name it and you can make it with this bread. Shape the dough into a loaf big enough for two to share or into several smaller, individual sandwich rolls (perfect for small-kid lunches). It is simple to make: Just mix the ingredients in an electric mixer, put the dough in a French bread pan, and let it rise. It bakes up to a nice light golden brown, and you can use it to make any sandwich you're hungry for. If you want to darken the crust color, spray the loaf with a *light mist* of canola oil (or canola baking spray) before you put it in the oven.

Loaves can be stored in refrigerator for up to three days or freezer for up to three weeks; wrap well in plastic wrap and then foil. Defrost in plastic wrap. Rewarm in 350°F preheated oven for 10–15 minutes; sprinkle bread with a bit of water and wrap in foil, but open the foil for the last five minutes.

* The recipe specifies Bread Flour Mix A, but you can also use Bread Flour Mix B, in which case the bread will be blander in flavor and lighter in color.

1½ cups Bread Flour Mix A* (see p. 8)

1 teaspoon xanthan gum

¾ teaspoon salt

2 tablespoons granulated sugar

1 packet (¼ oz.) of active dry yeast granules (not quick-rise)

1 teaspoon olive oil

¾ cup plus 1 tablespoon water, heated to 110°F

1. Spray 4-inch-wideFrench bread loaf pan(s) with baking spray and dust lightly with rice flour or sprinkle with cornmeal (spray and dust it over a paper towel if the pan has little holes in it).

2. Mix all dry ingredients in large bowl of electric mixer. Pour warm water (110°F) and olive oil into mixing bowl; mix until just blended. Scrape bowl and beaters and then beat at high speed for 2 minutes.

3. Spoon dough into prepared pan(s) and use a table knife or off-set spatula to shape into a baguette-shaped loaf (tube shape) about 11 x 2½ inches, two baguette-shaped loaves about 7 x 2½ inches (do not flatten dough), or three smaller loaves about 4½ x 2½ inches. Cover with a light cloth and let rise in a warm place (about 80°F) for 40–50 minutes or until dough has slightly more than doubled in size.

4. Place rack in lower third of oven. Preheat oven to 400°F while bread is rising (do not use a convection oven because it will brown the bread too quickly).

5. Bake bread in center of preheated oven for 35–45 minutes. When done, bread should have a hollow sound when tapped on the sides. Your instant-read thermometer should register 205–215°F. Bread

should be a light golden color. You can bake it longer to make a thicker crust; the color will deepen and the internal temperature will continue to rise. Remove bread from pan and cool on a rack at least 15 minutes before slicing. The crust will soften a bit after the bread cools, but you can easily recrisp it in the oven.

Cook's Note: Dry ingredients can be mixed ahead and stored in plastic containers for future use. Do not add yeast until just ready to bake bread.

RUSTIC FLAT BREAD
(FOCACCIA)

Makes one 8- or 9-inch round bread. Recipe can be doubled.

Bread can be prepared in advance: bake according to directions. Remove from oven and allow to cool on a rack. Wrap well in plastic wrap and then foil. Bread can be stored in refrigerator for up to three days or freezer for up to three weeks; wrap well in plastic wrap and then foil. Defrost in plastic wrap. Rewarm in 350°F pre- heated oven for 10–15 minutes; sprinkle bread with a bit of water and wrap in foil, but open the foil for the last five minutes.

Cook's Note: Dry ingre- dients can be mixed ahead and stored in plastic containers for future use. Do not add yeast until just ready to bake bread.

* The recipe specifies Bread Flour Mix A, but you can also use Bread Flour Mix B, in which case the bread will be blander in flavor and lighter in color.

Rustic flat breads can be found in cultures and cuisines around the globe. This one is more European in style, like the focaccia you find in Italian restaurants, specialty shops, and even grocery stores. I top mine in the classic way, with olive oil, fresh rosemary, and sea salt. But let your imagination go wild: sweet sautéed onion and peppers, fresh tomatoes, olives, a little cheese. Try your old favorites, or create new ones. You can also use this bread to make delectable panini or a sandwich (try grilled chicken with pesto mayonnaise). This very easy-to-make bread will become a favorite.

> $1\frac{1}{2}$ cups Bread Flour Mix A* (see p. 8)
>
> 1 teaspoon xanthan gum
>
> $\frac{1}{2}$ teaspoon salt
>
> 1 tablespoon granulated sugar
>
> 1 packet ($\frac{1}{4}$ oz.) of dry quick-rise yeast granules
>
> 1 teaspoon olive oil
>
> $\frac{3}{4}$ cup plus 1 tablespoon water, heated to 110°F
>
> Olive oil
>
> Fresh rosemary
>
> Sea salt

1. Spray an 8- or 9-inch round cake pan with baking spray and lightly dust with rice flour or sprinkle with cornmeal.

2. Mix all dry ingredients in large bowl of electric mixer. Pour warm water (110°F) and olive oil into mixing bowl; mix until just blended. Scrape bowl and beaters, and then beat at high speed for 2 minutes.

3. Spoon dough into prepared pan and spread it out to the sides with a spat- ula. Cover with a light cloth and let rise in a warm place (about 80°F) for about 40 minutes. Bread should be approximately double in height.

4. Place rack in lower third of oven. Preheat oven to 400°F while bread is rising.

5. Sprinkle olive oil over top and carefully spread it into a *thin* film over the entire surface of the bread (use your fingers to do this for best results). Sprinkle with rosemary and sea salt (or other toppings of your choice).

6. Bake 8-inch bread for 20–25 minutes, 15–20 minutes for 9-inch bread. Bread should be medium golden in color and cooked through. Remove bread from pan and cool on a rack for 15 minutes; slice and serve.

CHALLAH

I made a gallant effort to create gluten-free challah bread dough that I could braid, but doughs that were thick enough to braid were too dense and heavy to rise well. In the end, I sacrificed a "real" braid for taste and texture. My challah will not have the squishy feel of commercially made challahs made with highly refined wheat flour. Mine will be more like the homemade traditional challah I found recipes for in turn-of-the-century cookbooks (my favorite is *The Settlement Cook Book: The Way to a Man's Heart*, by Mrs. Simon Kander).

Take note: Allow the bread to rise slowly. Don't put it in a place that is too warm; the ideal temperature is about 80°F. A fast rise will contribute to an unstable bread that is likely to fall. The xanthan gum needs time to "set" in gluten-free breads. Also, try not to let the bread rise above the pan before you bake it, because this will also contribute to instability.

Makes one 1-lb. loaf.

> 3 large eggs (room temperature is best)
>
> 3 tablespoons canola oil
>
> 1¾ cups plus 2 tablespoons Bread Flour Mix A (see p. 8)
>
> 2 tablespoons sweet rice flour (see p. 6)
>
> 3 tablespoons granulated sugar
>
> 1½ teaspoons xanthan gum
>
> ½ teaspoon salt
>
> 1 packet (¼ oz.) active dry yeast granules (not quick-rise)
>
> ⅔ cup water, heated to 110°F
>
> 1 large egg, beaten (to glaze top of bread)
>
> Sesame or poppy seeds for top of bread, optional

1. Lightly grease a 9 x 5-inch loaf pan with cooking spray and dust with rice flour.

2. Mix eggs and canola oil together in a small bowl and set aside.

3. Mix all dry ingredients in large bowl of electric mixer. Pour warm water and egg and oil mixture into mixing bowl; mix until just blended. Scrape bowl and beaters, and then beat at high speed for 3 minutes.

4. Carefully spoon dough into prepared pan, creating a mound that is higher down than the middle and lower towards the sides (more like a large Italian bread). With a very sharp, pointed knife, start at the top left corner of the dough and draw a large, swirled, repetitive "S" pattern down the middle of the dough. Repeat the process starting from the other corner (essentially drawing a braid on the dough).

Wrap bread well in plastic wrap and then foil. Store in refrigerator for up to three days or freezer for up to three weeks; wrap well in plastic wrap and then foil. Defrost in plastic wrap. Rewarm in pre-heated 350°F oven for 10–15 minutes; sprinkle bread with a bit of water and wrap in foil, but open the foil for the last five minutes.

Cook's Note: Dry ingredients can be mixed ahead and stored in plastic containers for future use. Do not add yeast until just ready to bake challah.

Cover dough with a light cloth and let rise in a warm place for about 40–50 minutes (until dough is 1 inch from top of pan).

5. Place rack in center of oven. Preheat oven to 400°F while bread is rising (do not use a convection oven because it will brown the bread too quickly).

6. Lightly brush top of bread with beaten egg and sprinkle on sesame or poppy seeds, if desired (gently pat seeds into beaten egg so they will stay on). Bake bread in center of preheated oven for 10 minutes. Cover bread with aluminum foil and bake another 35–45 minutes. When done, bread should have a hollow sound when tapped on the sides. Your instant-read thermometer should register 205°F. Remove bread from oven and turn onto a rack to cool.

CHALLAH BREAD WITH RAISINS

After completing Step 3, add ½ to ¾ cup raisins to dough and mix on low speed until completely distributed.

BABKA (UKRAINIAN STYLE)

We always looked forward to Ukrainian Easter when I was young, because that is when we would receive a coveted Babka from John and Mary Fizer's kitchen. The Fizers always made so many Babka for the holiday that they baked some of them in coffee cans. The unique shape was only part of the charm; the egg-enriched, sweetened bread we loved to eat came studded with rum-infused golden raisins. This bread is delicious served with fresh, creamy butter and preserves for breakfast or brunch. Cut thick slices after it cools or toast it lightly for several days after.

Take note: Allow the bread to rise slowly. Don't put it in a place that is too warm; the ideal temperature is about 80°F. A fast rise will contribute to an unstable bread that is likely to fall. The xanthan gum needs time to "set" in gluten-free breads. Also, try not to let the bread rise above the pan before you bake it, because this will contribute to instability.

- ³⁄₄ cup golden raisins
- 1 teaspoon rum
- 2 large eggs and 2 egg yolks (room temperature is best)
- 2 cups Bread Flour Mix A (see p. 8)
- ¹⁄₃ cup granulated sugar
- 1¹⁄₂ teaspoons xanthan gum
- ¹⁄₂ teaspoon salt
- 1 packet (¹⁄₄ oz.) active dry yeast granules (not quick-rise)
- 3 tablespoons unsalted butter, melted and cooled slightly
- ²⁄₃ cup milk, heated to 110°F*

1. Lightly grease a 9 x 5-inch loaf pan with cooking spray and dust with rice flour.

2. Mix raisins and rum in a small bowl and set aside. Put eggs and egg yolks in a small bowl and set aside.

3. Mix all dry ingredients in large bowl of electric mixer. Quickly add eggs, egg yolks, warm milk, and butter to the bowl; mix until just blended. Scrape bowl and beaters, and then beat at high speed for 3 minutes. Add raisin and rum mixture and mix well. Spoon dough into prepared pan; cover with a light cloth and let rise in a warm place for about 50–80 minutes (until dough is about 1 inch from below top of pan).

4. Place rack in center of oven. Preheat oven to 400°F while bread is rising (do not use a convection oven because it will brown the bread too quickly).

5. Bake bread for about 10 minutes; remove from oven, cover bread with aluminum foil, return to oven, and bake another 40–45 minutes. Bread should have a heavy but hollow sound when tapped on the sides and bottom. Your instant-read thermometer should register about 205°F. Remove bread from oven and turn onto a rack to cool.

Makes one 1-lb. loaf.

Wrap bread well in plastic wrap and then foil. Store in refrigerator for up to three days or freezer for up to three weeks.

Cook's Note: Dry ingredients can be mixed ahead and stored in plastic containers for future use. Do not add yeast until just ready to bake babka.

IRISH SODA BREAD

Makes one 6½-inch loaf.

Irish Soda Bread is a classic favorite from across the sea. The original version was made simply, with flour, buttermilk, baking soda, and salt. At some point—and no one seems to know when—bakers added eggs, butter, raisins, and caraway seeds to add tenderness and flavor. My neighbor Madeline Van Duren has been making my family a loaf on Saint Patrick's Day for years, and we always looked forward to it. Several years after I could no longer eat gluten, I really started to miss her annual gift and asked her for the recipe. She happily gave it to me, and agreed to test my versions until I got it right. It took several tries, but I finally made a loaf that looked and tasted just like hers. I love to eat slices of this tender bread with coffee in the morning. It is delicious warm from the oven (see reheating instructions below) or toasted and served with fresh, sweet butter and fruit preserves.

1¾ cups Brown Rice Flour Mix (see p. 6)

2 tablespoons granulated sugar

2 tablespoons buttermilk powder

2 teaspoons baking powder

1 teaspoon baking soda

¾ teaspoon xanthan gum

¼ teaspoon salt

½ cup raisins

1 tablespoon caraway seeds

¾ cups water

3 tablespoons canola oil

1 large egg

Bread can be prepared in advance: bake according to directions. Remove from oven and allow to cool on rack. Wrap well in plastic wrap and then foil. Store in refrigerator for up to three days or freezer for up to three weeks; wrap well in plastic wrap and then foil. Defrost in plastic wrap. Rewarm in preheated 350°F oven wrapped in foil.

1. Preheat oven to 350°F. Position rack in center of oven. Lightly grease an 8-inch round cake pan with cooking spray and dust with rice flour.

2. Combine flour, sugar, buttermilk powder, baking powder, baking soda, xanthan gum, and salt in large mixing bowl. Mix in raisins and caraway seeds until well coated.

3. Combine water, oil, and egg in a small bowl and whisk until well blended.

4. Add water mixture to flour mixture all at once and mix until well blended (about 30 seconds). Use a rubber spatula to shape dough into a ball; dump the ball of dough into the middle of the prepared cake pan.

5. Use well-floured hands (rice flour) to carefully shape dough into a 6-inch to 6½-inch wide dome in the center of the pan. Pat extra flour

onto the top of the dome if needed in order to shape it. There should be about $\frac{1}{2}$ to 1 inch of space between the dome and the edges of the pan. The center of the mound of dough should be higher than the edges.

6. Use a very thin sharp knife to cut a cross in through the dough from edge to edge; cut through almost to the bottom of the pan.

7. Bake bread in center of preheated oven for 30–40 minutes until bread is a rich, dark golden brown, and a toothpick inserted in center comes out clean. Cool on a wire rack (do not slice bread when hot).

PIZZA CRUST

Makes one 12-inch
round pizza or two very
thin 9-inch round piz-
zas. Recipe can be dou-
bled.

This is the crust you have been waiting for. You won't even miss the wheat, and it's so good you will be able to serve it to anyone. It is a classic New York-style thin crust, but you could make it thicker by baking it in a smaller pan (be sure to adjust the baking time). Ideally, try to make the crust several hours or the day before you plan to use it. This gives the xantham gum time to set, and the crust will be crisp and chewy like one made with wheat. If you make the crust just before you use it, it will still be delicious and the texture will still be wonderful, but the crisp and chewy aspect won't be as pronounced. Prebaked crusts freeze well, so you can make several and store them in the freezer.

Cook's Note: Dry ingre-
dients can be mixed
ahead and stored in
plastic containers for
future use. Do not add
yeast until just ready to
bake pizza.

> 1 cup Brown Rice Flour Mix (see p. 6)
> $\frac{1}{2}$ cup millet flour*
> 1 teaspoon xanthan gum
> $\frac{1}{2}$ teaspoon salt
> 2 teaspoons granulated sugar
> 1 packet ($\frac{1}{4}$ oz.) of dry quick-rise yeast granules
> 1 teaspoon olive oil
> $\frac{3}{4}$ cup plus 1 tablespoon water, heated to 110°F
>   Cornmeal, optional

1. Generously spray pizza pan(s) (with ridged bottom, not smooth) or bottom of springform pan(s) (with ridged bottoms, not smooth) with cooking spray and lightly sprinkle cornmeal over entire pan (cornmeal is optional).

2. Mix all dry ingredients in large bowl of electric mixer. Pour olive oil and warm water (110°F) into mixing bowl; mix until just blended. Scrape bowl and beaters, and then beat at high speed for 2 minutes.

3. Spoon dough into center of prepared pan(s). Use a cake spatula to move dough from center to outer rim of pan using individual strokes; lightly dampen spatula with warm water as necessary. Try to arrange dough so that it covers entire pan in an even, thin layer. Cover with a light cloth and let rise in a warm place for 30–40 minutes. Pizza crust should approximately double in height.

4. Place rack in lower third of oven. Preheat oven to 425°F while pizza is rising.

5. Bake pizza in pan on rack of preheated oven for 15–16 minutes (12–14 minutes for 9-inch pizza). Pizza should be light golden in

color and cooked through. Remove from oven and cover with pizza topping of your choice (make sure topping is not too wet).

6. Leave pizza in pan and return to oven for an additional 10 minutes (8 minutes for 9-inch crust). Remove pizza from pan and place it directly on rack for six minutes (4 minutes for 9-inch crust) to finish baking. Remove from oven, let rest 3 minutes, slice, and serve.

For softer crust:
Put on pizza topping and return pan to rack in lower third of oven; bake 15–20 minutes, or until topping is cooked.

For very crisp crust:
Put on pizza topping, remove pizza from pan, and place pizza directly on rack in lower third of oven; bake 8–10 minutes (5–8 minutes for 9-inch pies) until topping is cooked and bottom is crispy.

To use a pizza stone:
Heat stone according to the manufacturer's directions and place pre-baked crust topped with sauce and cheese on preheated stone. Bake until crust is crisp and topping is cooked.

* ALTERNATIVE CRUST WITHOUT MILLET FLOUR (CRUST WILL SHRINK UP TO 2 INCHES)

1½ cups Brown Rice Flour Mix (see p. 6)
1 teaspoon xanthan gum
½ teaspoon salt
2 teaspoons sugar
1 packet (¼ oz.) of dry quick-rise yeast granules
1 teaspoon olive oil
¾ cup plus 1 tablespoon water, heated to 110°F
Cornmeal, optional

1. Follow directions for Pizza Crust, p. 186.

Pizza crust can be prepared in advance: Precook crust according to directions, but do not put on topping. Remove from oven and allow crust to cool on a rack. Wrap well in plastic wrap and then foil. Store in refrigerator for up to two days or freezer for up to three weeks. Defrost crust before topping with sauce and cheese.

Cook's Note: See page 156 for more information on pizza pans.

SOFT PRETZELS

Makes 6 pretzels.

I tried to make a good-tasting soft pretzel with my bread flour mix and various combinations of sweet rice flour for a very long time, but I couldn't get the right texture or taste until I replaced all the millet with sorghum in the flour mix. This recipe makes a delicious pretzel that you can munch on with a cold gluten-free beer when you're watching a ball game. The dough is also kid-friendly and easy to roll, so you can have a fun time making pretzels with any kids—large or small—you have around the house. Like all real homemade pretzels with wheat, expect them to look a bit different from the highly processed ones sold in stores, and remember that they're at their peak when warm from the oven. This is the only recipe in this book that uses the Pretzel Flour Mix.

Cook's Notes: Dry ingredients can be mixed ahead and stored in plastic containers for future use. Do not add yeast until just ready to bake pretzels.

Mustard dippers may want to reduce the amount of brown sugar to one tablespoon.

* If allergic to eggs, you might consider making plump pretzel logs or pretzel sticks, because without the egg wash, it is difficult to get the pretzel to stay together when boiled.

2 cups Pretzel Flour Mix: 1 cup sorghum flour, $\frac{1}{3}$ cup corn starch, $\frac{1}{3}$ cup potato starch, $\frac{1}{3}$ cup tapioca starch

2 tablespoons packed dark brown sugar

1$\frac{1}{4}$ teaspoon xanthan gum

1 teaspoon salt

1 packet ($\frac{1}{4}$ oz.) of active quick-rise dry yeast granules

1 teaspoon canola oil

$\frac{3}{4}$ cup water, heated to 110°F

6 cups water (for boiling pretzels)

1 teaspoon baking soda (for boiling pretzels)

1–2 tablespoons egg substitute or beaten egg*

Pretzel salt, sea salt or sesame seeds

1. Line large baking sheet with parchment paper.

2. Mix all dry ingredients in large bowl of electric mixer. Add oil and warm water to the bowl; mix until just blended. Scrape bowl and beaters and then beat at high speed for 2 minutes. Scrape all dough into large mound in the center of bowl. Dough will be thick.

3. Liberally flour hands with plain rice flour. Divide dough into six equal pieces and roll each piece into a ball (about 2 inch diameter). On a wooden board, roll or pat each ball out into a long strand of 14 inches (use a ruler) and form into a pretzel. First, form a letter "U." Pick up the top of left side of the "U" and bring it down to the right side of the bottom of the "U." Then, pick up the top of the right side and pull it down to the left side of the bottom of the "U." Carefully place the pretzel on baking sheet lined with parchment paper. Repeat with remaining dough to make six pretzels.

4. Brush tops and sides of each pretzel with beaten egg (including in between where the ends are attached to the rest of the pretzel, because the egg acts like glue). Cover with a light cloth and let rise in a warm place (about 80°F) for about 35–45 minutes (or until pretzels have doubled in size).

5. Lightly grease a large heavy baking sheet with baking spray. Combine 6 cups of water and 1 teaspoon baking soda in a 3-quart saucepan and bring to a rolling boil. Cut the large piece of parchment paper under pretzels into 6 smaller pieces so that each pretzel is on its own piece. Use the parchment paper to lift each pretzel and put it face down into the boiling water for 30 seconds (remove parchment paper). Use a pancake turner or slotted spoon to carefully remove pretzel and lay it on a paper towel. Pat dry and place pretzel face up back on greased baking sheet (replace paper towels as needed; if they are too wet, pretzels will stick). Repeat with remaining pretzels.

6. Place rack in center of oven and preheat oven to 425°F while pretzels are resting (cover with a light cloth).

7. Spray tops and sides of pretzels with canola oil cooking spray (this will help the pretzels to brown and give them a sheen) and sprinkle with salt or sesame seeds (pat seeds gently into cooking spray). Place in center of preheated oven and turn down oven to 400°F. Bake about 15–20 minutes, until pretzels have a hollow sound when tapped on top.

Best when eaten while warm from the oven. Can be stored in a tightly sealed container for one day and rewarmed in microwave, if necessary.

EGG BAGELS

Makes 8 small bagels.*

Crusty, chewy bagels seem like a distant memory to many people once they begin a gluten-free diet. The stretchy gluten so essential to a bagel's character is the very thing we must avoid. The seemingly simple bagel is complicated: it should have a slight cracking sound when you bite into the crust and a chewy interior. And it needs to taste good. My bread flour mix provides a good flavor to stand in for the flavor of wheat. A small amount of sweet rice flour combined with just the right amount of everything else helps with the chewiness; a finely-tuned baking technique helped with the rest. The recipe makes eight 3-ounce bagels, not the half-pound mammoths sold in bagel shops today. Traditional bagels were always around 4 ounces and were eaten no more than a few hours after they were made. These are delicious fresh from the oven or toasted, but you can store them in the freezer to enjoy another day (directions for storage on p. 191).

Cook's Note: Dry ingredients can be mixed ahead and stored in plastic containers for future use. Do not add yeast until just ready to bake bagels.

* *You can make larger bagels, but you will have to adjust the baking time (longer at 400°F).*

1 large egg (room temperature is best)

2 tablespoons canola oil

2¾ cups plus 2 tablespoons Bread Flour Mix A (see p. 8)

2 tablespoons sweet rice flour (see p. 7)

2 tablespoons granulated sugar

2 teaspoons xanthan gum

¾ teaspoon salt

⅔ cup plus 2 tablespoons water, heated to 110°F

1 tablespoon active dry yeast granules (not quick-rise)

Rice flour (about 1 heaping tablespoon, used to flour board)

8 cups water (for boiling bagels)

1 tablespoon granulated sugar (for boiling bagels)

2 tablespoons (or more) egg substitute or beaten egg

Sesame seeds, poppy seeds, caraway seeds, or coarse salt, bits of onion or garlic for topping

1. Lightly grease a large baking sheet with baking spray.

2. Mix egg and canola oil together in a small bowl and set aside.

3. Mix all dry ingredients in large bowl of electric mixer. Quickly add warm water and egg and oil mixture to the bowl; mix until just blended. Scrape bowl and beaters and then beat at high speed for 3 minutes.

4. Liberally spread rice flour over surface of a wooden board and lightly flour hands. Use a spatula to move dough out onto the

wooden board in a ball shape. Dough will be sticky. Roll dough around in the rice flour until it is lightly covered.

5. Divide dough in half; divide each half into four equal pieces with a small, sharp knife. Roll each with lightly floured hands to make eight balls of dough. Poke a hole through the center of each ball using one finger and then expand it with two fingers until it is 2 inches wide. The bagels should be ¾ to 1 inch thick. Place on prepared baking sheet, cover with a light cloth, and let rise in a warm place (80°F is ideal) for 1–1½ hours or until dough has slightly more than doubled in size.

6. Place rack in center of oven. Preheat oven to 425°F. Combine eight cups of water and 1 tablespoon sugar in a large 5-quart saucepan and bring to a rolling boil. Use a pancake turner to carefully move three bagels into water; boil for 2 minutes on each side. Remove the bagels with pancake turner and lay them on a paper towel. Pat dry and place bagels back on greased baking sheet. Repeat with remaining bagels (replace paper towels as needed so bagels do not stick).

7. Brush boiled bagels with beaten egg and sprinkle with seeds, salt, and so on. Pat seeds gently into egg so that they will stay on. Spray bagels lightly with cooking spray (it will give them a sheen). Bake in center of preheated oven for 10 minutes. Reduce oven temperature to 400°F for 15 minutes more, until bagels have a rich caramel color and are baked through. Remove bagels and cool on a rack. Serve warm.

Bagels can be prepared in advance. Bake according to directions. Remove from oven and allow to cool on a rack. Wrap well in plastic wrap and then foil to store in freezer for up to three weeks. Once frozen, bagels are best when defrosted (briefly in microwave, if necessary) and then toasted.

WALNUT BREAD

Makes one 9 x 5-inch loaf.

This fragrant quick-bread will win you over. It is the perfect choice if you are looking for something special to serve with a salad or cheese course at dinner. It has an uncommon crunchy texture and a warm, nutty flavor that's not too sweet. You can toast it right before you serve it or several hours before and then warm the pieces briefly in a microwave. Walnut Bread freezes well, so you can make it ahead of time and then pull pieces out of the freezer to toast when you need them. I leave it in chunks several inches wide, which I defrost and then slice; it stays a little fresher-tasting when left in larger pieces.

Walnut Bread can be prepared in advance: Bake according to directions. Remove from oven and allow to cool on a rack. Wrap well in plastic wrap and then foil. Store in refrigerator for up to two days or freezer for up to three weeks. Defrost and then toast bread slices.

* Cook's Note: Toast nuts on a baking sheet in preheated 350°F oven for 4–6 minutes.

    2 cups Brown Rice Flour Mix (see p. 6)

    $^1/_3$ cup granulated sugar

    1 tablespoon baking powder

    1 teaspoon baking soda

    $^3/_4$ teaspoon xanthan gum

    $^1/_2$ teaspoon salt

    1 cup milk less 1 tablespoon

    $^1/_3$ cup canola oil less 1 tablespoon

    1 large egg

    $^1/_2$ teaspoon pure vanilla extract

    2 cups shelled walnuts, toasted and coarsely chopped*

1. Preheat oven to 350°F. Position rack in center of oven. Lightly grease 9 x 5-inch loaf pan with cooking spray.

2. Combine flour, sugar, baking powder, baking soda, xanthan gum, and salt in a large mixing bowl.

3. Combine milk, oil, egg, and vanilla in a small bowl and whisk until well blended.

4. Add milk mixture to flour mixture all at once and mix just until moistened. Fold in toasted nuts. Spoon batter into prepared pan.

5. Bake 30–35 minutes or until a toothpick inserted in center comes out clean. Cool for 5 minutes in pan. Remove from pan and cool completely on a wire rack.

To make toasted Walnut Bread slices:
Place rack in lower third of oven and preheat to 375°F. Slice bread into $^3/_4$-inch slices. Arrange in a single layer on a baking sheet. Bake for 8–10 minutes or until browned. Turn slices over and bake another 8–10 minutes until other side is browned. Serve with salad or cheese course.

BUTTERMILK BISCUITS

When you're hungry for hot, buttery biscuits, nothing else will do. These Buttermilk Biscuits are crisp on the outside and tender on the inside. They are light but bursting with buttery flavor. Serve them hot from the oven with jam for breakfast, or use them to top a pot pie or fruit cobbler (add an extra tablespoon of sugar for a sweeter dessert biscuit). They are so delicious you can even serve them plain alongside soups and stews. Be sure to use extra-finely ground brown rice flour and sweet rice flour or your biscuits will be crumbly and not rise well. The grind of the flour will make a noticeable difference.

Makes five 2½-inch round biscuits. Recipe can be doubled.

3/4 cup Brown Rice Flour Mix (see p. 6)

1/4 cup sweet rice flour (see p. 7)

2 teaspoons granulated sugar

2 teaspoons baking powder

1/4 teaspoon baking soda

1/4 teaspoon xanthan gum

1 tablespoon buttermilk powder

1/4 teaspoon salt

5 tablespoons cold unsalted butter, cut into 5 slices

1 large egg white

3 tablespoons water

Biscuits can be stored in refrigerator for up to two days in an airtight container. Rewarm in 350°F preheated oven. Do not use a microwave.

1. Preheat oven to 425°. Position rack in center of oven. Grease small baking sheet with cooking spray and set aside.

2. Mix brown rice flour mix, sweet rice flour, sugar, baking powder, baking soda, xanthan gum, buttermilk powder, and salt in large bowl of electric mixer. With mixer on low speed, cut butter into flour mixture until mixture is crumbly and resembles coarse meal. Put mixture into a small bowl and set aside.

3. Beat egg white in the same large bowl of electric mixer until *very foamy*. Add water and flour mixture all at once, and mix at medium-low speed for 1 minute. Use lightly floured hands to pat out dough into a large 3/4-inch-thick round on lightly floured surface. Cut out biscuits with a 2½-inch round cookie cutter. Press dough scraps together and repeat.

4. Place baking sheet on center rack of oven and turn oven temperature down to 400°F. Bake 15–18 minutes or until medium golden brown. Serve immediately.

BREAD CRUMBS

Makes about 8 cups.

Bread crumbs are an important part of many dishes, and you probably won't want to be without them in your pantry. My simple recipe uses potato starch and corn starch to make an inexpensive, bland bread that is ground into almost eight cups of bread crumbs. (You do the math! Compare this to the price of gluten-free bread crumbs in the store.) Yeast flavors the bread, but baking powder is used for a quick rise. The loaf isn't really delicious to eat as bread, but it makes a fabulous bread crumb that you will love to cook with. You can also toast the crumbs in the oven (see Cook's Note at left) or toss them with herbs and spices to make flavored bread crumbs of your choosing.

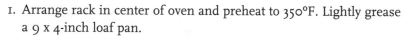

1 packet (¼ oz.) of dry quick-rise yeast granules

1 cup milk, heated to 105°F

1¼ cups potato starch

1¼ cups corn starch

1 teaspoon xanthan gum

1 tablespoon baking powder

½ teaspoon salt

2 tablespoons granulated sugar

1 large egg

¼ cup canola oil

Cook's Note: For toasted bread crumbs: Preheat oven to 325°F. Spread bread crumbs out on shallow baking pan and place in center of oven. Stir every few minutes until desired color is reached.

1. Arrange rack in center of oven and preheat to 350°F. Lightly grease a 9 x 4-inch loaf pan.

2. Stir yeast into warmed milk (105°F) and set aside.

3. Mix all dry ingredients together in bowl of electric mixer. Add egg, canola oil, and milk/yeast mixture to dry ingredients; mix until just blended. Scrape bowl and beaters and beat on medium speed for 1 minute. Dough will be thick.

4. Spoon dough into prepared pan and place on rack in center of oven. Bake 30–35 minutes or until toothpick inserted into center of loaf comes out dry. Your instant read thermometer should register 195°F, and your loaf will be a very light brown.

5. Remove bread from oven and turn onto a rack to cool completely. Cut into thin slices and grind in an electric blender or food processor until fine crumbs appear. Store in a tightly sealed container in freezer.

CHAPTER 10

Other Savories

BUTTERMILK PANCAKES
Buttermilk Waffles

SAVORY CREPES
Sweet Crepes

FRESH PASTA DOUGH

FLOUR TORTILLAS
Parathas

HERB BREAD STUFFING

POPOVERS

CHEESE PUFFS

ALTHOUGH MANY OF THE RECIPES in this chapter are not actually baked in an oven, they are made with flour batters or doughs and are among the many food items that those of us with a gluten intolerance come to miss over time. Even if you've survived without fresh pasta for five years, there comes a time when the longing to eat something you once loved overtakes you. The desire to eat something as simple as a flour tortilla or a really good pancake can start to pick away at you. Now, you can give into temptation. I've filled this chapter with easy-to-make recipes that will bring a smile to your face and happiness to your day. They are so basic that they can become a part of your weekly meals, and so delicious so you can serve them to anyone without explanation.

This chapter uses the following pans:
- 6 or 7-inch skillet or crepe pan
- Large 12-inch (or more) skillet for pancakes
- Waffle iron
- Well-seasoned cast-iron skillet or griddle for tortillas (or tortilla press)
- Popover pans or 12-cup muffin pan
- Large, heavy baking sheet for cheese puffs

THE LAST WORD ON SAVORY TREATS
- Set up before starting the recipe: assemble all ingredients.
- Measure carefully (see Chapter 3).
- Preheat the oven to the proper temperature (make sure the oven is calibrated correctly)
- Do not open the oven door more than necessary
- Use a timer because you can get distracted

BUTTERMILK PANCAKES

*Makes 12
4-inch pancakes or 3
6-inch waffles.*

If you miss the delicate flavor and texture of traditional buttermilk pancakes, try this recipe. Light and airy, without a trace of the grit, density, or aftertaste typically found in gluten-free pancake mixes, you'll be able to look forward to eating this classic breakfast treat once again. Even better, these flavorful pancakes are easy to make and look like their wheat counterparts. Heat up a little pitcher of maple syrup and make a batch this weekend.

Keep little bags of the recipe's premixed dry ingredients handy so you can quickly whip up a batch on a weekend morning.

1 cup Brown Rice Flour Mix (see p. 6)
2 tablespoons buttermilk powder
1 tablespoon granulated sugar
$\frac{1}{4}$ teaspoon salt
$1\frac{3}{4}$ teaspoons baking powder
$\frac{1}{2}$ teaspoon baking soda
$\frac{1}{4}$ teaspoon cinnamon (optional)
1 large egg, well beaten
1 tablespoon canola oil
$\frac{1}{2}$ cup plus 1 tablespoon water
$\frac{1}{2}$ teaspoon pure vanilla extract

1. Preheat large skillet over medium low heat.
2. Combine dry ingredients in a medium bowl and mix with a whisk. Add wet ingredients and whisk until well blended.
3. Brush skillet with butter. Pour batter (by $\frac{1}{4}$ cupful) onto heated skillet. Turn pancakes when bubbles on top surface start to pop. Finish cooking pancakes about 1 to 2 minutes more and remove from pan. (If the edges are flat when you cook them, the pan is too cool. If the pancakes brown before the little bubbles appear on the top and have time to pop, the pan is too hot.)

BUTTERMILK WAFFLES

Increase the 1 tablespoon canola oil to 2 tablespoons.

1. Preheat waffle iron.
2. Combine dry ingredients in a medium bowl and mix with a whisk. Add wet ingredients and whisk until well blended.
3. Pour about $\frac{2}{3}$ cup of batter into waffle iron and cook according to the iron manufacturer's directions.

SAVORY CREPES

The versatile crepe can help turn the simplest of ingredients into a special brunch, main course, or dessert. You can fill them with an wide variety of combinations: creamy chicken and mushroom, curried seafood, spinach and Gruyere, scrambled eggs with ham and cheddar, fresh strawberries and whipped cream, peaches and vanilla custard, or that famous classic, Crepes Suzette. These light, flavorful crepes take a lot less time to make than crepes made with wheat because you don't have to let the batter rest for two hours. They will be a welcome addition to your gluten-free repertoire.

- $\frac{1}{2}$ cup Brown Rice Flour Mix (see p. 6)
- $\frac{1}{8}$ teaspoon salt
- $\frac{1}{2}$ cup milk
- 2 large eggs
- 2 tablespoons unsalted butter, melted
  - Additional butter for pan

1. Preheat a 6-7 inch skillet/crepe pan over medium heat.
2. Combine all ingredients in a blender and mix well.
3. Brush skillet with additional butter. Pour batter (about 3 tablespoons) onto heated skillet with one hand; with the other hand, tilt the skillet so the batter completely coats the bottom (pour any extra batter back into the blender so the crepes are not too thick). Cook about 1 minute, until the underside is very light golden brown. Loosen the edges of the crepe with a spatula and turn it over in the skillet. Cook the other side about 30 seconds, until it is a spotty light golden brown. Slide crepe onto a plate and cover with foil.
4. Repeat Step 3 with remaining batter (be sure to brush skillet with more butter before you make each crepe).

SWEET CREPES

- $\frac{1}{2}$ cup Brown Rice Flour Mix (see p. 6)
- 1 tablespoon granulated sugar
- $\frac{1}{8}$ teaspoon salt
- $\frac{1}{2}$ cup milk
- 2 large eggs
- 2 tablespoons unsalted butter, melted
- 1 tablespoon rum, cognac, or liqueur
- $\frac{1}{2}$ teaspoon pure vanilla extract

Follow Steps 1–4 from the Savory Crepes recipe.

Makes 8–10 savory crepes and 12–14 sweet crepes.

Crepes can be held tightly covered with foil at room temperature for up to three hours.

They can be made one day in advance and refrigerated until ready to use; wrap in plastic wrap and then foil so they don't dry out. Crepes can be frozen for up to one week, although they will not be as flavorful; wrap in plastic wrap and then foil.

FRESH PASTA DOUGH

Makes about ½ pound. Recipe can be doubled.

Marcella Hazan was my inspiration for this pasta dough. Her recipe uses flour and eggs. Nothing more. I added a bit of xanthan gum and made a dough that is easy to roll, and delicious to eat. It is actually easier to make than pasta with wheat because it has no gluten to make it tough. As a result, you don't have worry about mixing it by hand. You also don't have to let the dough rest before kneading it, so the whole process takes less time. This recipe makes approximately six 6-inch round manicotti/cannonelli, or two 9x9-inch lasagna sheets (or cut to fit baking dish). The dough can be used to make ravioli and other filled pasta, and it can be used in a pasta machine. Take note: Fresh pasta cooks very quickly in boiling water.

Cook's Notes: Fresh pasta is best when eaten the same day. Rolled/cut pasta can be wrapped in cotton or linen dishtowel and left on a counter for up to two hours before it starts to dry out.

Rolled and cut dough can be stored in refrigerator for up to two days if well wrapped in plastic wrap and placed in a tightly sealed container. If making fettuccine, spaghetti, or pappardelle, etc., coil into little nests, allow to air dry for 15 minutes, and store in tightly sealed plastic bags.

* Be sure eggs are really large. Extra-large and medium eggs are sometimes put into containers marked "Large" when broken eggs are replaced at the store.

1 cup Brown Rice Flour Mix (see p. 6)
½ teaspoon xanthan gum
2 large eggs*
Brown Rice Flour Mix (for rolling out dough)

1. Mix flour and xanthan gum in large bowl of electric mixer. Add eggs and mix at medium speed for 2 minutes. Dough should be smooth, pliable, and hold together without being sticky. If it is really sticky, add a bit more flour. (This will depend on the dampness in the air, the size of the eggs, and how you mixed and measured the flour in the first place).

To make Manicotti/Cannelloni:
2. Divide dough into six equal pieces (12 if doubling recipe) and roll each piece into a ball using your hands. Place 1 level tablespoon of brown rice flour on a Silpat mat (or wooden board or a large sheet of wax paper). Gently cover one ball of dough with brown rice flour. Set it aside on a piece of wax paper or a small clean plate. Repeat with each of the five remaining balls. Spread any remaining flour over the surface of the Silpat mat.

3. If using a Silpat mat, fold mat in half and place one ball of dough so dough is sandwiched in the center between the top and bottom of the mat. Roll dough into a 6-inch round (sprinkle with extra flour if dough becomes too sticky). Dough should be so thin that you can see your hand through it. Place round of dough on a cotton or linen dishtowel. Cover with another towel. Repeat with remaining balls of dough. If using wax paper, place ball of dough on 1 piece of wax paper and cover dough with a second piece. If using a wooden board, be sure to use additional flour so dough will not stick when you roll it.

To make Lasagna:

2. Divide dough into two equal pieces (four if doubling recipe) and press into a thick square shape using your hands. Place 1 level tablespoon of brown rice flour on a Silpat mat (or wooden board or a large sheet of wax paper). Take one square and gently cover it with brown rice flour. Set it aside on a piece of wax paper or a small clean plate. Repeat with other square. Spread any remaining flour over the surface of the Silpat mat.

3. If using a Silpat mat, fold mat in half and place one square of dough so dough is sandwiched between the top and bottom of the mat. Roll dough into a 9 x 9-inch square (sprinkle with extra flour if dough becomes too sticky). Dough should be so thin that you can see your hand through it. Place square of dough on a cotton or linen dishtowel. Cover with another towel. Repeat with remaining square of dough. If using wax paper, place ball of dough on one piece of wax paper and cover dough with a second piece. If using a wooden board, be sure to use additional flour so dough will not stick when you roll it.

For Filled Pastas and Pasta Machine:

2. Divide dough into two equal pieces (four if you have doubled recipe). Follow your recipe directions for filled pasta or instructions for using pasta machine. You may need to hand roll the pasta a bit before putting it through the machine. Also, when using a pasta machine, you may have to add a bit more brown rice flour mix so the dough doesn't stick to the rollers of the machine (see Step 1, above). If the dough is cracking a bit at the edges, moisten it a bit with a few drops of water. Rolled dough should be so thin that you can see your hand through it. Moisten edges with a wet finger to make tortelloni, ravioli, etc.

Cook's Notes: Unrolled and uncut pasta dough can be stored in refrigerator overnight: roll dough into a large ball and wrap tightly in plastic wrap (press wrap onto surface of dough so there are no air pockets) and then wrap tightly in aluminum foil. Bring to room temperature before proceeding.

If you are well acquainted with how I develop and write recipes, you probably figured I'd test to find out if the pasta dough could be frozen—and you'd be correct. Even though it goes against my nature to offer up fresh-frozen pasta, I have to say that it froze beautifully. You can freeze the dough for up to three weeks without too much depreciation in taste and texture (it is a bit less tender). Wrap it really well in plastic wrap with no air pockets and then, in foil.

When making baked pasta dishes, brush baking dish lightly with olive oil.

FLOUR TORTILLAS

Makes six 6-inch
tortillas. Recipe can be
doubled.

Cook's Notes: The trick
to making a good flour
tortilla is to have your
pan hot enough so that
you can cook each tor-
tilla for about one
minute on each side—
enough to cook the
dough, have it bubble
with brown spots, and
not be overcooked.
When the tortilla is
cooked the perfect
amount of time at the
correct temperature, it
will be pliable, so you
can fold it. If over-
cooked, it will still taste
delicious, but it will be
harder and won't bend
as easily.

Tortillas are really best
when eaten immediate-
ly, but they can be
stored in the refrigera-
tor for three days. Cool
completely and wrap
tightly in plastic wrap
and then in aluminum
foil. Wrap in a damp
cloth or paper towel
and rewarm in
microwave.

Native Americans traditionally made tortillas with corn, but Spanish settlers to the New World began to make them with wheat in the border towns near what is now Texas and New Mexico. Home cooks originally used lard, and you can use it here for an authentic taste. But now "homemade" versions are more apt to be made with oil or shortening, and sometimes both, as I do here. In addition, when tortillas moved north of the border, baking powder was added to the recipe to help lighten the finished flat bread. Homemade flour tortillas were and still are vastly different from the mass-produced "flour tortillas" or wraps we see in gro-cery stores; tortillas sold in stores are designed to have a long shelf and remain pliable. This recipe makes pliable flour tortillas that taste nutty and delicious, and like the real homemade tortillas of the Spanish settlers, they are best when eaten hot off the skillet.

$^3/_4$ cup plus 1 tablespoon Bread Flour Mix A (see p. 6)

$^1/_4$ cup sweet rice flour (see p. 7)

$^3/_4$ teaspoon xanthan gum

$^1/_2$ teaspoon salt

$^1/_2$ teaspoon baking powder

2 tablespoons shortening

2 tablespoons canola oil `

$^1/_3$ cup water, heated to 110°F

Rice flour for rolling out dough

1. Mix flours, xanthan gum, salt, and baking powder in large bowl of electric mixer. Add shortening and mix until crumbly and resembling coarse meal.

2. Add oil and water and mix on low speed until dough holds together. Beat at medium speed for 2 minutes.

3. Heat a well-seasoned cast-iron skillet or griddle over medium-low heat until hot. (A well-seasoned cast-iron skillet will help to give your tortillas a great taste.) If you can use a real tortilla press, you won't have to turn the tortillas.

4. Divide dough into six equal pieces (or four pieces if you want larger tortillas), roll each piece into a ball using your hands and place it on a small sheet of plastic wrap. Place 1 tablespoon of brown rice flour on the small plate. Gently cover one ball with rice flour. Put it back on the plastic wrap. Repeat with each of the five remaining balls and then cover the balls with plastic wrap so they don't dry out.

5. Spread a little of the remaining flour from the plate over the surface of a small sheet of wax paper. Put a ball of dough on the wax paper and pat it into a 6-inch round with your fingers (sprinkle with a little extra flour if dough becomes too sticky). Turn dough over as you are patting so it won't stick. Peel dough off the wax paper and lay it in your palm. Carefully place it into the hot skillet. Cook tortilla about 1 minute, until it bubbles and puffs and bottom is browned in spots. Turn it over and cook it about another minute, until browned in spots (time depends on how hot griddle is). See Cook's Note on opposite page.

6. While tortilla is cooking, repeat Step 5 with next ball of dough and get it ready to go in the skillet. Remove tortillas as they cook and stack them in a linen kitchen or tea towel; keep them covered and warm. Serve immediately. Tortillas can be resoftened or rewarmed, if needed, by placing between damp cloth or paper towel in microwave.

PARATHAS

Indian parathas are traditionally made with a combination of whole-wheat and regular wheat flour, ghee (clarified butter), and water. A thin round of dough is brushed with ghee (or oil) and then folded in half. It is then brushed with more ghee (or oil) and folded into a triangle shape and rolled thin again before roasting in a hot pan where it puffs up a bit. The paratha is brushed with more ghee immediately after it is removed from the pan. With gluten-free flours, you can achieve a similar taste by simply brushing the finished flat bread made from the recipe above with a little ghee (or melted butter) immediately after you remove it from the hot pan. If you are concerned about having an authentic shape, pat it into a flat triangle instead of a circle.

Take note: if you substitute ghee/butter for the oil and shortening in the above recipe, it seems to makes the flat bread "heavy" and a bit oily, but it still tastes good. Better to brush it on after it is cooked.

HERB BREAD STUFFING

Serves 6. Recipe can be doubled.

* You can make Sandwich Bread (see p. 158) or you can use fresh, top-quality bread that is not purchased frozen. (However, Whole Foods does sell a frozen sandwich bread that works well for this purpose.) The small, hard-frozen rice breads will not make a good stuffing.

** More Than Gourmet® makes a delicious assort-ment of high-quality con-centrated stock and glaces. Almost all of its stocks and glaces, except its classic veal demi-glace, are gluten-free. You can reach the com-pany at 800-860-9389 or on the Internet at www.morethangourmet. com.

After I became gluten intolerant, I struggled with what to do about making my family's "must-have" stuffing. Make two turkeys? (I did that one year.) Make two stuffings out of the bird? (I did that for two years.) But there was really only one good solution—make a gluten-free stuffing so good that I wouldn't have to apolo-gize to the wheat eaters around the table. Luckily, current cooking lore has made it acceptable for cooks to offer stuffing baked outside the bird, which is a good thing, because it is close to impossible to control the texture of gluten-free bread stuffing cooked in a turkey. My simple recipe can provide a foundation for you to make your family's "must-have" stuffing by adding your own touches (see Cook's Note on opposite page). Be sure to follow the directions for toasting a high quali-ty sandwich bread in the oven first—it is a critical step.

6 cups gluten-free "plain white bread" cubes** (see p. 158)

$3/4$ cup celery, chopped

$3/4$ cup onions, chopped

6 tablespoons unsalted butter or margarine

$3/4$ teaspoon dried sage

1 teaspoon dried thyme leaves

1 teaspoon dried marjoram leaves

1 teaspoon demi-glace (optional)**

Salt and freshly ground pepper, to taste

1 cup low-sodium chicken broth (add another $1/4$ cup for a moister stuffing)

1 large egg (optional)

3 tablespoons butter or margarine cut into thin slices (for top of stuffing)

1. Preheat oven to 325°F. Position rack in center of oven. Remove crusts from bread and cut into $1/2$-inch cubes. Spread bread cubes on a large baking sheet and bake until cubes are dried out and golden. Allow to cool thoroughly. (Bread cubes can be prepared two days in advance. Store in a tightly sealed container or plastic zip-lock bag in refrigerator.)

2. Preheat oven to 350°F. Lightly spray an 8 x 8-inch baking dish with cooking spray.

3. Melt butter in medium skillet over medium heat. Add onions and celery, sage, thyme, and marjoram; mix well and sauté until tender.

Stir in demi-glace (if using) and mix to combine. (Vegetable/herb mix can be prepared 2 days in advance. Store in a tightly sealed container in refrigerator.)

4. Put bread cubes in a large mixing bowl. Stir in onion and celery mixture. Combine broth and egg and beat well with a whisk. Add broth mixture to bread cubes and mix in gently. Allow mixture to sit until all moisture is absorbed (about 15 minutes).

5. Spoon stuffing mixture into greased 8 x 8" baking pan and cover with foil. Bake, covered, for 20 minutes. Remove foil, dot with thin slices of butter across top of stuffing, and bake an additional 20–30 minutes until top is golden brown and a little crisp.

Store any leftovers tightly covered in the refrigerator. Can be rewarmed in microwave or conventional oven.

Cook's Notes: For variation, add about 1 cup cooked, crumbled sausage and $\frac{1}{2}$ cup chopped apples, or 1 cup dried fruit, and/or 1 cup cooked chestnuts (high-quality jarred chestnuts are good for this). Adjust spices and herbs to suit your family's preferences. If your family likes a cornbread stuffing, see the Cornbread recipe on p. 21.

POPOVERS

Makes 8 popovers.

Popovers rise like magic in the oven. Crisp on the outside, tender and mostly hollow on the inside, they "pop" while baking until they are three times their original size. My gluten-free version takes a lot less time to make than those made with wheat because you don't have to let the batter rest. In no time at all, you'll have eight delectable chef hat-shaped popovers to bring to your table. The trick to getting a good rise is to have the milk and eggs at room temperature. I recommend buying the popover pans if you are a popover lover, that way your popovers will look and taste authentic. If you use a regular 12-cup muffin pan, the recipe will make ten smaller popovers.

1 cup milk (room temperature)

3 large eggs (room temperature)

3 tablespoons unsalted butter, melted

¾ cup Brown Rice Flour Mix (see p. 6)

⅛ teaspoon xanthan gum

¼–½ teaspoon salt

Best when eaten immediately. Popovers can be made several hours ahead and reheated in a preheated 375°F oven for 10–15 minutes.

1. Preheat oven to 400°F. Position rack in center of oven. Spray popover pans with cooking spray.

2. Combine milk and egg in a blender and mix until frothy. Add melted butter, flour, xanthan gum and salt. Blend 1 to 2 minutes until batter is the consistency of heavy cream.

3. Divide batter between eight popover pan cups. Put pans in oven and reduce temperature to 375°F. Bake 45–50 minutes until popovers have risen and are brown and crusty. Quickly open oven and use a pointy, sharp knife to cut a slit in each popover to release the steam. Bake 5–10 minutes more. Popovers should be brown and crisp on the outside and tender inside. Remove popovers from pan (you may need to run a sharp knife around the edges to loosen them) and serve immediately.

CHEESE PUFFS

Make a batch of these cheese puffs for your next gathering, and watch them disappear before you even set them down. Cheese Puffs smell so good when they're baking in the oven that your guests will be circling around your kitchen waiting for them to come out. Add your favorite cheese to this puff pastry dough, pipe it onto a cookie sheet, and then into the oven it goes. You can make the puffs ahead of time and simply reheat them for more effortless entertaining; just follow the directions for reheating below.

$\frac{1}{2}$ cup Brown Rice Flour Mix (see p. 6)

$\frac{1}{4}$ teaspoon xanthan gum

$\frac{1}{8}$ teaspoon salt

    Dash finely ground pepper

    Pinch nutmeg (optional)

$\frac{1}{4}$ cup unsalted butter, cut into 4 pieces

$\frac{1}{2}$ cup fat-free milk

 2 large eggs

$\frac{1}{2}$ cup packed, grated Swiss, Gruyère, Cheddar, and/or Parmesan cheese

Makes 24 cheese puffs, 1 $\frac{1}{2}$ inches diameter. Recipe can be doubled.

Cook's Note: Soak saucepan in ice-cold water for easy clean-up.

1. Preheat oven to 400°F. Position rack in center of oven. Line a large, heavy baking sheet with parchment paper.

2. Combine flour, xanthan gum, salt, pepper, and nutmeg (if using) in small bowl and set aside.

3. Bring butter and milk to a boil in a 1-quart saucepan over medium heat. Try not to allow too much milk to evaporate. As soon as milk mixture boils, remove pan from heat and add flour mixture all at once. Use a soup spoon to stir vigorously to combine. The dough should come together in a tight ball.

4. Return the pan to medium heat and cook, stirring constantly, until dough has a smooth appearance and oil from the butter begins to glisten on the surface (about 1 minute). Bottom of pan will be coated with a thin film of dough, and temperature inside the dough (taken with an instant-read thermometer) should be 140°–150°F. (Use a thermometer—don't guess until you've done it many times!)

5. Transfer dough to large bowl of an electric mixer. Begin to beat dough at medium speed while adding eggs one at a time; allow first egg to be fully absorbed and the dough to become smooth and shiny before adding second. After each addition, dough will separate into

slippery little lumps before coming back together. Beat until dough is very smooth in consistency and a very pale yellow color, about 2–3 minutes. Beat cheese into the warm dough.

6. Use a pastry bag with a $\frac{1}{2}$-inch smooth, round opening at the tip. Fill pastry bag with warm dough. Squeeze dough onto prepared baking sheet, making circular mounds 1 inch in diameter and $\frac{1}{2}$-inch high at highest point. You can also use a soup spoon to drop small mounds of dough onto the baking sheet. (Easier than above, and takes less time, but cheese puffs will not be uniform. Don't worry— no one will notice.) Space mounds 2 inches apart. Be sure to tap down any pointy dough tips that result from pulling away the pastry bag. Sprinkle each cheese puff with a pinch of additional cheese if desired.

7. Place baking sheet on center rack in oven and bake about 20 minutes or until dough rises and turns medium golden brown. Turn oven temperature down to 300°F but do not open door. Bake another 5–10 minutes. Puffs are done when they have doubled or tripled in size, are a rich golden brown, and are firm and crusty to the touch. Remove baking sheet from oven and pierce side of each puff with a sharp knife to allow steam to escape.

To use immediately:
Serve cheese puffs immediately or at room temperature.

To use within 24 hours:
Store in an airtight container at room temperature. Puffs will soften. Recrisp in preheated 350°F oven.

To freeze for use within 2 weeks:
Store in an airtight container and freeze for up 2 weeks. Puffs will soften. Defrost and recrisp in preheated 350°F oven.

MEASUREMENTS/EQUIVALENTS

APPROXIMATE MEASUREMENTS

1 lemon = 3 tablespoons juice

1 lemon = 1 teaspoon grated peel

1 orange = $\frac{1}{3}$ cup juice

1 orange = 2 teaspoons grated peel

1 pound unshelled walnuts = $1\frac{1}{2}$ to $1\frac{3}{4}$ cups shelled

1 pound unshelled almonds = $\frac{3}{4}$ to 1 cup shelled

8 to 10 egg whites = 1 cup

12 to 14 egg yolks = $1\frac{1}{2}$ cups

EQUIVALENTS

3 teaspoons = 1 tablespoon

2 tablespoons = $\frac{1}{8}$ cup

4 tablespoons = $\frac{1}{4}$ cup

8 tablespoons = $\frac{1}{2}$ cup

16 tablespoons = 1 cup

5 tablespoons + 1 teaspoon = $\frac{1}{3}$ cup

12 tablespoons = $\frac{3}{4}$ cup

4 ounces = $\frac{1}{2}$ cup

8 ounces = 1 cup

$\frac{5}{8}$ cup = $\frac{1}{2}$ cup + 2 tablespoons

$\frac{7}{8}$ cup = $\frac{3}{4}$ cup + 2 tablespoons

16 ounces = 1 pound

1 ounce = 2 tablespoons fat or liquid

2 cups = 1 pint

2 pints = 1 quart

1 quart = 4 cups

speck = less than $\frac{1}{8}$ teaspoon

INDEX

A
Almond milk, 12
Almonds
    Biscotti, 124
    Butter Cookies, 118
    Crisps, 123
    Mandelbrot, 126
Angel Food Cake, 62
Apple Cider Doughnuts, 153–154
Apples
    Cinnamon Muffins with Streusel
      Topping, 24–25
    Crisp, 138
    Custard Cake with Fruit, 73–74
    Pie with Crumb Topping, 91–92
    Rustic Tart, 94–95
    Sour Cream Coffee Cake, 75–76
Authentic Foods®, 7, 17

B
Babka, 183
Bagels, 190–191
Bananas
    Cream Pie, 103
    Nut Muffins, 27
Biscotti
    Almond, 124
    Hazelnut, 125
Black and White Cookies, 127–128
Blueberries
    Lemon Pound Cake, 82
    Muffins, 22
Bob's Red Mill® brown rice flour, 9
Bob's Red Mill® oatmeal, 123
Boston Cream Pie, 103
Bread Flour Mixes, 6, 7–9. *See also* Gluten-
    free flours
Bread puddings
    Coconut, 142
    Pumpkin with Caramel Sauce,
      140–141
Breads, 155–157
    Babka, 183
    Basic Sandwich, 158–159
    Bread Crumbs, 194
    Buttermilk Biscuits, 193
    Buttermilk Sandwich, 159
    Challah, 181–182
    Cinnamon, 162–163
    Cinnamon Raisin, 163
    Cinnamon Raisin English Muffins, 170
    Cranberry Nut, 30

    Egg Bagels, 190–191
    English Muffins, 170
    French-Italian, 171
    Golden Italian with Raisins and
      Fennel, 176–177
    Hamburger and Hot Dog Buns,
      168–169
    Herb Stuffing, 202–203
    Irish Soda, 184–185
    Lemon Poppy Seed Tea Loaves, 34
    Lemon Walnut Tea Loaves, 34
    Multigrain Artisan, 172–173
    Multigrain Sandwich, 160–161
    Orange Juice, 35
    Orange Juice Pecan, 35
    Pecan Raisin Artisan, 174–175
    Pumpkin Bread, 31
    Rustic Flat, 180
    "Rye," 164–165
    Submarine Sandwich, 178–179
    Triple Ginger Tea Loaf, 32–33
    Walnut, 192
Brown Rice Flour Mix, 6–7
Brownies, 133
Butter Cookies, 110–111
Buttermilk Biscuits, 193
Buttermilk Pancakes/Waffles, 196
Buttermilk Sandwich Bread, 159

C
Cakes, 43–44
    Angel Food, 62
    Carrot, 67–68
    Chocolate Fudge, 57–58
    Chocolate Sponge or Jelly Roll, 65–66
    Classic Cheesecake, 72
    Coconut Layer, 52–53
    Crumb, 77–78
    Custard with Fruit, 73–74
    European-Style Coffee Cake, 83–84
    Flourless Chocolate, 61
    German Chocolate, 59–60
    Gingerbread, 69
    Hazelnut, 54–56
    Lemon Layer, 48–49
    Lemon Pound, 81–82
    Maple Walnut, 50–51
    New York Cheesecake, 70–71
    Sour Cream Coffee, 75–76
    Vanilla (Butter) Layer Cake, 47
    Vanilla Cupcakes, 46
    Vanilla Pound, 79–80

    Vanilla Sponge or Jelly Roll, 63–64
    Yellow Layer, 45
Cannelloni dough, 198–199
Caramel sauce, 140
Carrots
    Carrot Cake, 67–68
    Carrot Spice Muffins, 29
Celiac disease, 3–4
Challah, 181–182
Cheese Puffs, 205–206
Cheesecakes
    Classic, 72
    New York, 70–71
Cherries, Custard Cake with, 74
Chocolate chips
    Chocolate Chip Cookies, 107
    Chocolate Chip Muffins, 23
    Chocolate Chip Pound Cake, 79–80
    Chocolate Ricotta Muffins, 28
    Chocolate Shortbread Cookies,
      115–116
    German Chocolate Cake, 59–60
Chocolate extract, in Chocolate
Doughnuts, 151–152
Chocolate, melting of, 14
Chocolate, semi-sweet
    Chocolate-Filled Butter Cookies, 111
    Chocolate Peanut Butter Balls, 129
    Cream Pie, 98–99
    Flourless Chocolate Cake, 61
    Glaze, 148
    Sauce, 144
Chocolate, unsweetened
    Brownies, 133
    Chocolate Fudge Cake, 57–58
Cinnamon Bread, 162–163
Cinnamon Raisin Bread, 163
Cinnamon Raisin English Muffins, 170
Cinnamon Rolls, 38–39
Classic Cheesecake, 72
Cocoa
    Chocolate Shortbread Cookies,
      115–116
    Chocolate Sponge Cake or Jelly Roll,
      65–66
    Cream-Filled Chocolate Cookies,
      108–109
Coconut
    Bread Pudding, 142
    Carrot Cake, 67–68
    Carrot Spice Muffins, 29
    Cream Pie, 100–101

Layer Cake, 52–53
Lemon Coconut Muffins, 26
Macaroons, 120
Shortbread Cookies, 114
Cookies, 105–106
Almond Biscotti, 124
Almond Butter, 118
Black and White, 127–128
Butter, 110–111
Chocolate Chip, 107
Chocolate-Filled Butter, 111
Chocolate Peanut Butter Balls, 129
Chocolate Shortbread, 115–116
Coconut Macaroons, 120
Cream-Filled Butter, 111
Cream-Filled Chocolate, 108–109
Gingerbread Men, 122
Gingersnaps, 121
Hazelnut Biscotti, 125
Linzertorte, 117
Mandelbrot, 126
Oatmeal, 123
Pecan Butter, 119
Shortbread, 113–114
Sugar, 112
Cornmeal
Cornbread Muffins, 21
Lemon Cornmeal Scones, 37
Lemon Shortbread Cookies, 114
Cranberry Nut Bread, 30
Cream cheese
Classic Cheesecake, 72
European-Style Coffee Cake, 83–84
Frosting, 68
New York Cheesecake, 70–71
Cream-Filled Butter Cookies, 111
Cream-Filled Chocolate Cookies, 108–109
Cream Puffs, 143–144
Vanilla Filling for, 145
Crepes, 197
Crumb Cake, 77–78
Cupcakes, Vanilla, 46
Custard Cake with Fruit, 73–74

D
Doughnuts
Apple Cider, 153–154
Chocolate, 151–152
Old-Fashioned Buttermilk, 149–150

E
Eclairs, 146–148
Vanilla Filling for, 145
Egg Bagels, 190–191
Egg substitutes, 12

English Muffins, 170
Equipment, 14
European-Style Coffee Cake (Cheese-Filled), 83–84

F
Flour Tortillas, 200–201
Flourless Chocolate Cake, 61
Focaccio, 180
French-Italian Bread, 171
Frostings
Chocolate, 128
Chocolate, for doughnuts, 152
Coconut, 53
Cream Cheese, 68
German Chocolate, 60
Lemon Buttercream, 49
Maple Buttercream, 51
Vanilla, 128
Vanilla, for doughnuts, 150
Fruit Crisps, 139
Fruit Pies, 93
Fruit Tarts, 103

G
Gelatin, 13
German Chocolate Cake, 59–60
Ginger
Gingerbread Cake, 69
Gingerbread Men, 122
Gingersnaps, 121
Oatmeal Cookies, 123
Triple Ginger Tea Loaf, 32–33
Gluten, 4
Gluten-free flours
baking with, 11–12, 14–15
measuring and mixing, 9–10
purchasing and storing, 10
recipes for, 6–9
Golden Italian Bread with Raisins and Fennel, 176–177
Ground nut flour, 8
Guar gum, 10–11

H
Hamburger Buns, 168–169
Hazelnuts
Biscotti, 125
Cake, 54–56
Herb Bread Stuffing, 202–203
Hot Cross Buns, 40–41
Hot Dog Buns, 168–169

I
Ice Cream Sandwiches, 136–137

Icing. See Frostings
Ingredients
to have on hand, 15–16
measuring of, 13
Irish Soda Bread, 184–185

J
Jelly rolls
Chocolate, 65–66
Vanilla, 63–64

K
Key lime
Pie, 97
Squares, 135

L
Lasagna dough, 199
Lemon rind/lemon extract
Coconut Muffins, 26
Cornmeal Scones, 37
Layer Cake, 48–49
Lemon Squares, 134–135
Poppy Seed Muffins, 26
Poppy Seed Tea Loaves, 34
Pound Cake, 81–82
Shortbread Cookies, 114
Walnut Tea Loaves, 34
Linzertorte Cookies, 117

M
Mandelbrot, 126
Manicotti dough, 198–199
Maple Walnut Cake, 50–51
McCanns® Irish Oatmeal, 123
Millet flour, 9, 10
More Than Gourmet®, 202
Muffins, 19–20
Apple Cinnamon, 24–25
Banana Nut, 27
Blueberry, 22
Carrot Spice, 29
Chocolate Chip, 23
Chocolate Ricotta, 28
Cornbread, 21
English Muffins, 170
Lemon Coconut, 26
Lemon Poppy Seed, 26
Peach Ginger, 25
Pumpkin, 31
streusel topping for, 23, 25
Multigrain Artisan Bread, 172–173
Multigrain Dinner Rolls, 167
Multigrain Sandwich Bread, 160–161

N
New York Cheesecake, 70–71

O
Oatmeal Cookies, 123
Old-Fashioned Buttermilk Doughnuts, 149–150
Orange juice
    Cranberry Nut Bread, 30
    Orange Juice Bread, 35
    Orange Juice Pecan Bread, 35

P
Pancakes, 196
Parathas, 201
Pasta Dough, 198–199
Peaches
    Ginger Muffins, 25
    Summer Fruit Crisp, 139
Peanut butter, in Chocolate Peanut Butter Balls, 129
Pears
    Custard Cake with Fruit, 73–74
    Pear Crisp, 138
Pecans
    Butter Cookies, 119
    Orange Juice Bread, 35
    Pie, 96
    Raisin Artisan Bread, 174–175
Pies, 85–86. See also Tarts
    Apple with Crumb Topping, 91–92
    Boston Cream, 103
    Chocolate Cream, 98–99
    Coconut Cream, 100–101
    Fruit, 93
    Key Lime, 97
    Pecan, 96
    Traditional Crust for , 87–88
    Vanilla Cream Filling, 102
Pizzas, 155–157
    Crust, 186–187
    gluten-free flours for, 9
Plums, in Rustic Tart, 95
Popovers, 204
Poppy seeds
    Lemon Muffins, 26
    Lemon Pound Cake, 82
    Lemon Tea Loaves, 34
Pretzels, 188–189
Profiteroles, 144
Pumpkin puree
    Pumpkin Bread or Muffins, 31
    Pumpkin Bread Pudding with Caramel Sauce, 140–141

R
Raisins
    Challah with, 182
    Golden Italian Bread with Fennel and, 176–177
    Hot Cross Buns, 40–41
    Irish Soda Bread, 184–185
    Lemon Cornmeal Scones, 37
    Pecan Artisan Bread, 174–175
    Traditional Scones, 36
Raspberry preserves, in Linzertorte Cookies, 117
Refrigeration, 13
Rice flour, 13
Rice milk, 12
Ricotta cheese, in Chocolate Muffins, 28
Rolls
    Multigrain Dinner, 167
    Traditional Dinner, 166–167
Rustic Flat Bread, 180
"Rye" Bread, 164–165

S
Savories, 195
    Buttermilk Pancakes, 196
    Buttermilk Waffles, 196
    Cheese Puffs, 205–206
    Flour Tortillas, 200–201
    Fresh Pasta Dough, 198–199
    Herb Bread Stuffing, 202–203
    Parathas, 201
    Popovers, 204
    Savory Crepes, 197
    Sweet Crepes, 197
Scones
    Lemon Cornmeal, 37
    Traditional, 36
Shortbread Cookies, 113–114
Soft pretzels, 188–189
Sour cream
    Coffee Cake, 75–76
    Crumb Cake, 77–78
Soy milk, 12
Streusel topping, 23, 25
Stuffing, Herb Bread, 202–203
Submarine Sandwich Bread, 178–179
Sugar alternatives, 12–13
Sugar Cookies, 112
Sweet Crepes, 197
Sweet rice flour, 7

T
Tarts, 85
    Berry, 103
    Chocolate Shell Crust, 90

Rustic Apple, 94–95
Rustic Plum, 95
Shell Crust, 89
Tea loaves. See Breads
Teff flour, 8
Tortillas, 200–201
Traditional Scones, 36
Treats, 131–132
    Apple Cider Doughnuts, 153–154
    Apple Crisp, 138
    Brownies, 133
    Chocolate Doughnuts, 151–152
    Coconut Bread Pudding, 142
    Cream Puffs, 143–144
    Eclairs, 146–148
    Ice Cream Sandwiches, 136–137
    Lemon Squares, 134–135
    Old-Fashioned Buttermilk Doughnuts, 149–150
    Profiteroles, 14
    Pumpkin Bread Pudding with Caramel Sauce, 140–141
    Summer Fruit Crisp, 139
    Vanilla Filling, 145
Triple Ginger Tea Loaf, 32–33

V
Vanilla (Butter) Layer Cake, 47
Vanilla Cream Pie Filling, 102
Vanilla Cupcakes, 46
Vanilla Filling, 145
Vanilla Pound Cake, 79–80
Vanilla Sponge Cake or Jelly Roll, 63–64

W
Waffles, 196
Walnuts
    Apple Cinnamon Muffins with Streusel Topping, 24–25
    Banana Nut Muffins, 27
    Carrot Cake, 67–68
    Carrot Spice Muffins, 29
    Cranberry Nut Bread, 30
    Lemon Walnut Tea Loaves, 34
    Linzertorte Cookies, 117
    Mandelbrot, 126
    Sour Cream Coffee Cake, 75–76
    Walnut Bread, 192

X
Xanthan gum, 10–11

Y
Yellow Layer Cake, 45